ROYALIST NEWARK, 1642–1646

Sieges and Siege Works

Stuart B. Jennings

'This is the Century of the Soldier', Fulvio Testi, Poet, 1641

Helion & Company

Helion & Company Limited
Unit 8 Amherst Business Centre
Budbrooke Road
Warwick
CV34 5WE
England
Tel. 01926 499 619
Email: info@helion.co.uk
Website: www.helion.co.uk
Twitter: @helionbooks
Visit our blog https://helionbooks.wordpress.com/

Published by Helion & Company 2024
Designed and typeset by Mach 3 Solutions (www.mach3solutions.co.uk)
Cover designed by Paul Hewitt, Battlefield Design (www.battlefield-design.co.uk)

ISBN 978-1-804515-48-8

British Library Cataloguing-in-Publication Data.
A catalogue record for this book is available from the British Library.

For details of other military history titles published by Helion & Company Limited
contact the above address or visit our website: http://www.helion.co.uk.

We always welcome receiving book proposals from prospective authors.

Contents

Acknowledgements

I would first like to acknowledge the advice and support of my commissioning editor, Charles Singleton, and the expertise of the team at Helion & Company who transformed my manuscript into this book.

I am very much indebted to Glyn Hughes and Kevin Winter at the National Civil War Centre, Newark, who worked closely with me in identifying and supplying images for this book and allowed access to primary sources in their collection. Kevin took the time to read through the manuscript, suggesting alterations and corrections, and both Glyn and Kevin jointly wrote the Preface to this book.

I have been researching and writing about Newark for over 25 years, and many individuals and groups have contributed their advice and support over this time. Amongst the large list, I need to especially thank Professor Martyn Bennett, Professor Andrew Hopper, Dr David Appleby, Dr Ismini Pells and the numerous students who have contributed to my thinking via the lectures and tutorials I delivered. Finally, I need to thank the staff at Nottinghamshire Archives, who have generously supported my journey through the archive sources over the decades.

This volume is dedicated to all who made the vision of a National Civil War Centre at Newark a reality: employees, volunteers, academics, Newark and Nottinghamshire Local Governments and the National Lottery Heritage Fund. It has been an exciting journey that I have been proud to take a part in.

Timeline for Key Events Involving Newark over the Course of the First Civil War, 1642–1646

1642

10 January – King Charles I leaves London as unrest against him grows, and he begins to rally his supporters. The King does not return to his capital until his trial in 1648/1649.

11 July – Charles is at Newark and addresses the gentry and freeholders of the county.

17 August – Charles stays overnight at Newark before travelling to Nottingham, where he will raise his standard.

22 August – The King raises his standard at Nottingham, a time-honoured symbol for retainers and feudatories to assemble for military service. Gervase Hollis comes into town with soldiers he raised at Newark, as does William Staunton with his servants and tenants from the parish of Staunton.

13 September – The King leaves Nottingham for Derby and then on to Shrewsbury, taking Royalist gentry and troops raised in Nottinghamshire with him.

23 October – The Battle of Edgehill. Both Hollis and Staunton, with their soldiers raised in Newark and Nottinghamshire, are at the battle.

12 November – The Battle of Brentford. William Staunton is present with his Nottinghamshire troopers.

Early November – Lincolnshire Parliamentarians make an attempt to enter Newark. Town citizens, rallied by Edward Twentymen (from 1644 captain of the town regiment), drive them away.

Late November – William Staunton is sent back to Newark with the rank of colonel and a commission to raise a regiment of foot, alongside his troop of horse.

18-23 December – Between these dates, Sir John Henderson arrives at Newark with around 4,000 horse to secure the town as a garrison for the King.

1643

January – Henderson begins initial work on constructing basic town defences beyond the ruinous medieval stone walls.

27 February – First siege of Newark by Parliamentarian forces under the command of Major General Ballard.

9 March – Parliamentarian forces under the command of Lord Willoughby of Parnham advance towards Newark, being intercepted and dispersed by troops from the town led by Captain Charles Dymock.

Early March – Charles Cavendish is sent by the Earl of Newcastle with his regiment of horse to strengthen Newark.

23 March – Henderson and Cavendish, with Newark forces, storm Grantham, taking prisoners.

Early April – Newark forces capture Stamford and Peterborough.

11 April – The Battle of Ancaster Heath, where Newark forces under the command of Cavendish rout Parliamentarian forces under the command of Lord Willoughby.

9 May – Oliver Cromwell arrives with his regiment at Sleaford to assist Lord Willoughby's Lincolnshire forces.

13 May – The Newark Horse under Cavendish attack a detachment of Lincolnshire Parliamentarians at Belton, killing 70 soldiers. Later that day, Willoughby and Cromwell halt Cavendish's forces at the Battle of Grantham. Royalists are able though to make strategic retreat back to Newark.

End of May – Newcastle sends two regiments of foot to Newark from his Northern Army in anticipation of the Queen's arrival.

16 June – Queen Henrietta Maria arrives at Newark with an army of 5,000 men. She remains in the town until 3 July.

21 June – Newark forces make an unsuccessful attempt to capture the Parliamentarian town of Nottingham.

28 July – The Battle of Gainsborough. Parliamentarian forces under the command of Lord Willoughby surprise and take the town on 20 July. Cavendish, with forces from Newark, lays siege to the town. Sir John Meldrum and Oliver Cromwell come to the Willoughby's aid and defeat the Newark forces, killing the Royalist Commander Charles Cavendish. The Earl of Newcastle arrives with his Northern Army to turn the defeat into a victory for the Royalists.

September – Sir Richard Byron is appointed the governor of Newark.

13 September – Newark forces under the command of Richard Byron attack Nottingham and occupy the town for five days. Parliamentarians under the command of Colonel John Hutchinson maintain control of the town castle.

11 October – The Battle of Winceby. Newark forces under Sir William Widdrington are defeated by a coalition of forces under the commands of the Earl of Manchester, Oliver Cromwell and Thomas Fairfax.

27 November – The Newark Horse raid Melton Mowbray in Leicestershire, capturing many soldiers as well as members of the Parliamentarian committee for the county.

December – The Marquis of Newcastle and his Northern Army overwinter in quarters around his country home at Welbeck.

1644

Early January – Newcastle leaves Nottinghamshire to return north in anticipation of the invasion of Scottish forces now allied with Parliament.

1644

12 January – The Newark Horse raid Grantham and Sleaford and surprise elements of Cromwell's regiment quartered at Waddington and Harmston.

16 January – 3,000 soldiers from Newark under Sir Charles Lucas make another attempt upon Nottingham but are driven out by the Parliamentarian troops.

17 February – Newark troops under Colonel Rowland Hacker make another unsuccessful attempt to capture Nottingham.

29 February – The second siege of Newark by Parliamentarian forces under the command of Sir John Meldrum.

21 March – Prince Rupert arrives at Newark with troops drawn from numerous Royalist garrisons. A stunning military victory over Meldrum brings the second siege to an end.

27 March – Rupert and his forces leave Newark. Local Royalists are once again able to take control of large parts of Lincolnshire.

2 July – The Battle of Marston Moor, outside York. The Duke of Newcastle and Prince Rupert's forces are routed by an alliance of Parliamentarian and Scottish forces. The Northern Royalist Army ceases to exist. Troops previously quartered at Newark are present at the defeat.

4 August – The Newark Horse under Colonel Eyre successfully attack detachments of the Earl of Manchester's army quartered in and around Tuxford. They gain both plunder and colours.

October – Troops from Newark and its satellite garrisons gathering in the vicinity of Belvoir to ride to relieve the Crowland garrison are attacked and routed by Parliamentarians.

18 November – Newark forces quartered outside of the town are attacked and defeated by Parliamentarians under the command of Colonel Rossiter.

December – The Newark garrison is closely monitored by both Nottinghamshire and Lincolnshire Parliamentarian horse regiments.

1645

January – The Newark Horse commanded by Colonel Eyre attack and surprise two troops of Nottinghamshire Horse quartered at Southwell. Sir Richard Willis is appointed the governor of Newark.

28 February – Sir Marmaduke Langdale, with 1,500 Royalist horse, defeats Colonel Rossiter's Parliamentarian force outside Melton Mowbray and marches on to Newark, breaking the blockade of the town.

March – Extensive work on strengthening Newark's defences begins and continues to November, when the third and final siege of the town begins.

30 April – A raiding party from Newark attacks Trent Bridge at Nottingham and captures the fort there, which it holds for over a month.

30 May – The King and his army storm the Parliamentarian town of Leicester. Sir Richard Willis, with 1,200 Newark Horse, takes part in the storming.

June – The 140 carts of plunder and arms taken at Leicester are escorted back to Newark by 400 of the Newark Horse.

14 June – The King's main field army is defeated by the New Model Army under Thomas Fairfax at the Battle of Naseby. Eight hundred of the Newark Horse are attached to Rupert's regiment of Bluecoats in the reserve. Most of the Newark Horse appears to have escaped with the King and returned back to Newark.

18 June – The Newark Horse raiding party under Captain Wright defeats a Parliamentarian force of 200 at Riby in Lincolnshire.

16 July – Newark forces retake possession of Welbeck Abbey, the home of the Duke of Newcastle.

1 August – The Newark Horse raid and destroy Torksey House, Lincolnshire, held by soldiers for Parliament.

27 August – Charles arrives at Newark with the remainder of his horse and stays in the town until 3 November.

10 September – Prince Rupert surrenders the city of Bristol to Thomas Fairfax.

16 October – Rupert arrives at Newark to defend his actions at Bristol to the King. Charles orders him to remain at Belvoir Castle, but the prince ignores the command and rides into the town with Willis and the town mayor. Charges against Rupert are dismissed.

26 October – To defuse growing tensions within the Newark garrison, the King dismisses Willis and appoints John Lord Bellasis as the new governor.

27 October – Rupert takes offence at the dismissal of his friend Willis, and, along with Willis, Gerard, Prince Maurice and supporters, he leaves Newark and applies to Parliament for passes to go overseas.

3 November – Parliamentarians storm Newark's satellite garrison at Shelford, killing 140 of the defenders and its governor. Charles leaves Newark to ride to Oxford as the storming was occurring.

9 November – The example of Shelford encourages the Royalist garrison at Wiverton to surrender on terms.

Mid-November – The governor of Newark sends two-thirds of the garrison's horse to the Royalist garrison at Lichfield in anticipation of the forthcoming siege.

22 November – Parliamentarians under Poyntz fail to storm Belvoir Castle. The decision is made to leave a small besieging force whilst Poyntz goes with the rest of the Northern Association Army to the developing siege at Newark.

25 November – Scottish forces under the command of General Leven arrive to the west side of Newark and swiftly take control of the island opposite the castle and town. This marks the official beginning of the third and final siege.

December – Three hundred Royalists sally out of Newark and attack the quarters of Colonel Rossiter.

1646

January – A large force of the Newark garrison sallies out and attacks General Poyntz's quarters, taking many prisoners and almost capturing Poyntz before returning to the town.

2 March – Plague reappears in Newark after disappearing over the harsh winter.

5 March – Newark forces attack the Scottish forces on the island opposite the town.

28 March – The first summons to surrender is issued to the Newark garrison.

5 May – Charles surrenders himself to the Scottish army outside Newark. He orders Lord Bellasis to surrender the town on the best terms that he can achieve for his soldiers and the town.

6 May – Articles of surrender are signed.

8 May – Royalist soldiers march out of Newark, leaving their weapons behind a day earlier than expected because of the plague. The majority return to their homes, as there are few other Royalist garrisons to go to.

List of Abbreviations

The following abbreviations are used in the Notes.

BL – British Library
CCC – Calendar of the (Proceedings of the) Committee for Compounding
CSPD – Calendar of State Papers Domestic
EEBO – Early English Books Online, <https://proquest.libguides.com/eebopqp>
HC Journal – Journal of the House of Commons
HL Journal – Journal of the House of Lords
HMSO – His/Her Majesty's Stationery Office
NA – Nottinghamshire Archives
NCWC – National Civil War Centre – Newark Museum
NUMD – Nottingham University Manuscripts Department
RCHM – Royal Commission on Historical Monuments
TNA – The National Archives
TT – Thomason Tracts

Preface

When we started to explore the possibility of restoring the Grade II Star Old Magnus Buildings into a National Civil War Centre – Newark Museum (NCWC), we established an academic panel who could help direct us to the stories we should be telling, check our interpretation for accuracy and ensure we were not perpetuating old stereotypes and clichés. One of the first to join the panel was Stuart Jennings, who had already published *These Uncertaine Tymes*, about the civilian experience of the First Civil War in Newark, in 2009.

Since those initial meetings in 2012, Dr Jennings has become a personal friend as well as a friend and advocate for NCWC, which opened in May 2015. He is always happy to assist in enquiries from members of the public when we do not have the depth of knowledge to be able to fully answer. Dr Jennings was also instrumental in urging us to arrange the return of over 90 documents from the 1640s that had been on loan to Nottinghamshire Archives. He had worked on these documents whilst researching *These Uncertaine Tymes*, and they are now available to researchers in the place they were produced, during the time Newark was besieged by Parliamentarian and later Scots forces. They provide a fascinating glimpse into how daily life carried on.

We are now proud to be asked to write this Preface to Dr Jennings' new book on the military aspects of Newark's prominent role in the First Civil War (1642–1646). The town became known as 'The Key to the North' due to its key strategic location at the crossroads of the Great North Road and the Fosse Way and was the last crossing point of the River Trent before it became tidal. As you will discover, it was visited on numerous occasions by King Charles I and his wife, Queen Henrietta Maria, and was the site of a quarrel between Charles I and his nephew Prince Rupert, who was also the town's saviour in 1644. A visit to Newark can take in many of the buildings and fortifications where the events described in Dr Jennings' book took place. At NCWC, we hope to let visitors find out more about not only local events but also wider national and international events related to the Civil Wars. The story we tell would undoubtedly be poorer without Dr Jennings and our other academic panel members' input.

The last in-depth book about Newark's role in the Civil War was the 1964 HMSO publication *Newark on Trent: The Civil War Siegeworks*, although there was a booklet by Tim Warner published by Nottinghamshire County Council in 1992. Much has changed over the intervening years, not least the opening of NCWC, so we are delighted that a new account of Newark's crucial part in the Civil Wars is being written, and there could be no better person to take on that job than Dr Stuart Jennings.

We look forward to continuing our friendship with Dr Jennings and thank him for his continued support of NCWC.

Glyn Hughes – Exhibitions and Collections Manager, National Civil War Centre – Newark Museum

Kevin Winter – Exhibitions and Collections Officer, National Civil War Centre – Newark Museum

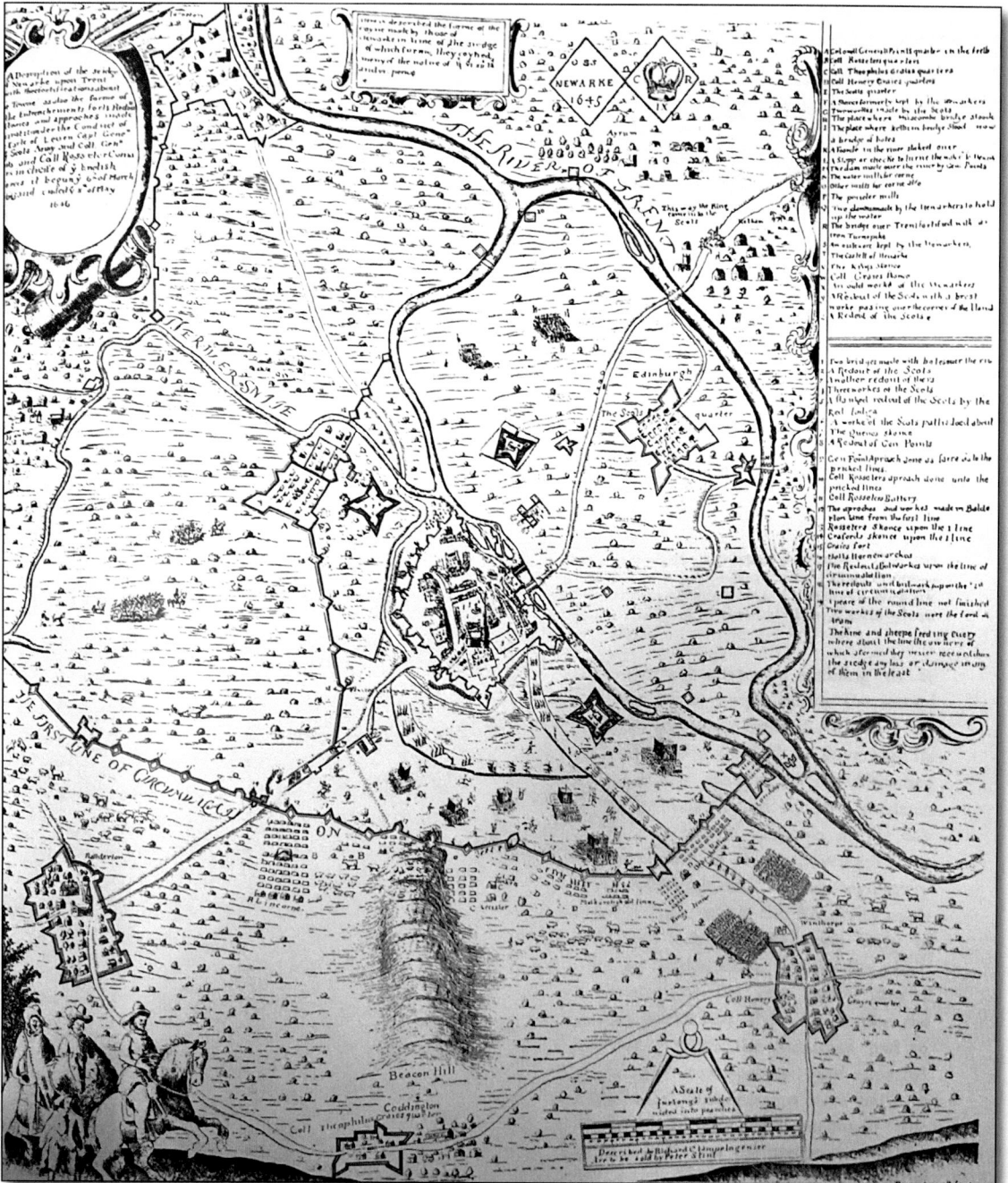

Plate of the final siege works around Newark, drawn from a copy in the British Museum taken from Cornelius Brown, *A History of Newark-on-Trent* (1907). (National Civil War Centre)

Introduction

The motto on the coat of arms of Newark reads, '*Deo Fretus Erumpe*', which literally translates as 'trust God and sally forth'. These were words that the mayor of Newark spoke to the governor of the town garrison after he had received instructions from his King to surrender the town on 6 May 1646. The town had previously endured two sieges and was by then nearly six months into a third siege. Provisions were becoming increasingly limited, but ammunition was in plentiful supply, and the will to continue was there for the soldiers as well as certain sections of the civilian population. There was a real concern for the defenders that the King's instruction, conveyed to the town by the besiegers, might limit any terms they could obtain for the safety of soldiers and officers as well as the security of the civilians and their property within the town. It is not surprising then that John Lord Bellasis, the military governor, read the King's letter to the town corporation with tears in his eyes.

The articles of surrender finally signed later that evening proved to be more generous than all had expected, and the presence of a serious outbreak of plague within the town ensured that they were meticulously observed. It was probably the presence of this pestilence that guaranteed the survival of many of the town's civic and ecclesiastical records from over the period of the war, the survival of a number of the siege works and the partial slighting of Newark's castle. The western curtain wall of the castle, looking out over the River Trent, survived almost to its full height, and the shell of the impressive twelfth-century gatehouse, which acts as a sentinel over the river crossing, is almost complete, with only the roof and floors missing.

Newark coat of arms with the motto '*Deo Fretus Frumpe*', which means 'trust God and sally forth'. (Reproduced under the Creative Commons Licence, copyright J. Hannan-Briggs)

Situated where the Great North Road and the Fosse Way cross the River Trent, Newark was an important link between the north of the country with London and the south. Secured early in the war by the Royalists and turned into a garrisoned town, it became a strategic communications centre between the King's headquarters at Oxford and the main Royalist northern base at the city of York. It also became a considerable thorn in Parliament's side, with the many horse regiments based there at different times (often identified generically as the 'Newark Horse') raiding and collecting contributions across much of the East Midlands right up until the final siege. It also supplied both men and materials for three of the main Civil War battles fought in England, the Battles of Edgehill, Marston Moor and Naseby.

The town of Newark provides, even up until the present day, an excellent case study for Civil War sieges and their works. Apart from the remains of the works that can still be seen on the ground, there also survives two contemporary plans of the final works, one compiled by the Royalists at Newark, which can still be viewed at the National Civil War Centre (NCWC), and the other compiled for the besieging Parliamentarian forces by Richard Clampe and now in the possession of the Ashmolean Museum in Oxford.[1] The Newark map was drawn on Vellum and is 30in by 31in. At the bottom of the map, the title reads:

> The siege of Newark by the English and Scotch Armies consisting of sixteene thousand men which continued twenty and six weekes, and was surrendered the eight of May 1646, by his Ma[jest]ies Command to the Committe of both Kingdomes for the Parliament.

Map legend on the map of the Newark defences, 1646. (National Civil War Centre, Newark, with permission)

The map is neither dated nor signed, but the details upon it are such that it must be contemporary to either the siege or the immediate aftermath and the surrender of the town. The Parliamentarian siege map was surveyed by the engineer Richard Clampe, who had served initially under the command of the Earl of Manchester and later under Sir Thomas Fairfax, with the New Model Army. The dimensions of the map are 20in by 17in. The address of the printer given on the map shows that it must have been printed before 1650, and the map is illustrated with pictures of incidents from the siege, including the hanging of a spy.[2]

Newark's tenacious commitment to the Royalist cause became a matter of concern for the victorious Parliamentarians but of considerable pride for both the town and those who supported the Royalist cause. After its surrender in May 1646, Parliament ordered Francis Thornhagh and John Hutchinson, with their regiments, to carefully monitor and police the town, and it appears troops were stationed there until after the execution of Charles I in 1649, as bills of payment for those soldiers still survive amongst the

---

1 A full review of the surviving siege works was undertaken in the early 1960s; see Royal Commission on Historical Monuments [RCHM], *Newark on Trent: The Civil War Siegeworks* (London: HMSO, 1964).

2 Peter Young, *Civil War England* (London: Longman Group, 1981), pp.88–90.

Borough Miscellaneous papers.[3] During the Rule of the Major Generals in 1655, Edward Whalley was appointed to oversee the East Midlands region. His family roots lay at Screveton, a village just under 10 miles away from Newark, and so his local connections enabled him to keep a close watch of the town, but he also spent periods of time accommodated in Newark.[4]

Interest in and admiration for Newark over the period of the Civil War begins to appear both in publications and private diaries from an early date. John Evelyn wrote in his diary as early as 1654 of Newark as that 'brave Towne and Garrison'.[5] Just over 50 years later, Daniel Defoe published praise for Newark's history when he wrote of the town:

> At Newark one can hardly see without regret the ruins of that famous castle, which maintained itself through the whole civil war in England, and keeping a strong garrison there for the king, cut off the greatest pass in the north that is in the whole kingdom; not was it taken, 'till the king, pressed by the calamity of his affairs, put himself into the hands of the Scots army, which lay before it, and then commanded the governor to deliver it up, after which it was demolished, that the great road might lie open and free.[6]

The nineteenth century witnessed several local histories published about the history of Newark. This renewed interest coincided with the publication of a number of diaries and memoirs that mentioned the role of Newark during the Civil War, amongst which were the diaries of Henry Slingsby and John Evelyn as well as the *Memoirs* of Lucy Hutchinson. The first significant volume was Dickinson's *History of Newark*, published in 1806. One of the town's most important historians was Cornelius Brown, who published his *Annals of Newark* in 1879 and later his two-volume history of Newark-on-Trent in 1904. Both men began the task of identifying both local and national records that were created at the time of the Civil War. C. H. Firth's edition of Lucy Hutchinson's *Memoirs*, published in 1906, contained extensive footnotes and 37 appendices that linked her narrative to records that survived in The National Archives (TNA). All these resources provided an extensive foundation both for their works and for future research. The surviving archaeological remains in and around the town received extensive surveying and description in the early 1960s by the Royal Commission on Historical Monuments (RCHM).[7]

The current author has been researching and writing about the history of Newark during the Civil War period for over 25 years and, over that time, has published a book, a book chapter and four peer-reviewed academic papers, adding further details to our knowledge about the town. What follows is an

3   National Civil War Centre – Newark Museum (NCWC): NEKMS 2021.19.12–13: Newark Borough Miscellaneous Papers.

4   Christopher Durston, *Cromwell's Major-Generals: Godly Government during the English Revolution* (Manchester: Manchester University Press, 2001), pp.39–43.

5   E. S. de Beer (ed.), *The Diary of John Evelyn* (Oxford: Oxford University Press, 1959), p.347.

6   Daniel Defoe, *A Tour through the Whole Island of Great Britain* (London: Penguin, 1971).

7   All these works are referred to throughout the following narrative and are listed in the Bibliography at the end of the book.

attempt to combine in a single narrative the historical and archaeological information garnered over the generations right up until to the present day. Wherever it is possible, contemporary reports and eyewitness accounts have been incorporated into the narrative. These primary sources are reproduced with original spellings retained, but punctuation is sometimes inserted to aid the reading of them.

1

Newark in the Seventeenth Century

Church, Road and River Crossings at Newark

The tower and spire of St Mary Magdalene at Newark are visible for many miles over the flood plains of the River Trent. Standing at 232ft (71m), it is claimed to be the fifth highest parish church spire in England. In good weather, the towers of Lincoln Cathedral (20 miles), Southwell Minister (8.5 miles) and Belvoir Castle (14.2 miles) can be seen from it.[1]

It was from this tower that John Twentyman watched the lifting of the second siege of Newark by Prince Rupert in 1644. The full panoply of the battle unfolded before him on Beacon Hill, which lay beyond the town's Civil War defences. In the seventeenth century, this was the town's only parish church and was one of the largest parish churches in England, a source of great pride to the town. It was, and still is, a beautifully decorated medieval church built using the proceeds of trade that flowed through the town from the thirteenth century to the fifteenth century. The five bells that resided in the tower in the seventeenth century directed the life, business and worship of the town.[2] In 1642, Charles Handley had been paid 3s 4d 'for ringing 4 and 6 a clocke bell [and] tolling to prayers', and this tradition continued right through the Civil War.[3]

The spire was an important aid to travellers in the seventeenth century, acting as a guide and sentinel to the place where the Fosse Way, running from Exeter to Lincoln (18 miles from Newark), and the Great North Road, running from London (125 miles) via York (81 miles) and then on to Edinburgh, met. Newark had acquired a bridge over the River Trent by the year 1204, which flowed to the west of the town, and, in the seventeenth century, this was the last bridge over the river before the Humber estuary. Technically, there were two bridges, as just before the town the river split into two separate branches,

---

1   Brenda M. Pask, *Newark Parish Church of St. Mary Magdalene* (Newark: District Church Council of St. Mary Magdalene, 2000), p.174.
2   Pask, *Newark Parish Church*, p.184.
3   Nottinghamshire Archives (NA): PR/24810: Newark Churchwarden Accounts, 1642.

Image of St Mary's Church, Newark, from *The Illustrated London News*, 1853. (Author's collection)

which rejoined farther north of the town, forming an island between the branches. The bridge from Newark took you onto the island, and another at Muskham took the traveller over the second arm of the river. The Newark Bridge, at this time, was constructed of timber and underwent major repairs in 1627 and then again in 1653 once the Civil War had ended.[4] There were also a number of places where ferries might be taken to cross the river, but these were much less reliable and were often limited in the winter months by the flow of the river. The River Trent was a significant contributor to the

---

4   Anon., *Calendar of State Papers Domestic* [*CSPD*] (London: HMSO, 1860–1897), 1653–1654, p.19.

wealth of the town, being navigable southwards to Nottingham and north up to the Humber estuary and Hull. Newark thrived on trade, with products from farming, such as wool, leather and hides, coupled with the traffic of corn and coal along the river, all bringing considerable income into the town. Travellers and merchants often passed through the town on the way to Lincoln or York and could break their journey by staying at one of the several inns in the town.[5] All these factors were to make the town an important place to occupy and control for both parties once the Civil War began in 1642.

Town, Medieval Walls and Gates

'Prospect of Newark from Hawton Way' by Richard Hall, 1676. Plate taken from Robert Thoroton's *Antiquities of Newark* (1677). (Author's collection)

At the start of the seventeenth century, Newark still possessed its medieval walls and gates, though in places the walls were in a ruinous state and there had been ribbon development of houses beyond them alongside the roads leading out of the town. The gates in the walls provided access into the town, but their narrow entrances and the very confined streets within the walls caused considerable congestion, especially on market days. It was in these narrow, crowded streets by the town gates that the poor tended to dwell. Outdoor earth privies serving several households, hen coops and other animals kept in small pens added to the overall squalor of these districts, making them excellent breeding grounds for disease. The situation was to get worse over the period of the Civil War, as houses beyond the town's defensive circuit were demolished and their occupants were moved into the town, forcing many of the poorer to move into these districts. The two poorest districts were Barnby Gate and North Gate, both of which were adjacent to the final outer defences constructed in 1645. As late as the 1664 Hearth Tax

---

5   Stuart B. Jennings, *'These Uncertaine Tymes': Newark and the Civilian Experience of the Civil Wars, 1640–1660* (Nottingham: Nottinghamshire County Council, 2009), p.6.

returns, these two districts still showed the largest numbers of households in Newark exempt from paying the tax because of their poverty.[6]

It was often in these overcrowded areas that the saltpetre men were particularly active both over the 1630s and during the Civil War, causing both a nuisance and a lot of angst amongst its inhabitants. Saltpetre (potassium nitrate) was an essential ingredient in the manufacture of gunpowder in the early modern period. It had been a royal monopoly since the sixteenth century, and, as the use of cannons, muskets and firearms became increasingly essential for modern armies, obtaining large quantities of it became crucial. Saltpetre was a by-product of bird droppings and human urine, and government officials (saltpetre men), under the royal prerogative, had authority to enter any property they chose to dig and remove the soil from henhouses and privies. Although they were not supposed to remove soil from buildings occupied by people, saltpetre men felt that the royal monopoly gave them a degree of autonomy to dig where they wanted. It was areas where there were large numbers of inhabitants of low social status that the saltpetre men generally targeted, as their status meant they could object the least. In 1638, saltpetre men in certain parts of England even had the audacity to dig up floors of churches 'because women pisse in their seats which causes saltpetre'.[7] They were unlikely to have gained permission to do so at Newark church, though. The policy of William Laud, Archbishop of Canterbury, to bring uniformity and beauty to the fabric of all churches in the 1630s meant that, between 1636 and 1637, the churchwardens at Newark had paid out over £240 to make the pews 'seemly and uniform' and repave an estimated area of 3,200 square feet of the church floor.[8] Local saltpetre men would have faced the wrath of both the town and ecclesiastical authorities trying to undo this costly renovation. As the Bishops' Wars transitioned into the Civil War between 1640 and 1646, the demand for saltpetre became even more essential, especially to meet the Newark garrison's requirements for gunpowder. For the citizens of Newark, the disruption and upheaval of this period must have been considerable. A testimony to the ongoing work of the saltpetre men, and their continued unpopularity, can be found in the constable's accounts for the neighbouring parish of Upton, where, in 1645, they spent 1s plying the saltpetre official with ale and then proceeded to hand over a bribe of 5s 6d for the 'salt peeter man to goe from our towne'.[9]

In 1642, Newark was a town of predominately timber-framed houses with thatched roofs, though a privileged few still possessed large gardens. Fire was a regular concern for the town authorities. Despite the close proximity of the river, there were regular instructions to its citizens to keep fire buckets by their front doors. The corporation constantly monitored the condition of the town's fire-fighting equipment, which was stored at the parish church.

---

6   Jennings, *These Uncertaine Tymes*, pp.76–77.

7   David Cressy, 'Saltpetre, State Security and Vexation in Early Modern England', *Past and Present*, 212 (2011), pp.73–111.

8   Pask, *Newark Parish Church*, p.77.

9   Martyn Bennett (ed.), *A Nottinghamshire Village in War and Peace: The Accounts of the Constables of Upton, 1640-1666* (Nottingham: Thoroton Society, 1995), p.32.

An inventory of the equipment kept there in 1629 lists, 'three draggs, twelve buckets and a pole to pull them downe', all essential if or when the thatched roofs caught fire.[10] Summer was always a vulnerable time, as the dry weather tended to make the thatch more combustible. The equipment and the fire watches were to become even more essential components of civic life over the period of the Civil War. Within the medieval walls of the town, there were only three stone-built buildings: the castle (see below), the parish church and the sixteenth-century Magnus Schoolroom. During the Civil War, the castle and schoolroom would become essential as secure places of storage for munitions and provisions, especially during bombardments. The church was spared and retained for worship, but there is evidence to suggest that, during the third and final siege, part of the roof may have been stripped of its lead in order to make musket balls.[11] Beyond the walls just above the North Gate of the town lay the Spittal, a stone-built residence of the Countess of Exeter that, by 1644, had become nothing more than a shell and was finally demolished in 1645 to build the King's Sconce.[12]

Newark Castle

1769 print of the west curtain wall of Newark Castle. Engraver unknown. (Author's collection)

Newark Castle was actually a fortified Bishop's Palace built early in the twelfth century for Alexander Bishop of Lincoln to command this important crossing from the north of England. By the Reformation, it had reverted to royal control but had been leased out by the Crown to a succession of wealthy tenants before Charles I bestowed it upon his bride, Henrietta Maria,

---

10   Nottinghamshire Archives (NA): DC/NW/3/1/1: Newark Borough Corporation Minutes.
11   Jennings, *These Uncertaine Tymes*, p.113.
12   Alfred C. Wood, *Nottinghamshire in the Civil War* (Wakefield: S. R. Reprint, 1971), pp.40–41.

as a wedding gift in 1625. Throughout much of the sixteenth century, a succession of aristocratic tenants had spent large sums of money turning the castle into a luxurious home. William Cecil, Lord Burghley, spent large sums of money inserting extra fireplaces and large windows as well as turning its big chambers into smaller apartments for accommodation. In 1607 alone, he had spent £400 on the fabric of the building. All these alterations were to have significant consequences for the building's defensive capabilities. The large oriel window inserted into the curtain wall on the west side of the castle would have been little use against cannon fire from an enemy on the island opposite, as happened in 1646. Complaints about the castle's military potential had been expressed to Henry VIII as early as 1539, when he was informed that it had 'scant lodgings for a 100 men and no water'.[13] Although it was luxurious enough to entertain both James I and Charles I on visits to the town in the first part of the century, it was by then no longer adequate to accommodate a large number of soldiers, such as would have been required for a garrison.

Inns, Taverns and Mills

For brewing and milling, access to an adequate supply of water is essential. For every pint of beer brewed, it has been estimated that up to 90 litres of water were required, and beer was a staple part of the diet of most people in seventeenth-century England.[14] Likewise, for a watermill to function, a constant flow of water is required to drive the mechanical process. Newark was fortunate in having an ample supply of running water, as there was the River Trent bordering the town on the west side and the River Devon, which joined the Trent just to the south of the town. During the Civil War, these two rivers were to become an integral part of the defensive network around the town.

Situated, as it was, adjacent to the Great North Road and the Fosse Way, over the sixteenth century, Newark increasingly became a service centre not only for travellers but also for the surrounding parishes, as they came into the town on the market days of Wednesday and Friday. Amongst the surviving corporation miscellaneous papers, there exists a list of 'Brewers and Tipplers' within the town in 1609. This lists 54 Brewers and 24 tippling houses within Newark.[15] Alongside these, there were numerous taverns and inns, some of which are still standing in the town, that provided accommodation for travellers. During the period of the Civil War, when few travelled far because of the conflict, a number of the inns in Newark became accommodation for

---

13 Stuart B. Jennings, 'Controlling Disease in a Civil-War Garrison Town: Military Discipline or Civic Duty? The Surviving Evidence for Newark-upon-Trent, 1642–1646', in D. J. Appleby and A. Hopper (eds), *Battle-Scarred: Mortality, Medical Care and Military Welfare in the British Civil Wars* (Manchester: Manchester University Press, 2018), pp.42–44.

14 Anon., 'The Main Ingredient in Beer is Water', *BWT* (2018), <https://www.bwtshop.co.uk/the-main-ingredient-in-beer-is-water/>, accessed 7 Sept. 2022.

15 R. F. B. Hodgkinson (ed.), *Extracts from the Records of the Borough of Newark-upon-Trent* (Newark: Newark Herald, 1921), p.21.

officers and soldiers at the Royalist garrison and, as will be shown later, in some cases could be associated with particular regiments.

At the start of the seventeenth century, there were a growing number of mills for grinding corn and fulling cloth along the Rivers Devon and Trent. As early as 1534, a surviving lease records that Anthony Foster was running five corn mills and two fulling mills, and, by 1700, the figure had risen considerably.[16] Once the town was garrisoned in 1642, alongside these mills would also appear a number of mills for milling gunpowder, which also required large amounts of water to extract the saltpetre from the earth gathered from the privies and chicken coops. Although originally these mills largely lay beyond the town walls, as the war progressed, they were brought within the circuit of the earthwork defences.

Demographics of Newark in the Seventeenth Century

Estimating the population of the town of Newark in the seventeenth century is fraught with difficulty because surviving documents from the period are usually more concerned with taxation than the size of the population. The Nottinghamshire historian Professor A. C. Wood estimated that 70 burials recorded in the parish registers for the period of 1599–1600 would suggest a population of over 2,000 at the start of the century.[17] Other work on a larger sample of the parish register data has yielded an estimated population of around 2,774, but the multiplier used in this calculation is now generally thought to be too high. The best that can be assumed about the town's population is that it lay between 2,000 and 2,400 people for the first part of the seventeenth century. Once the garrison was established at Newark in 1642, the population of the town doubled overnight, and, in 1643, with the arrival of the Queen and her army, the population almost quadrupled. The town and surrounding parishes had to struggle to accommodate and provide for these extra bodies, and, in 1642, it began from a very vulnerable position. The fact that they managed to do so is a testimony to the resilience of Newark and its people.

The 1630s proved to be a time of demographic and economic hardship for Newark. There was a succession of bad harvests recorded across much of the country, with 1630 being described as a bad harvest and 1632 and 1637 as 'deficient harvests'. Of the remaining years of the decade, six were classed as 'average', and only 1639 was described as a 'good harvest'.[18] Such low yields led to a decline in the grain trade along the River Trent, causing hardship for Newark's merchants. It unfortunately also coincided with the departure of a number of gentry from the town. Alongside these harvest deficits, mortality

16   M. W. Barley, 'Newark in the Sixteenth Century', *Transactions of the Thoroton Society*, 53 (1949), pp.16–17.

17   Alfred C. Wood, 'A Note on the Population of Nottingham in the 17th Century', *Transactions of the Thoroton Society of Nottinghamshire*, 40 (1936), pp.109–13.

18   W. G. Hoskins, 'Harvest Fluctuations and English Economic History, 1620–1759', *The Agricultural History Review*, 16:1 (1968), pp.15–31.

rates for adults within Newark increased. The mean average of deaths per year for the 1620s had been just below 52, but, for the 1630s, this rose to 70.9, although the latter part of the 1630s did witness a significant improvement in mortality rates. The loss of these adults would have had a dramatic impact upon the size of the town's population. The years 1631–1635 also saw the total number of children buried amount to 420, giving a mean annual average of 84, far in excess of anything experienced in the decades prior to the Civil War and this was only for a five-year period.[19] These economic and demographic hardships, coupled with growing rates of taxation, through ship money and coat and conduct levies for the Bishops' Wars, meant that a phenomenal effort and sacrifice had to be made by the civilians of Newark to support the Royalist cause after 1642.[20]

Newark Borough Corporation

Until 1547, the town of Newark was part of the manor owned by the Bishops of Lincoln, with the Guilds of Corpus Christi and Holy Trinity having considerable authority over the day-to-day affairs of both the church and town.[21] An exchange of land with the Crown in that year brought it under the remit of the king, Edward VI, and, within two years, a first Charter of Newark was issued at Westminster, with corporate responsibility within the town being granted to an alderman and 12 assistants. A fifth charter issued in 1626 changed the post of alderman into that of mayor, and his 12 assistants became 12 aldermen. The charter also allowed for the appointment of a town recorder. By 1640, most of the town's economic and public affairs fell clearly within the jurisdiction of this corporation, consisting of mayor and aldermen.

Election to the post of alderman was confined to the 13 members of the corporation, and, by the middle of the seventeenth century, it had become, in effect, a self-perpetuating oligarchy. The Civil War and interregnum (1640–1660) certainly challenged this oligarchy but never really dismantled it. The post of alderman, whilst underlining social status within the town, could be quite onerous, and so a series of heavy fines, or even a short period of imprisonment, could be imposed on those who refused to take up office when elected or failed to attend to their duties. The post of alderman was usually granted for life unless the individual left the town or 'in respecte of sickness and other weaknesse in bodie' was unable to continue.[22]

The establishment of trade, the appointment of freeman and the oversight of apprentices within Newark all fell under the remit of the corporation. Anyone who moved into the town and sought to establish a trade had to pay the sum of £5 as a bond. Apprentices, on the completion of their training, were obliged to appear before the mayor and alderman to swear an oath of

---

19   Jennings, *These Uncertaine Tymes*, pp.63–65.
20   For the civilian experience of the war, see Jennings, *These Uncertaine Tymes*.
21   Much of what follows is derived from Jennings, *These Uncertaine Tymes*, pp.10–11.
22   NA: DC/NW/3/1/1: Borough Minutes, entries for 3 January 1636 and 27 March 1640.

allegiance to the king and affirm their consent to abide by the rules of the borough and pay all tolls as required. Then, and only then, would they be recorded as a freeman and allowed to practice their trade.

The borough corporation shared control of the town with the Lord of the Manor, which, as we have seen, was the Crown. Profits from certain fairs and the right to force all inhabitants of the town to take their grain for milling at the lord's mills all belonged to the Crown. Ownership of the manor belonged from 1625 to Charles I, and later Queen Henrietta Maria, up until the execution of Charles in 1649. For the Crown, the manor proved to be a considerable source of income, but surviving records suggest that it rarely interfered with the mayor and aldermen's administration of town affairs, as long as it continued to receive its dues and payments.

The fact that the town had a long, close and agreeable relationship with the Crown for nearly two decades before the Civil War began might possibly be one factor that contributed to its commitment to the Royalist cause. By 1642, the corporation had long been used to running its own affairs, but surviving evidence from the years 1642–1646 strongly suggests that, apart from the period of the governorship of Sir Richard Willis, the relationship between the military and civic authorities was amicable and worked well. The civilian experience of the Civil War within Newark has been explored elsewhere in an earlier publication, so this book will now focus on the military history of the town over the course of the First Civil War.[23]

Newark and Ship Money

During a period in which Charles I governed the country without calling a Parliament (1629–1640), the Crown's need to raise finances led to a number of perceived innovations to extract payments for the royal coffers. The most controversial and significant of the King's impositions, increasingly so as the decade progressed, was the extension of the ship money levy from seaports to all English counties from 1635. This levy had initially been imposed just on ports and coastal counties to finance the navy. The first writ of 1635 saw Newark being assessed at £110, and surviving evidence shows that the town had been able to meet this.[24] By 1637, the town was economically struggling, and, by 18 September, it had only been able to meet £50 of the £120 levy, though, by the end of the first quarter of 1638, the outstanding amount had been reduced to £20.[25]

A nationwide economic hardship, coupled with lower naval requirements than expected, meant that the levy set by the Crown in 1638 was considerably lower. Newark was required to raise the sum of £45, but even this proved difficult to meet from within the town. The corporation took the unprecedented action of petitioning the Star Chamber, as there was no

---

23   See Jennings, *These Uncertaine Tymes*.

24   M. D. Gordon, 'The Collection of Ship-Money in the Reign of Charles I', *Transactions of the Royal Historical Society*, 4 (1910), pp.142–62.

25   Anon., *CSPD*, 1637, 18 September 1637, p.423.

Parliament to approach, seeking a further reduction. In this, they complained 'Of being over-rated towards the business of shipping, viz. smallness of trade; the poorness of the people; the absence of gentlemen and able men that dwelt there and contributed to former taxes but are now removed, that £45 considering the weak estate of the town is more than double the proportion laid on other towns in that country'.[26]

Sir Francis Thornhagh, then Sheriff of Nottingham, was instructed by the Privy Council to examine the circumstances around Newark's petition, but that did not stop a further levy of £120 being set for Newark in 1639. The Sheriff reported back to the Privy Council, 'I took into consideration the poor estate of Newark and in accordance with your former directions … have eased the town of £40 and imposed it upon the body of the county'.[27]

Across most of the country, including Newark, very little of the 1639 levy was collected as political events unfolded. The Bishops' War with Scotland and the summoning of a Parliament by the King halted the collection of ship money.

Ship money has often been spoken of as one of a number of catalysts that sparked the descent into civil war. In Newark, it certainly created hardship and disaffection within the town, but it proved to have little long-term effect on its subsequent allegiance to the King once his standard was raised in Nottingham in 1642.

The economic and social developments within the town over the 1630s, whilst shared with many other communities across England, give little hint of its subsequent commitment to the Royalist cause over the course of the Civil War.

---

26   Anon., *CSPD*, 1639, 8 May 1639, p.134.
27   Anon., *CSPD*, 1639–1640, 8 May 1639, p.134.

2

The War Begins: From the Raising of the Royal Standard (1642) to the First Siege (27 February 1643)

All of the nobility and the gentry, and their dependants were generally for the king ... The greatest family was the Earl of Newcastle.[1]

On 22 August 1642, Charles I raised his royal standard at Nottingham Castle. This was a rallying call to all his supporters to assemble for military service and, as such, amounted to a declaration of war against Parliament. The reality was that these two protagonists had been at loggerheads since 1640, and outbreaks of violence and manoeuvring had been happening around England weeks before this event. Lucy Hutchinson's comments at the beginning of this chapter reflect how she witnessed the situation in her own county of Nottinghamshire.

The Road to War

For 11 years from 1629, Charles I had managed to rule his kingdom without a Parliament. Over this period of 'personal rule', a growing angst grew across the country, focusing particularly on issues such as taxation, religion and what was perceived as arbitrary justice being dispensed via the Star Chamber. It was the war with Scotland, fuelled by the arbitrary introduction of a new prayer book into that kingdom, that became the issue necessitating the recall of Parliament by the King. He needed to raise both money and provisions for his army, which would be best achieved via an elected Parliament. The Short Parliament – so called because it only sat for three weeks (13 April–5 May 1642) – proved to be more concerned with redressing grievances caused by

---

1   Neil H. Keeble (ed.), *Memoirs of the Life of Colonel Hutchinson* (London: J. Dent, 1995).

A true and exact Relation of the

manner of his Maiefties fetting up of His
Standard at *Nottingham*, on Munday the
22. of Auguſt 1642.

Firſt, The forme of the Standard, as it is here figured, and who were pre-
ſent at the advancing of it

Secondly, The danger of fetting up of former Standards, and the damage
which enſued thereon.

Thirdly, A relation of all the Standards that ever were ſet up by any King.

Fourthly, the names of thoſe Knights who are appointed to be the Kings
Standard-bearers. With the forces that are appoynted to guard it.

Fifthly, The manner of the Kings comming firſt to *Coventry*.

Sixtly, The *Cavalieres* reſolution and dangerous threats which they have
uttered, if the King concludes a peace without them, or hearkens unto
his great Councell the Parliament : Moreover how they have ſhared
and divided *London* amongſt themſelves already.

Nottingham.

London, printed for *F. Coles.* 1642,

1642 tract describing the raising of the royal standard entitled 'A true and exact Relation'. (Author's collection)

the King's personal rule than in voting funds to fight against the Scots. In fact, a number of members of Parliament (MPs) probably sympathised with the Scots for resisting such an arbitrary imposition upon their church. The King swiftly dissolved this Parliament, but the deteriorating situation during the Second Bishops' War resulted in the Scottish army invading northern England and occupying Newcastle at the end of August 1640. Charles urgently needed to call a second Parliament to raise the necessary funds required to pay off the Scottish army so that it left England and returned back to Scotland. Thus, what came to be known as the 'Long Parliament' (1640–1660) was convened at Westminster on 3 November 1640.

The dire financial straight that the King found himself in, coupled with the growing distrust of the King's motives and actions by a majority of MPs, resulted in a growing and increasingly bitter rift between the Crown and Commons. As the acrimony increased, so also did the growing crowds assembling outside Westminster to expressly support the Commons. As a result, Charles became progressively concerned both for his and his family's safety, and so, on 10 January 1642, he left London and was not to see his capital again until his trial in 1649. Over the next seven months, the increasing attempts of Parliament, under the leadership of John Pym, both to protect its own rights and privileges as well as to curtail the King's command of the military and his appointment of court officials began to stimulate both concern and growing support for the King amongst some of the gentry. By August, the King found himself back in Nottingham, and war was formally declared. This is where the account of Newark's part in the First Civil War begins.

Raising the Royal Standard and the Early Months of the War

It remains unclear why Charles chose Nottingham to be the place where he raised his royal standard. As the quote by Lucy Hutchinson at the start of this chapter clearly demonstrates, the county was one of divided loyalties. The response to the summons in the city of Nottingham was very disappointing for the King. The strength of support for Charles across England tended to be focussed in the north-west, the Devonian peninsula and Wales. It may be that the King believed that the town was the nearest place to London where he could safely muster his supporters. He may also have chosen the town of Nottingham, as it was accessible from the Humber estuary by the River Trent, where he hoped further support would arrive from. Generally, across the county though, even those who were later to become firm supporters of either protagonist, the majority response was to hold back from making an instant commitment and hope that an accommodation between Charles and his Parliament might still be arrived at. Parliament was not too impressed with those who even initially rallied to the King at Nottingham. A contemporary Parliamentarian tract of the time notes, 'His Majesties Army doth not consist of above four thousand Horse and Foot, and many of the Horses very unserviceable, and the men the very scumme of the Countrey, being for the greatest leud and idle persons.'[2]

Given that many of the gentry in Nottinghamshire rallied to the standard in August, the comments about the serviceability of the horse and the status of their riders seem to be a piece of Parliamentarian propaganda that failed to hit the mark for the county. The Battle of Edgehill on 23 October 1642 was to shatter the hope of any negotiated settlement being reached before major violence occurred, though talks both nationally and within Nottinghamshire continued to December.[3]

---

2   John Brown, *His Majesties Resolution Concerning the Setting Up of His Standard at Nottingham* ... (London: J. Hansott, 1642).

3   Wood, *Nottinghamshire in the Civil War*, pp.23–28.

Newark and the villages around it proved to be an exception to this general trend. Both Lord Newark (Henry Pierrepont), the lord lieutenant of the county, and the Sheriff of Nottingham (Sir John Digby) proved to have some sympathy for the King, and this was transformed into loyalty when they attempted to rally the local militia to unsuccessfully seize the main part of the county magazine (some of it was at Newark) then mainly based at Nottingham. On 11 July 1642, Charles was at Newark with the Sheriff and Lord Newark to address the gentry and freeholders of the town. The King's speech reflected his perception of the loyalty of the town. In his address, Charles said, 'I go to other places to confirm and undeceive my subjects, but I am come here only to thank and encourage you. I ask nothing of you (although your demeanour gives me good evidence that you are not willing to deny) but to preserve your own affections for the religion and law establish.'[4]

The reason for Newark's staunch royalism has long been a matter of conjecture. The most likely explanation lies in the fact that the Crown was a principal landowner both in and around the town. At the Reformation, control of Newark Castle had reverted back to the monarch, who had rented it out to a series of tenants into the early years of the seventeenth century. In 1625, Charles had presented the castle to his Queen, Henrietta Maria, as a wedding gift.[5] Both James I, and more frequently his son, Charles I, had often visited Newark, and the latter, it was claimed, was apparently well liked by the townspeople.[6]

Charles returned to his base at York later that same day after addressing the gentry and freeholders, but Lord Newark stayed on to address the trained bands that he had summoned to assemble at Newark on 13 July. Technically, Parliament had withdrawn his appointment as lord lieutenant of the shire, but Lord Newark drew attention to the royal commission of array confirming his appointment. The trained bands obeyed and turned out on this occasion, but they proved to be less responsive at the raising of the standard.

On 22 August, the gentry, their tenants and freeholders of land around and within Newark proved to be much more responsive to the summons of their King. William Staunton of Staunton-in-the-Vale, a parish that lay just six miles to the south of Newark, came to Nottingham with his sons, servants and tenants. They were to form the core of the troop of horse he was to command throughout the Civil War. Later, whilst based at Newark, Staunton was issued with a commission to also raise a regiment of foot. His troop of horse later had the task of collecting the assessment to provision his soldiers from villages around Nottinghamshire.[7] John the future Lord Bellasis, who held land in Holme (six miles north of Newark), joined the King at Nottingham with some of his tenants. Lord Bellasis was to be the

---

4   Wood, *Nottinghamshire in the Civil War*, p.16.

5   Jennings, 'Controlling Disease', p.42.

6   Tim Warner, *Newark: Civil War and Siegeworks* (Nottingham: Nottinghamshire County Council, 1992), p.7.

7   Martyn Bennett, Stuart Jennings, and Martin Whyld, 'Two Military Account Books for the Civil War in Nottinghamshire', *Transactions of the Thoroton Society of Nottinghamshire*, 100 (1996), pp.107–21.

My Lord Newarks
SPEECH
To the Trained-bands of
Nottingham-shire at *Newark,*
13. July 1642.

Concerning His MAIESTIES
Commiffion of Array.

LONDON,
Printed by *Edward Griffin.* 1642.

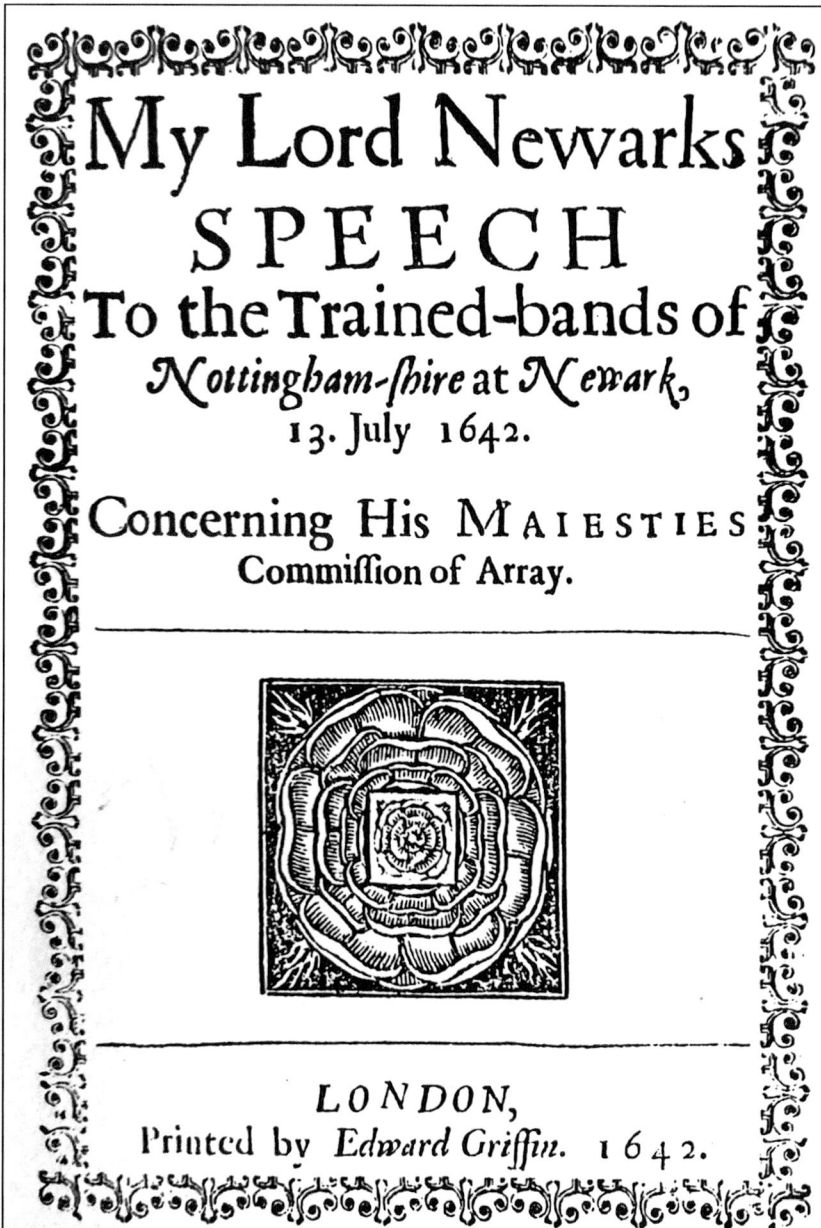

Lord Newark's speech to the trained bands assembled at Newark, 1642 pamphlet. (Author's collection)

final governor of the Newark garrison before it was ordered to surrender by the King in 1646. Gervase Holles arrived at the standard with an equipped company of soldiers he had recruited at Newark. His cousin William also rallied to the King and was later to be slain at Newark in March 1644.[8] The Byron family of Newstead Abbey were also with the King at Nottingham, with the second son, Sir Richard Byron, going on to serve as a future governor of the Newark garrison from the end of 1643. All the above and their recruits

---

8   Wood, *Nottinghamshire in the Civil War,* p.219.

were at the Battle of Edgehill on 23 October. This was to leave the town of Newark devoid of many of its most active Royalists for the next three months.

Of the 35 individuals who were nominated to serve on the Nottinghamshire Royalist commission of array in 1642, research by Professor Bennett went on to show that only nine could be deemed to have been active within the county over the duration of the war. From the beginning of 1643, these individuals, drawn predominantly from the upper ranks of Nottinghamshire's gentry, were based at Newark and remained there throughout the course of the war. Eight of the nominees went on to serve the Royalist cause beyond the boundaries of Nottinghamshire, whilst Parliamentarians captured another two early on in the war, and so they were unable to function. William Staunton, also an appointee, was at Newark for most of the war, where he served as the colonel of a regiment of foot and a troop of horse, so military matters probably limited his functioning as a commissioner.[9] Being local to the Newark region, most of Staunton's soldiers and troopers were probably recruited locally from 1642 onwards, and so he was fulfilling this aspect of the role of a commissioner. The primary function of the commission of array was to sustain the Royalist war effort in the county by raising men, finance and provisions for the King's cause. They also probably oversaw, or mediated, where there was controversy between the civilian authorities and Royalist commanders as well as supervised the allocation of parishes to particular Royalist regiments within the county for the collection of contribution, either in money or goods. This will be explored further later in the book (see Chapter 6).

John Twentyman

Amongst the Mellish papers at the Nottingham University Manuscripts Department, there is to be found a copy of the memoirs of a John Twentyman. The original document has long since gone missing, but thankfully a copy was made in the early nineteenth century. The Twentyman family at Newark was an influential family within the town, with one of the family (an earlier John Twentyman) delivering a Latin oration to the future James I on 21 April 1603 as he journeyed from Scotland to take possession of the English throne.[10] It was probably over the early period of the Civil War, after the Battle of Edgehill, that an event occurred at Newark that is only found mentioned in John Twentyman's account:

> Our familie was loyall & true to his late Majestie Charles the First & gave the decision to make that Town of Newarke a Garrison. Thus two troopes of Horse came from Lincoln under command of them who were for the Parliament, & faced the Towne upon Beacon Hill, it was reported in the town that they would come and plunder the towne.

9   Martyn Bennett, *In the Midst of the Kingdom: The Royalist War Effort in the North Midlands, 1642-1646* (Warwick: Helion & Company, 2021), pp.41–42, 52.

10   Jennings, *These Uncertaine Tymes*, p.6.

One of my uncles having been Ensign to Captain Rossell & an old drum being in the House, but the head broken, my Grandmother charged my uncle Edward Twentyman upon her blessing to take it out & commanded Edward Foster her grandchild to beat an alarm & see who would stand for king Charles & their own Defence.

They came together unanimously with forks and spitts & what weapons they had, for very few guns were among them & resolved to defend themselves as well as they could & upon what notice or feare I know not those Troopes withdrew & made no attempt.[11]

This episode probably reflects the uncertainty and unpreparedness of Royalists across the county as a whole from August to November 1642. In Lincolnshire and Derbyshire, Nottinghamshire's neighbouring counties to the east and west, supporters of Parliament were already taking the initiative in organising. That the ordinary citizens could be rallied under the command of a former solder is itself a testimony to the town's willingness to defend itself and a growing sympathy for the King's cause. The Twentyman manuscript goes on to inform us that 'my uncle Edward Twentyman was the Eldest or first Captain [of] that [the town] Regiment & died of a Gangrene which followed upon butting of his Toe a little before the surrender'. His burial was recorded in the parish register on 2 March 1646, and his will also survives.[12]

Newark Post Edgehill until the End of 1642

After the Edgehill campaign was over, the Sheriff of Nottingham, Sir John Digby, returned to the county with the intention of securing it for the King. He based himself at Newark and called on 10 December for all the justices of the shire to attend a meeting at Newark, with the intention of securing 'the peace of the county, security of their estates, and such like fair pretences'. According to Lucy Hutchinson, this was a trap to seize those who had roundhead inclinations. Being forewarned, John Hutchinson and others did not attend but set about securing the town of Nottingham for Parliament.[13] With troops sent from Derbyshire by Sir John Gell, according to Lucy Hutchinson, John Hutchinson threw up defences around the city whilst his brother, George Hutchinson, raised a town regiment of around 700 men. Realising their predicament, the authorities in Newark sent to the Earl of Newcastle, commander of the Royalist Northern Army, a request for help. Recognising the importance of Newark as a bridge between Oxford and York, Newcastle acted quickly and sent Sir John Henderson with soldiers

---

11 Nottingham University Manuscripts Department (NUMD): Me LM 11: Mellish Papers, Twentyman Manuscript. See Appendix I.

12 Nottinghamshire Archives (NA): PR/27256–257: Newark Parish Registers, Nottinghamshire Wills, 1640–1660, Will of Edward Twentyman. See also Jennings, *These Uncertaine Tymes*, pp.46–47.

13 Keeble (ed.), *Memoirs of Colonel Hutchinson*, pp.100–01.

to establish a garrison. Henderson arrived at Newark before Christmas. According to the newssheet *Special Passages* for 27 December–3 January 1643, 'There came into this town [Newark] this week 4000 men of my Lord Newcastle and to them the Sheriff of Notts. brought in 400 more and one Butler a lawyer brought in 100 more.'[14] Professor Wood identified this Butler as a Robert Butler of Southwell, Nottinghamshire (which lay six miles away from Newark).[15] The arrival of Henderson at Newark not only strengthened the resolve of the town's residents but also had a positive impact on Royalist sentiment in the adjacent county of Lincolnshire. Having such a strong garrison nearby, a number of the gentleman of that county moved to Newark and established a base there. By January, these Lincolnshire Royalists, supported by troops provided by Henderson, began to recruit both men and money to create their own regiments from the Kesteven district of that county. These new regiments were often based at Newark during the war and, on occasion, formed an integral part of the Newark Horse.[16]

The arrival of Henderson and his troopers would have come as a relief to the inhabitants of Newark, who had apparently nailed their colours to the Royalist cause by December, but it would have also introduced them to a problem that was to beset the town for the whole of the period of the Civil War, that of logistics. As we have seen in the previous chapter, the population of the town was just over 2,000 people, and, within the circuit of its medieval walls, there were only three stone buildings: the castle, the church and the Magnus school. The rest of the town consisted mainly of timber-framed houses with thatched roofs. Being on a major travel route, there were a number of coaching inns, but these were generally occupied either by Royalist officers, the accounts of William Staunton's regiment record that their commander was based 'at the Hart' (the White Hart) inn,[17] by members of the commission of array who were based at the town or by gentry from neighbouring counties.

Apart from the church, which was used continuously throughout the Civil War, the other two stone buildings would have been used for storage of munitions and provisions, as they were less susceptible to the risk of fire. Where, then, were the ordinary soldiers accommodated and the horses of the cavalry, of which there could be thousands, stabled? The amounts of horse dung alone would have required regular clearance, for which there are some payments recorded in the regimental accounts of William Staunton. The most obvious answer is that soldiers were quartered in the homes of Newark citizens. We are given glimpses of this fact in the churchwarden accounts of Newark.[18] When a soldier died in the home of a citizen, perhaps from wounds, the wardens stepped in to pay for the inkle and shroud to bury them when the householder was too poor to meet the cost. Where the soldiers were buried is a matter we shall return to later.

---

14   British Library (BL): Thomason Tracts (TT): E84 (6).

15   Wood, *Nottinghamshire in the Civil War*, p.217.

16   Clive Holmes, *Seventeenth-Century Lincolnshire* (Lincoln: Society for Lincolnshire History and Archaeology, 1980), pp.162–63.

17   Bennett, Jennings, and Whyld, 'Two Military Account Books', pp.107–21.

18   NA: PR/27256–257: Newark Parish Registers.

The White Hart Inn at Newark.
(Author's photograph)

By the end of the year, the Parliamentarian newspaper *Weekly Intelligencer* described the situation in Nottinghamshire as:

> … in Nottinghamshire the Cavalliers doe make a party, having possessed themselves of Newark-upon-Trent, and put 400 men in the Castle, and command the passage there over the river. Col. Henderson commands in Chief, the Lo. Chaworth, Sir Jo. Digby and divers Lincolnshire and Nottinghamshire Malignants do flock thither to their assistance. Mr Hutchinson, a Gentleman of integrity and honesty, offers great aid to Nottingham. The Cavalliers of Newark make incursions into Lincolnshire, and fetch men out of their beds, but the E. of Lincolne, Sir Edw Ascough, and Mr Grantham are there with 1500 men to defend that county.[19]

---

19   Early English Books Online (EEBO), *The Kingdomes Weekly Intelligencer: Sent Abroad to Prevent Mis-Information, 27 December to 3 January 1642–1643*. See also Cornelius Brown, *A History*

First Siege of Newark, 27 February 1643

At the start of the new year, Sir John Henderson found himself in charge of a garrison that possessed few defensive works. The old stone town walls still surrounded Newark, but, in many places, they were in a ruinous state and would be of little use against cannons and could be easily stormed. Houses had long been built beyond the town walls, and ribbon developments along roads to the north, south and west of the town put many households beyond Newark's defensive circuit. January and February were not the best time of the year for any sort of construction work, but Sir John, being an experienced soldier, recognised the necessity of starting work immediately.

Newark was fortunate for the first few weeks of 1643, in that Newcastle and the Royalist Northern Army were based not too far away at Pontefract. This discouraged Parliamentarian forces in Nottinghamshire and Lincolnshire from moving against the town. Newcastle's instruction had been to march south to join up with the King's forces at Oxford as soon as it was possible, and many of the cavalry that came with Henderson were in fact part of the proposed vanguard for that venture. As often throughout the war, Newark's fortunes were shaped by events beyond the county border. Newcastle had sent Sir William Savage to secure Yorkshire by taking the last remaining towns sympathetic to Parliament before he advanced. Initially, Savage enjoyed some success, occupying Leeds and Wakefield, but, on 23 January 1643, his gains were cancelled when Parliamentarian forces under the command of Sir Thomas Fairfax retook these towns and drove Savage back towards the Royalist northern base at York. Newcastle had no option but to move back towards York to consolidate his hold on the county, and with him went many of the cavalry that were based at Newark. Henderson remained at Newark as its governor, but his garrison now only consisted of local volunteers who had come into the town over the past few weeks.[20]

By the start of February, John Twentyman observed of the town's defences as they then stood: 'they made a garrison of it, takeing in only the round of the Town & leaving out Milngate & the best streete for building Northgate with the Earle of Exeter's House. And most pitifull works they were, very low and thin & a drie ditch which most men might easily leap upon the East & South'.

In such circumstances, with few Royalist soldiers and inadequate defences, it was an

Portrait of William Cavendish, Earl (later Duke) of Newcastle. Engraver Thomas Phillibrown, c. 1845. (Author's collection)

of *Newark-on-Trent: Being the Life Story of an Ancient Town* (Nottingham: Nottinghamshire County Council, 1995), vol. II, p.60.

20   Samuel R. Gardiner, *History of the Great Civil War, 1642–1649* (Moreton-in-Marsh: Windrush Press, 1991), vol. I, pp.87–88.

excellent opportunity for Parliamentarian forces in the East Midlands to move against the town and take this important centre of communications and crossing over the River Trent.

According to Lucy Hutchinson, the Nottingham committee first proposed the idea of a united campaign against Newark. She wrote:

> the gentlemen there considering that would be easier to prevent Newark from being made a fortified garrison than to take it when it was so, they sent over to Lincoln and Derby to propound the business to them, where it was at length, about Candlemass [2 February 1643], agreed and appointed that the forces of Nottingham and Derby should come on their side of the town, and those of Lincoln on the other.[21]

The fact that the decision was taken 'at length' suggests that Parliamentarians at Nottingham made the initial suggestion towards the end of January, after Newcastle had withdrawn his forces. The forces from Nottingham and Derby were to assemble to the south of Newark with those from Lincoln to the north.

Portrait of Lucy Hutchinson, authoress and wife to Colonel John Hutchinson. Engraver unknown. (Author's collection)

Command of this joint venture against Newark was given to Major General Thomas Ballard. As commander of the Lincolnshire forces, the largest component of the joint force, Ballard was an experienced soldier who, after service at the Battle of Edgehill, had been promoted from the rank of colonel for his service. On paper, he was clearly the most experienced of the officers. Initially, it had been arranged that the forces of Derby, Nottinghamshire and Lincolnshire were to rendezvous within a mile of Newark on 25 February, but, for reasons that remain unclear, Ballard delayed moving the Lincolnshire forces into position. It was not until 27 February that Ballard and his force moved into position. According to Royalist propaganda, the total size of the Parliamentary forces amounted to 6,000 men and 10 pieces of ordinance, but Lucy Hutchinson put the number nearer to 2,000.[22] It is more difficult to estimate what the size of the forces within Newark was at this time, especially as Newcastle had removed from the town most of his cavalry to go with him back into Yorkshire. If Colonel William Staunton had returned back to Newark immediately after the battle at Brentford and started immediately raising local volunteers for his growing foot regiment, the forces under Henderson's command would have been nearly comparable with those of the Parliamentarians. Unfortunately, the surviving evidence is not substantial enough to be certain about this.

---

21   Keeble (ed.), *Memoirs of Colonel Hutchinson*, p.102.
22   Wood, *Nottinghamshire in the Civil War*, p.240.

Henderson had some intelligence of this planned attempt on Newark and drew up what cavalry he had on Beacon Hill, hoping to halt the attack before it reached the town's weak defences. His lack of artillery, plus Ballard's delay in arriving, forced him to retire this force back behind his defences.[23] This meant that the fight for Newark would be brought right into the town itself.

On the morning of Tuesday, 28 February, the Parliamentarian commanders made the decision to storm the Royalist defences, though it was later claimed that Ballard had not been too enthusiastic about this plan. The Lincolnshire forces left their overnight base at the Spittal, the ruined stone shell of the Countess of Exeter's home just outside the North Gate of Newark, and attacked the Royalist defences. They were initially successful in advancing to within pistol range of the defences and engaging the defenders in a musket fight. An additional attack on the eastern side of the defences led to sections of the Parliamentarian force gaining entry into the town and fighting their way along Balderton Gate to make a deep incursion into Newark, with one contemporary source claiming that they got as far as the Beaumond Cross. Here, they encountered a stiff resistance from the Royalist defenders, where Henderson had concealed men and a cannon in barns to engage them. Although outnumbered, the Royalists managed to drive them out of the town. Rather than risk sending in reinforcements, Ballard made the decision to withdraw his attackers.[24] To the south of the town, the Nottinghamshire and Derbyshire troops had also managed to occupy a ditch within pistol shot of the town works. Here, they encountered intense musket fire and were unable to advance any farther. By late afternoon, other sections of the Parliamentarian army moved round to join the forces of John Hutchinson and Sir John Gell at the ditch in the hope that their combined numbers might overwhelm the Royalists. Henderson, discerning their plan, moved more of his men to this part of the defences, and an intense exchanged of musket fire lasted here for around three hours.

At 6:00 p.m., Henderson sallied out through the North Gate with large numbers of his defenders and managed to break the Parliamentarian ranks, capturing three guns that they left behind at the Spittal. These proved to be a much-needed resource for the Royalists at Newark at this time. The next day, though the Nottinghamshire and Derbyshire forces were willing to make another attempt, Ballard refused, and so the besieging forces returned back to their respective counties. According to a Royalist pamphlet, only one soldier of the Newark garrison was killed in this action, and 'but few' were injured. It goes on to claim that 200 Parliamentarians were slain and many, including Ballard, were injured. In the sortie out of Newark led by Henderson at the end of the day, 60 of the enemy's soldiers were captured, and some of them were claimed to be 'French papists'.[25]

---

23 Jennings, *These Uncertaine Tymes*, pp.22–23.

24 Malcolm Fox, *Newark in the Civil War* (Newark: Newark and District Council, 1985); Wood, *Nottinghamshire in the Civil War*, p.41.

25 Bodleian Library: Peter Heylyn, *A Brief Relation of the Remarkable occurrences in the Northern parts: viz. The Landing of the Queenes Maiestie In the Bay of Burlington: And the repulse given unto the Rebels of the Town of Newark, 'both signified by severell Letters on the same day, being Friday March 1642'* (March 1642/1643); Warner, *Civil War and Siegeworks*, pp.10–11.

Twentyman, ever the contemporary witness to events in Newark at this time, gave his own detailed and dramatic description of events that happened during this first short siege:

> The Parliament forces came against it under the command of Major Generall Ballard, who had served in forreign warrs & such were so renowned that they were thought able to do wonders among us in the beginning of our unhappy discords. Sir John Henderson a Scotchman who had also been abroad in forreign service was then Governor of the Town. The Parliament's forces came to the Spittle or towards it, which occasioned both it and Norgate to be sett on fire. Then they made some attempt to enter at Balderton Gate, but were beat off & the Towns-men won 2 or 3 little peices from them which greatly encouraged them. They attempted some other parts of the town, but not in diverse places at once, for they within had so few guns that they were forced who had them to run with them to the place of assault as Colonell Henderson ordered and directed who rode upon a white horse & encouraged the soldiers & kept in continuall motion upon his horse that the enemie might not take mark at him. Low & bad (as I have said) works. God at this time preserved the Town, for the Parliament forces drew off & went away & they imputed the not winning of the Town at this time to the trechery of Major General Ballard.

Colonels John Hutchinson of Nottingham and Sir John Gell of Derby were united in their assessment that the failure of the siege was the sole responsibility of Ballard, who dithered in his actions. In her *Memoirs*, Lucy Hutchinson was even more critical in her assessment of Ballard's actions.[26] The Nottinghamshire committee sent two gentlemen to lodge a formal complaint to Parliament about Ballard's poor decisions and actions and sought his removal.[27] According to the *Perfect Diurnall*, Ballard was sent from Lincoln to be tried before the Earl of Essex for his conduct.[28] Later in the war, Ballard was to change sides and join the Royalists.

An interesting surviving testimony to the suddenness of this first siege can be found in the constable's accounts for the village of Upton. The village of Upton lies just over six miles to the north-west of the town and is fortunate to possess a complete set of constable accounts for the period of the First Civil War. A short time before the siege, the constables had laid out 2s when 'wee went to Newarke concerning the continuing of the army [Henderson's forces] there'. Five entries later, the accounts record the expense of a further 1s 'when we were at the Battle of Newark'. It would appear that the constables found themselves trapped in the town and unable to leave as the siege began.[29]

Although this first siege was of short duration, the fighting actually came right into the town, but little evidence survives to analyse the amount of collateral damage inflicted upon it. In the papers of the Committee for

26 Keeble (ed.), *Memoirs of Colonel Hutchinson*, pp.103–04.
27 Anon., *Journal of the House of Commons, 1643–1644 [HC Journal]* (London: HMSO, 1802), vol. III, 30 March 1643.
28 BL: TT: *Perfect Diurnall* (April 3–10 1642).
29 Bennett (ed.), *Accounts of the Constables of Upton*, pp.10–11.

Collection of seventeenth-century shot and musket balls found in and around Newark. (Author's collection)

Compounding, there survives a petition to the commissioners from Thomas Atkinson in late April 1646 that adds a little more detail. Atkinson was a leading Royalist supporter and the tenant keeper of the White Hart Inn during the first siege of 1643. He asserted that, during the fighting of the siege, the inn was hit by a 'grenado', stating:

> On or about which time the said town of Newark was besieged by the Parliaments forces and through a bumball or granado shott which came from the besiegers a great part of the said howse was blowne upp and some were there slaine and others mortally wounded and your orator himself wounded and his wife and many small children in great danger of being slaine likewise by shott your orator was damnified in his goods and estate in that part of the howse so as aforesaid blowne upp £300 or near thereabouts.[30]

Atkinson claimed to be an ideal tenant and that the owner of the property refused to make the building safe, forcing him and his family to move away from the inn. The damage could not have been that extensive though, for, by 1645, Colonel Staunton and some of his officers appear to have made it their own quarters. It has been argued that it was probably the south part of the

---

30   Anon., *Calendar of the Proceedings of the Committee for Compounding etc., 1643-1660* [CCC] (London: HMSO, 1889–1892), part II, p.1225.

south range of the inn that possibly contained the stables and the drinking room that may have been damaged.[31]

A further attempt on Newark was made on 9 March by Lincolnshire forces, possibly in an attempt to redeem their earlier failure. Their force was 2,000 strong and commanded by Lord Willoughby of Parham. Henderson, according to a Parliamentarian newssheet, sent out from Newark a force of 1,200 foot and 300 horse under the command of Captain Charles Dymock. These figures were probably inflated for propaganda purposes, but they do suggest that Henderson risked a large section of his forces within Newark for this attack. After a sharp encounter, the Parliamentarians claimed that the Newark Horse broke, leaving their foot exposed. This claim was again probably propaganda, as Gervase Holles, who was in Newark at that time, claimed that Willoughby's attack was halted and his forces were dispersed. Had the Newark forces taken such a defeat, it is difficult to understand why the Parliamentarians did not begin the siege again, especially as they had seen their enemy's strength even more diminished.[32]

Despite the fact that Parliamentarians had achieved superiority across Lincolnshire and Derbyshire and even managed, under John Hutchinson, to take control of the county town of Nottingham, Newark had survived the first six months of the Civil War. Over the next six months, the garrison was to find even greater stability and prominence as the Earl of Newcastle moved south to begin his siege of Hull and the close proximity of the Royalist Northern Army strengthened its position. At this stage of the war, no one at Newark, both civilian and soldier, could have foreseen that the conflict would last for a further three years and that the town would experience a further two sieges, each being longer and more severe than its predecessor.

---

31   This whole episode is explored in some detail in John Samuels, F. W. B. Charles, Adrian Henstock, and Philip Sidall, "'A Very Old and Crasey Howse": The Old White Hart Inn, Newark, Nottinghamshire', *Transactions of the Thoroton Society*, 100 (1996), pp.19–54.

32   BL: TT: *Perfect Diurnall* (March 13–20); Wood, *Nottinghamshire in the Civil War*, p.42, footnote 2.

3

Securing the Garrison, 1643

Charles Cavendish and the Formation of the Newark Horse

As the Royalist forces under the command of the Marquis of Newcastle began to gain the upper hand against Sir Thomas Fairfax's Parliamentarian forces in Yorkshire, Newcastle decided in early March to send his commander of horse, Charles Cavendish, and the regiment he had raised in the north to the garrison at Newark. Cavendish was instructed to coordinate with both Lincolnshire and Newark Royalists, all nominally under the command of their Colonel General Henry Hastings, who later became Lord Loughborough, to create a mobile cavalry force that would later come to be known as the 'Newark Horse'. Such was Cavendish's reputation and charisma that the King's commissioners for Nottinghamshire and Lincolnshire petitioned Charles for him to be appointed as commander of the forces of those two counties and given the rank of colonel general. This request was to be granted by the King.[1]

Within days of Cavendish's arrival at Newark, he, along with Sir John Henderson, led a large force from the town into Lincolnshire. On 23 March, they stormed the town of Grantham and captured a number of prisoners. The Royalists then went on to destroy the fortifications and left it as an open town. In the process of doing this, they also obtained from the town money and provisions for their needs. By early April, the Royalist forces of Newark had added Stamford and Peterborough to their list of taken towns, and their cavalry had even appeared before the walls of Lincoln.[2] As the Royalist force under Cavendish began to march towards the port of Boston, they were intercepted on 11 April at Ancaster Heath by a force of 1,500 Parliamentarian troops under the command of Lord Willoughby of Parham, who attempted to block their progress. The Royalists easily routed their enemy, driving them off the field of battle, and were able to return to Newark with their plunder and provisions.

Parliament was clearly concerned both by the defeat of Willoughby and the free range of activity that the Newark Royalists appeared to enjoy

---

1   Charles H. Firth, 'Charles Cavendish', in L. Stephen (ed.), *Dictionary of National Biography* (London: Smith, Elder and Co., 1887), vol. IX, p.343.

2   Holmes, *Seventeenth-Century Lincolnshire*, p.163.

across Lincolnshire. They ordered Cromwell of the Eastern Association, Captain Hotham with some of his Yorkshire recruits and soldiers from Nottingham to rendezvous at Sleaford with the intentions of intercepting a Royalist convoy of munitions then making its way south from York to the King at Oxford and afterwards coordinate an attack on the garrison of Newark. Unfortunately, Cromwell got delayed in taking the Royalist garrison at Crowland in Lincolnshire and did not arrive at Sleaford until 9 May 1643, by which time it was too late to intercept the Royalist convoy. They therefore advanced quickly towards Grantham and easily reoccupied the town, which had not been garrisoned, but then, for no apparent reason, remained in the town a further two days. This delay gave Cavendish and Henderson time to plan and implement a counterattack against this combined force. Early in the morning of 13 May, Cavendish made a surprise attack on some of the Lincolnshire Parliamentarian soldiers, then quartered in the village of Belton, killing 70 and taking 40 prisoners according to Royalist accounts.

Oliver Cromwell. Image from *Tyler's History of Scotland* (William MacKenzie, 1880), engraver unknown. (Author's collection)

The bulk of the Parliamentarian forces that were quartered in and around the town of Grantham were quickly warned of events at Belton and marched out to confront the Newark cavalry. In the growing dusk of a May evening, a confused military action took place. The Parliamentarian soldiers under the command of Captain John Hotham made little or no impression on the Royalist left wing, but Oliver Cromwell led his regiment against the right wing and drove the Royalists off the field. Despite Cromwell's assertion of a great victory, the reality was that the Newark forces were able to make a strategic withdrawal back towards Newark whilst the combined forces of Parliament withdrew towards Lincoln.[3] Over the months of April and May, in a remote part of Lincolnshire, two reputations were beginning to be shaped: that of the Newark Horse and, just as importantly, that of a middle-aged Parliamentarian colonel called Oliver Cromwell.

The Parliamentarian forces, assembled at Spalding, had only done part of the task they were called to do. In response to a plea from John Hutchinson, governor of Nottingham Castle, they were then to make their way to that town to strengthen its defences against a potential attack from the Royalist forces of the Earl of Newcastle. By the time that Lord Thomas Grey, Oliver Cromwell, Sir John Gell and Sir John Hotham, with their forces, had assembled at Nottingham on 24 May, the situation had changed considerably. On 21 May 1643, Sir Thomas Fairfax achieved a major victory over Royalist

---

3   Holmes, *Seventeenth-Century Lincolnshire*, pp.166 67.

forces at Wakefield, and, sensing that his rear was now exposed, Newcastle had to return to York with most of his army.[4] The situation was now reversed, but the various Parliamentarian commanders failed to come to an agreement about what to do with their combined force. There were two options open to them. The first was a march up north to join up with Fairfax and continue the fight against the Royalist Northern Army of Newcastle. Fairfax had a desperate need for additional cavalry in his force, and this combined force at Nottingham had plenty to offer. But Grey, Gell and possibly Cromwell were loath to leave their respective areas of Leicestershire, Derbyshire and the Eastern Association vulnerable to further attacks by local Royalists in their absence. A more promising opportunity, which, according to Lucy Hutchinson, gained the approval of John Hutchinson, Francis Thornhagh and Oliver Cromwell, was an attack on Newark itself, which had recently been reduced in strength when Newcastle returned to York. The situation was to change quickly though for Newark at the end of May, when Newcastle felt able to send two regiments of foot back to Newark, possibly in anticipation of the Queen's journey south.[5] The arrival of these additional Royalist forces at the town meant that the various Parliamentarian commanders failed to come to an agreement on a unified strategy and, slowly over the next few weeks, they began to drift back to their respective areas. Newark Royalists now held sway across much of Nottinghamshire, and again the local Parliamentarians had failed to capitalise on an opportunity.[6] The one positive outcome for Parliament over this period of indecision at Nottingham was that suspicions were raised about the loyalty of John Hotham to the Parliamentarian cause, and both Hutchinson and Cromwell made complaints about his conduct to the Committee of Safety. This resulted in both his father, Sir John, and John himself being arrested and taken to London in June 1643.

It was between June and September 1643 that Sir Richard Byron of Strelley replaced Sir John Henderson as governor of the town of Newark, a post he was to retain until January 1645. Byron had proved himself to be a capable soldier and commander to the King as they fought together at the Battle of Edgehill in 1642. Coming from an influential Nottinghamshire family, he was deemed to be the most capable individual to safeguard and secure the town over the difficult times that lay ahead. On 29 May 1643, the garrison at Newark held a great muster that recorded the presence of 38 troops of horse and dragoons, amounting to around 2,000 men under arms.[7] This muster was probably held before the arrival of the foot regiments sent by Newcastle, and this combined concentration of troops was almost certainly put together to cover Henrietta Maria as she prepared to march through the county on her journey towards the King at Oxford. Newark was by then a very formidable Royalist presence across the Midlands region.

---

4   Wood, *Nottinghamshire in the Civil War*, pp.44–46.

5   Wood, *Nottinghamshire in the Civil War*, p.46.

6   Keeble (ed.), *Memoirs of Colonel Hutchinson*, pp.107–08.

7   Warner, *Civil War and Siegeworks*, p.13.

Queen Henrietta Maria at Newark (16 June–3 July 1643)

When the Civil War broke out in 1642, Queen Henrietta Maria went overseas to the Netherlands to sell both her own jewels and some of the crown jewels, raising money to purchase weapons and munitions for her husband's army. On 20 February 1643, she landed at Bridlington with these munitions and some professional mercenaries, with the intention of taking these down to join the King at Oxford.

The crossing by ship from the Netherlands had been very rough, and, on landing, ships loyal to Parliament had bombarded the Queen and her party, so she remained in Bridlington for a few days to recover. On 5 March 1643, the Queen and the munitions were escorted safely to York, which was the base for the Royalist forces in Yorkshire. Here, the Marquis of Newcastle lavishly entertained her. By the start of June, Royalist successes in the Midlands and Newcastle's growing strength across the north were deemed to make it relatively safe for the Queen to begin her journey south towards Oxford to join her husband. She left the city of York on 4 June with both the munitions she had purchased abroad and an army of nearly 5,000 men, most of whom had been raised by Newcastle across the north and equipped by the Queen.[8] She reached Newark on 16 June 1643, where Sir Charles Cavendish greeted her on behalf of the garrison and the bell ringers were paid 5s 'to celebrate the queene's arrival'.[9] In spite of being anxious to be reunited with the King, Henrietta Maria was to remain at the town until 3 July.

The arrival of nearly 5,000 troops at Newark, a town of only just over 2,100 civilians and a garrison of around 2,000 soldiers, was to create tremendous pressures on both accommodating and feeding the new arrivals, not only for Newark but also for all the villages around the town. The constable for the parish of Upton in 1643 was James Bloomer, and his accounts record the additional costs visited upon the parish whilst the Queen was present at Newark that were paid alongside the regular contributions it had to make of money and materials, such as pease, oats and hay, to sustain the garrison at Newark. Below are some of the details of moneys and goods laid for the 'her she Generalissimo', as the Queen affectionately termed herself, as she led her army south to join the King.

Queen Henrietta Maria. Engravers Richard Earlom and Charles Turner, 1815. (Author's collection)

---

8   'Yorkshire 1643', *Civil War Petitions*, <https://www.civilwarpetitions.ac.uk/?s=yorkshire+1643>, accessed 25 Aug. 2022.

9   NA: PR/24810: Newark Churchwarden Accounts, 1643.

Payments Made by the Upton Constables during the Queen's Stay at Newark

Note	Amount
Payed to George Ward & Richard Ward for going to Newarke with Pease, when the queene was there	4d
The next day when I went for money for pease and sackes I spent	8d
Payed to John Chapell for carrying strawe to Newarke	2s
Spent I went a bout it	6d
Payed for twooe capons more than ye king's price	6d
When I went to carry provisions for the queene spent	4d
When we went to put in the catalogue of the Warrant of Array spent	1s 2d
Spent when I went to Morton concerning the Draught to go with the Queene	4d
Spent when the Morton men came to Upton to consider with the Neighbours about ye Draught	8d
Spent at the time when I went to Newarke to see what time the Draught should goe	4d
Spent of the souldiers when the[y] went to Newarke when the Queene was there, being called in by warrant	1s 8d

The first thing to notice about these entries is that they list the charges, totalling 8s 8d, for the delivery of goods and services to Newark, not the actual value of the goods themselves. The total expenditure for Upton constables in 1643 was to be £8 8s 6d. For the town of Newark and larger villages, the burden of levies would have been considerably larger. This pattern was repeated across all the parishes that fell within the orbit of Newark's influence during the Queen's stay. The commissioners of array based at Newark would periodically call in the constables of the various parishes with their accounts to check that goods and cash payments collected as contribution agreed with their accounts. The warrant of array listed by the constables may well have been an additional check to verify that the levies for the Queen's stay at Newark were being met. The fact that the constables had to pay out an additional 6d for two capons sent to Newark suggests that the price paid by the royal warrant was considerably less than the value that the market would have paid for them. As Henrietta Maria travelled south towards Oxford with her army, she augmented her force by using conscripts levied by the commissioners of array, and the last five entries are related to meeting this conscription. The constables often chose those conscripted, and, unless they had money to pay for someone else to go in their place, they had little choice in the matter other than running away.[10] Not all that joined Henrietta Maria were conscripts, though. A witness to the presence of the Queen at Newark recorded that 'the courtesy of her behaviour while she stayed at Newark brought a great increase to her forces, in so much that she had not arms enough for the men'.[11]

The Queen was extremely protective of the men and munitions she was taking down to Oxford, but, on 21 June, she allowed some of her men to join others from the Newark garrison in an attack on the Parliamentarian

---

10   Much of the above is derived from Bennett (ed.), *Accounts of the Constables of Upton*, pp.10–13, 132–33.

11   Brown, *History of Newark*, vol. II, p.62.

The house that Queen Henrietta Maria occupied during her stay at Newark in 1643. (Author's photograph)

stronghold of Nottingham. The size of the Royalist force is estimated between 2,000 and 3,000, though one account puts it to be as many as '3,000 horse and 4 or 5 regiments of foot', which is most certainly an over-estimation since it would have virtually emptied the Newark garrison.[12] Lucy Hutchinson suggested the reason for the attack was to cover the passing of the Queen out of Newark and on to Ashby-de-la-Zouch, but, as she did not leave the county until 3 July, this was not correct.[13] Although cannon was fired at the Royalists, killing a few soldiers, and the Nottinghamshire Horse then rode out to face them, no major battle took place. The Royalist forces were not strong enough to take the town and castle, and the Parliamentarians were not strong enough to take their enemy on in a pitched battle. According to the Royalist newssheet *Mercurius Aulicus*, the force from Newark took 80 prisoners and killed

---

12   Royal Commission on Historical Manuscripts, *The Manuscripts of His Grace the Duke of Portland, Preserved at Welbeck Abbey* (London: HMSO, 1891–1919), vol. I, p.120; Wood, *Nottinghamshire in the Civil War*, p.48, suggests a total of 2,000.

13   Keeble (ed.), *Memoirs of Colonel Hutchinson*, p.109.

50 Parliamentarians.[14] Amongst the Royalist casualties was a 'Baron of Dohna' who had probably come over from Europe with the Queen and was subsequently buried at Newark.

On 27 June 1643, Henrietta Maria wrote to the King from Newark, informing him that she would bring with her to Oxford 3,000 foot, 30 companies of horse and dragoons, six pieces of cannon, two mortars and 150 wagons. She went on to claim that she would leave behind for the safety of Nottinghamshire 2,000 foot, arms for 500 more men and 20 companies of horse under Sir Charles Cavendish.[15] It is possible that the 2,000 foot she left behind under Cavendish were those regiments sent to the town by Newcastle at the end of May to prepare the garrison for the Queen's arrival. The logistics of quartering, feeding and coordinating such a large body of men for nearly a month safely in and around the garrison of Newark must have been considerable, yet little evidence survives to explain how this was achieved. Even so, when the Queen came to leave Newark, the leaders of the town tried to persuade her to remain a little longer to help them take the town of Nottingham. Henrietta Maria was sympathetic to their pleas but explained that her first duty was to her husband, the King, and she had to get these resources quickly and safely to him at Oxford. For the town of Newark though, the time of the Queen's presence with them was looked back upon with gratitude and pride.

Battle of Gainsborough, 28 July 1643

Lying just over 25 miles north of Newark, on the opposite bank of the River Trent, the town of Gainsborough was another important crossing place over the River Trent before it reached the Humber estuary. Although it did not acquire a bridge until the end of the eighteenth century, the ferry there provided a direct route from Lincolnshire into Yorkshire. For both protagonists during the Civil War, it was viewed as an important strategic gain. Parliamentarians in Lincolnshire and the Eastern Association valued it as a direct route to their major garrison and armoury at Hull. Royalists at Newark viewed it as a useful base from which to launch raids deep into Lincolnshire. It would also provide a direct route for the Royalist forces under the Earl of Newcastle in the north to advance southwards towards London. In 1643, it did just that as Newcastle had a bridge of boats built for his army to cross the river to retake Gainsborough from the Parliamentarian forces then based there.

It was the Royalists who took the first action to secure the town. In March 1643, Sir John Henderson sent a strong force of troopers from Newark to demand the surrender of the town. The civil authorities within the town

---

14   Early English Books Online (EEBO), *Certaine Informations*, 3–10 July. See also C. H. Firth (ed.), *Memoirs of the Life of Colonel Hutchinson by His Widow Lucy* (London: George Routledge & Sons, 1906), p.404.

15   Brown, *History of Newark*, vol. II, p.62; England and Wales. Sovereign, *The King's Cabinet Opened, or, Certain Packets of Secret Letters & Papers* (London: Robert Bostock, 1645).

quickly agreed, and soldiers were stationed there to make it a Royalist base. During May–June, the Royalists at Gainsborough, along with troops from Newark, raided persistently across north Lincolnshire and even managed to intercept a shipment of gunpowder on its way to the Parliamentarian garrison at Rotherham.[16] The Royalist forces of the Earl of Newcastle were subsequently able to storm and capture Rotherham on 4 May 1643. Parliament ordered that something had to be done about this disruptive Royalist presence at Gainsborough, but, with the Queen and her forces at Newark until the first week of July, local Parliamentarians felt unable to attempt anything until she had moved on.

The Royalist hold on north Lincolnshire was further strengthened at the start of July when Robert Pierrepont, Earl of Kingston, was appointed lieutenant general of the Royalist forces across Lincolnshire, Rutland, Huntingdonshire, Cambridge and Norfolk. He made the town of Gainsborough his base of operations. Kingston was alleged to be one of the wealthiest men in Nottinghamshire but had held out as long as he could from deciding which side in the war to support. His eldest son, Lord Newark, had sided with the King almost immediately, but his two younger sons William and Francis Pierrepont both fought for Parliament. According to Professor Wood, this was not a straightforward case of a family being divided 'by the sword' but possibly 'a matter of policy' seeking to protect the family estate.[17] Whether this was the case or not, it appears a harsh analysis, as the commitment of the four to their respective causes was never doubted and was to cost the father his life. Kingston is alleged to have brought to the King's aid several thousand armed men.[18]

The Royalist ascendency was quickly shattered once the Queen had left Newark. On 20 July 1643, Lord Willoughby of Parham surprised the garrison at Gainsborough with a night attack on the town before 'it was fully fortified'. According to Lucy Hutchinson, the Royalists in the town 'Disputed it as long as they could, but being conquered were forced to yield; and the Earl himself retreated into the strongest house, which he kept till it was all on flame round about him, and then giving himself up only to my lord Willoughby'.[19] After his surrender, Kingston was sent down-river in a pinnace as a prisoner to Hull but was killed by a cannon ball that was fired at the boat by Royalists on the riverbank.

An act of clever strategy had enabled Willoughby to take the town, but holding on to it was to prove much more difficult. As he later wrote, 'the same day I took it I was beseaged before night, and there kept in some 10 days before I had any release'.[20] Gainsborough was too important a base for the Royalists to leave in Parliamentarian hands. Newcastle therefore ordered Sir Charles Cavendish, who had just returned to Newark after escorting the

---

16   Ian Beckwith, *The Book of Gainsborough* (Buckingham: Barracuda Books, 1988), pp.36–37.

17   Wood, *Nottinghamshire in the Civil War*, p.50.

18   David Lloyd, *Memoirs of the Lives, Actions, Sufferings & Deaths of Those Noble, Reverend and Excellent Personages …* (London: Samuel Speed, 1668), p.435.

19   Keeble (ed.), *Memoirs of Colonel Hutchinson*, p.109.

20   John West, 'Oliver Cromwell and the Battle of Gainsborough, July 1643', *Cromwelliana* (1993), p.10.

Queen to Oxford, to take as many troops as could be spared from Newark to begin a siege of the town whilst he marched southwards with the Northern Army to join him. For over four days, the Newark troops implemented a siege on the town. Meanwhile, Parliament acted quickly to support Willoughby and ordered Sir John Meldrum to march from Nottingham and join up with Cromwell, who was then moving up from the Eastern Association with 600 horse. Cromwell wrote, 'I marched after the taking of Burleigh House upon Wednesday to Grantham where I met about three hundred horse and dragoons from Nottingham, with these by agreement we met the Lincolners at North Scale.'[21] In total, Meldrum's relief force (he was the commander of this combined force but largely ignored by Cromwell in his subsequent reports) amounted to 22 troops of horse and three or four companies of dragoons, possibly amounting to around 1,200 men.[22]

As the combined Parliamentarian relief force reached the village of Lea, which lay a mile and a half to the south of Gainsborough, they encountered a forlorn hope of Royalists that consisted of about a 100 horse. After a brief skirmish, these were driven back to join the main body of Sir Charles Cavendish's force. This had been drawn up at the top of a steep hill on the outskirts of the town, which today is known as 'Foxby Hill'. This consisted of three regiments of horse in the front, with Cavendish's own horse regiment in reserve. In total, this consisted of around 30 troops of horse and dragoons. The hill was extremely steep and was pitted with rabbit warrens, making it difficult terrain for the Parliamentarians to attack up, but they felt they had no choice but to do so. This they prepared to undertake led first by the Lincolnshire forces, then Meldrum, with the Nottinghamshire Horse with Cromwell and his troops at the rear. Before the Parliamentarians had properly drawn up in formation though, on the difficult terrain, the Royalist horse advanced upon them.

On 31 July 1643, Cromwell delivered a full account of the battle to the Committee of Association then sitting at Cambridge. It is this report that gives us the most detailed, though not unbiased, account of what follows:

> … in such order as we were, we charged their great body, I having the right wing. We came up horse to horse, where we disputed it with our swords and pistols a pretty time, all keeping close order, so that one could not break the other. At last they a little shrinking, our men perceiving it, pressed upon them, and immediately routed this whole body, some flying on one side, others on the other of the enemy's reserves; and our men pursuing them, had chase and execution about six miles …[23]

In the excitement of a broken enemy fleeing, Cromwell kept his head and ordered three of his troop to remain with him, watching carefully what

---

21 Firth (ed.), *Memoirs of Colonel Hutchinson*, p.129, footnote 1.
22 Stuart B. Jennings, *A Very Gallant Gentleman: Colonel Francis Thornhagh (1617-1648) and the Nottinghamshire Horse* (Warwick: Helion & Company, 2022), pp.42–45.
23 S. C. Lomas (ed.), *The Letters and Speeches of Oliver Cromwell, with Elucidations by Thomas Carlyle* (London: Methuen & Co., 1904), vol. I, pp.141–42.

Cavendish did with his reserve so as to respond accordingly. His account continues, 'At last the General charged the Lincolners, and routed them. I immediately fell on his rear … which did so astonish him, that he gave over the chase, and would fain have delivered himself from me, but I pressing on forced them down the hill, having good execution of them'.

At the foot of the hill, there lay a patch of swampy ground by the side of the River Trent. Into this morass, the Royalists fled, struggling both against the mud and the pursuing enemy. Cavendish was knocked from his horse by a blow to the head, and, as he lay stunned on the ground, Thomas Berry, Cromwell's captain lieutenant, stabbed him through the chest. It was to take Cavendish two painful hours before he died of his wound.[24]

With the Royalist forces driven from the field, Meldrum was able to send a convoy of provisions and munitions into the town to restock the garrison stores, and he left some additional troops to strengthen Willoughby's forces. As this provisioning was taking place though, Meldrum and Cromwell received information that a small force of horse and foot had been observed approaching the town. Assuming this was nothing more than a detachment of the original Royalist force, they sent 600 of Lord Willoughby's foot to intercept them. To the shock of the infantry sent to stop them, they discovered not a detachment of Cavendish's original force but the whole of the Northern Army, under the command of the Earl of Newcastle, approaching the town to recapture it. They were too late to save the deceased Cavendish's force but were now able to reverse the Parliamentarian victory. Meldrum and Cromwell had to devise a safe withdrawal of their forces sent to relieve the town back towards Lincoln. This they were able to do, as much to the credit and military skill of Sir John Meldrum, Major Whalley and Captain Ayscoghe as well as Oliver Cromwell, who figures prominently in many accounts of the battle.

Gainsborough ultimately proved to be a success for the Royalists, and, with Newcastle's forces being once again in the North Midlands for a while, local Royalist garrisons, especially that at Newark, were to thrive. It came at a tremendous cost to the region's Royalists though, with both Sir Charles Cavendish and Robert Earl of Kingston killed. The Parliamentarian forces within Gainsborough were besieged once again by the army of Newcastle and finally surrendered on 30 July. Within a few days of this, Newcastle was also able to capture and garrison the county town of Lincoln, which lay just over 25 miles to the south-east of Gainsborough. Newark and the Royalist cause in the region had reached the zenith of its success in the Civil War.

Strengthening of the Defences at Newark, 1643

The short siege at the start of 1643 had clearly shown the Royalist defenders at Newark just how inadequate the town's defences were, with Parliamentarian soldiers being able to break through them and enter the town. With the

---

24   See accounts of the battle in Peter Young and Richard Holmes, *The English Civil War: A Military History of the Three Civil Wars, 1642–1651* (London: Eyre Methuen, 1974), pp.151–53, and Jennings, *A Very Gallant Gentleman*, pp.42–46.

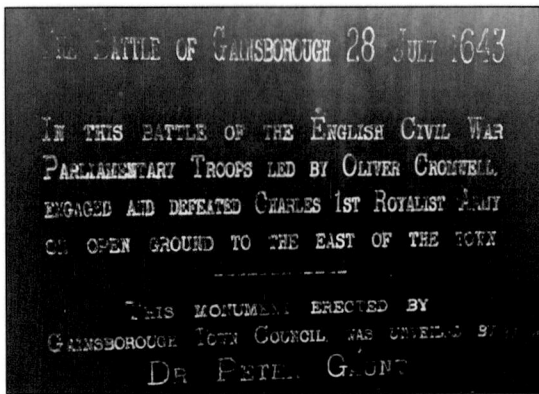

Above: Plaque on the Gainsborough memorial. (Author's photograph)

Right: Monument to the Battle of Gainsborough on Foxby Hill, up which the Parliamentarians charged the Royalist forces. (Author's photograph)

warmer, dryer weather of summer then approaching, when the water table and the River Trent levels were lower, this proved to be an ideal time to strengthen the defences considerably. Much of this work probably happened after the Queen had left the town on 3 July and Newcastle had returned to the region to secure the town at Gainsborough. John Twentyman gave a short account of the work in his memoirs:

> After this they began to make new works very high and strong & set up a great skonse in my Dove Coate Close called the King's Skonce, a footstep whereof is seen by the ditch left in it & at this time they secured the street called Milngate. These works were begun when his Majesties Forces were Masters of the Field, & according to humane judgment (but the Lord ruleth over all, & further appeared in his anger gainst us for our sins) they might have marched to London, into the associate Counties & have placed the king in his throne.

The site of this 'King's Skonce' is not known today, but it is not to be confused with the King's Sconce built in 1645 just outside the North Gate of the town. It is interesting to note that this defensive work was constructed on the close that belonged to Twentyman. The Mill Gate area of the town was important for the security of the town in any possible future sieges because it contained both the flour and later powder mills that served Newark.[25] Alongside the sconce, new ditches were dug, ramparts were heightened, sharpened stakes

---

25   RCHM, *Newark on Trent*, pp.29–31.

were fixed projecting horizontally to make scaling difficult, and double rows of sharpened stakes were fixed on top of ramparts that were most vulnerable. It is also claimed that concealed pits, known as 'pitfalls', with wooden stakes at their bottom were dug in front of some of the defences. The River Trent and the castle curtain wall on the west side of the town meant that this approach already had strong protection.[26] To secure the island formed by the two branches of the river to the west of the town, the fort at Muskham Bridge was strengthened, and a smaller subsidiary earthwork at Crankley Lane was thrown up. Situated on a high deposit of river gravel, thus sparing the town from flooding, this gravel, along with wooden piles driven into it, gave the ramparts additional strength to withstand artillery fire.

Much of the construction of this work, as with even more work during 1645, was undertaken by men conscripted from the surrounding villages on both sides of the river. The constable's accounts for Upton in 1643, which lay to the west of the town across both branches of the river, record expenses incurred for parishioners conscripted to do this, even noting the cost of taking the ferry across to Farndon to get to Newark:

> Payd for boting the men over when we went to the works – 4d.
> For going with the Ditchers to Newark – 6d.
> For boting the workmen when the[y] went to ye works – 2d.[27]

The Thorpe-by-Newark constable's accounts, a village five miles from Newark, contain the following entry for 1643: 'It[e]m p[ai]d for the making of tenne yeards of the workes at the Garrison of Newarke £2. 3s. 10d.'[28] The few surviving records from this period show that not only the labour but also some of the financial costs of the works appear to have been met by neighbouring parishes.

Newark Forces Attack Nottingham, September 1643

The success at Gainsborough and the strengthening of the defences around Newark should have been a foundation for even greater victories for Royalists within Nottinghamshire, but, according to Twentyman, poor military decisions taken elsewhere across the country meant that they were unable to capitalise on this potential: 'They might have marched to London, into the associate Counties & have placed the king in his throne. But his Majestie with his army set down before Glocester & the Duke of Newcastle with his besieged Kingston upon Hull, where both suffered much losse, gave advantage to the Parliament to recruit their Forces & were compelled to leave them.'

---

26   Warner, *Civil War and Siegeworks*, pp.11–12.
27   Bennett (ed.), *Accounts of the Constables of Upton*, pp.12–13.
28   Nottinghamshire Archives (NA): PR/5767: Thorpe-by-Newark Account Book of Parish Officers including Constable's Accounts.

Artistic impression of Nottingham Castle in the sixteenth century from *The Illustrated London News*, 1878. Engraver unknown. (Author's collection)

Newcastle had issued a summons to Colonel Hutchinson to surrender Nottingham to him on 6 August 1643, which the colonel declined to do. There was subsequently no attempt by the Duke to pursue this further, and, by the end of the month, he and his forces were outside the city of Hull, ready to begin a siege there. Even though he had left the county, the Newark garrison had been rejuvenated by Newcastle's intervention and were able to raid across the county right up to the walls of Nottingham itself. On 18 September, 600 Royalists under the command of Sir Richard Byron, governor of Newark, actually entered Nottingham by a mixture of subterfuge and stealth. According to Lucy Hutchinson, they were let into the town by 'Alderman Toplady, a great malignant, having the watch', and no alarm was given to the castle.[29]

The force from Newark quickly and quietly took control of the town but made no attempt on the garrison within the castle; instead, they turned to plundering the homes of those in Nottingham who were identified as supporters of Parliament. It was fortunate for the Parliamentarians that the Royalists did not make a concerted attempt to take the castle because, contrary to instructions issued by its governor, the majority of its soldiers and officers had left the garrison to sleep in their own homes in the town. When the governor of the castle, John Hutchinson, awoke next morning, he discovered not only the Royalists in the town but that he had only 80 men in

---

29   Keeble (ed.), *Memoirs of Colonel Hutchinson*, pp.124–26.

the castle to defend it.[30] He managed to get a messenger out through a sally port to take a message calling for help to Parliamentarians in Leicester and Derby. For five days, the Royalists from Newark remained in Nottingham, looting without hinder, though, according to Lucy Hutchinson, ordinance at the castle was able to fire out at them, killing some of the soldiers and a few of the civilians. Over the five days, a number of the Parliamentarian soldiers who were sleeping in the town when the Royalists first got into it were able to sneak back into the castle, doubling Hutchinson's force to around 160 men.

After five days, the Royalists withdrew from the town once a relief force was known to be coming to help the castle, but they left behind 25 men who were captured. The Royalists had established a fort at Trent Bridge and left the then Captain Rowland Hacker with 80 men to garrison it after their withdrawal. This fort was to considerably limit movement into and out of the town and travel up the River Trent, and Colonel Hutchinson was not able to recapture it until after heavy fighting and bombardment over the period of 9–13 October. On entering the fort on the morning of 13 October, they discovered that the Royalists had slipped away overnight, destroying two arches of the bridge to hinder any pursuit.[31] The Royalist garrison at Newark had proven yet again that it was a real threat to Parliamentarian hegemony across the region, even when Newcastle and his army were no longer in the area.

Battle of Winceby, 11 October 1643

The month of October proved to be one of considerable setbacks for the Royalist garrison at Newark. It began with a defeat on the battlefield and ended with the loss of Lincolnshire to the Parliamentarians. Newcastle's failure to set up a close siege of Hull contributed significantly to the catalogue of disasters that happened next.

On 20 September 1643, Willoughby and Cromwell were able to cross the River Humber and enter Hull for a conference with Lord Fairfax, the Parliamentarian commander. As a result, it was agreed that Sir Thomas Fairfax would be sent across the river to Lincolnshire with 25 troops of horse to join up with Cromwell. The force sent by Newcastle to intercept this party proved to be inadequate to prevent this escape. In August 1643, the Earl of Manchester had been appointed commander of the Eastern Association, with the brief from Parliament to move north into Lincolnshire to block any attempt by Newcastle to move southwards towards London. Initially, he was tied up with the siege of King's Lynn, which fell on 16 September. At this point, he moved on to Boston, having sent a further 500 soldiers to enter Hull to aid its defence. At Boston, Manchester, Cromwell and Fairfax met up, creating an army of 6,000 foot and 1,500 horse.[32]

---

30   Wood, *Nottinghamshire in the Civil War*, p.57.

31   Wood, *Nottinghamshire in the Civil War*, p.59.

32   Young and Holmes, *English Civil War*, pp.154–56.

Engraving of Thomas Lord Fairfax dated 1807. Engraver Bocquet. (Author's collection)

The combined forces of Parliament under the command of Manchester arrived before the Royalist garrison at Bolingbroke Castle on the evening of 9 October and issued a summons to surrender. This was rejected, and skirmishes immediately began the next day.[33] The siege had to be quickly broken off, as Manchester received information from a cavalry detachment of Sir Thomas Fairfax that they had encountered the vanguard of an approaching Royalist force. The approaching Royalist force consisted of around 2,000 horse and 800 dragoons under the command of Sir William Widdrington, who had been appointed the senior Royalist commander by Newcastle after the death of Sir Charles Cavendish. With him were Sir John Henderson and a number of horse from the Newark garrison. Their combined force was considerably smaller than that of Manchester's, but they sought only to force Manchester to break off the siege. In some accounts, Henderson is identified as the commander, but this was not the case, and, according to the memoirs of Twentyman, there was a degree of friction between him and Widdrington. Henderson had proven to be a brave and efficient governor at Newark, and this possibly coloured Twentyman's memory and account: 'the Lord Witherington would needes encounter them, though Sir John Henderson was utterly against it who was comander in cheife, untill the other provoked him by telling him he was a coward, & then his judgment yeild to his reputation & honour, but the victory soon fell to the Parlimenteers'.

The Parliamentarian victories at Winceby are often seen as the first significant military triumph of Oliver Cromwell, not least by Cromwell himself, but, as we shall see, the significant contributions were made by Manchester and Fairfax. It was Manchester who decided to break the siege to confront the Royalist army – Cromwell had advised against the plan, claiming that his horses were exhausted.[34]

The two armies met near the village of Winceby, six miles from Bolingbroke, and both drew up on the crest of opposite hills about 600 yards apart. The Royalists, including those from Newark, placed their dragoons in the van, with their horse divided behind them in three divisions. Sir William Saville commanded the right wing, with Henderson and the Newark Horse on the left. The third division was kept in reserve under Widdrington. The Royalists made the first move, and the battle degenerated into a ferocious melee occurring between the ridges in the landscape, with Cromwell having his horse shot from under him and, before gaining another mount, getting knocked over the head. This took him out of action for quite a while. Fairfax

---

33   'The Siege of Bolingbroke Castle', *Heritage Lincolnshire*, <https://www.heritagelincolnshire.org/resources/the-siege-of-bolingbroke-castle>, accessed 3 and 5 Sept. 2022.

34   Young and Holmes, *English Civil War*, p.155.

won the day by surveying the landscape and discerning a way to secretly get round the Royalist army and attack it from the rear. This caught the Royalists by surprise, and their horse broke, racing from the field of battle in all directions to escape. A number were caught at a gate that opened inwards towards them, and a great slaughter occurred there as the Parliamentarian horse caught up with them. To this day, the place is still known as 'Slash Hollow'. Total casualties estimated for the battle were 1,000 Royalists and 20 Parliamentarians, but the latter figure is probably a gross underestimate for propaganda purposes.[35]

The defeat was costly, but worse was to follow for the garrison at Newark. Manchester was able to march northwards, and Lincoln surrendered to him on 20 October. On 20 December, Parliamentarian forces led by Sir John Meldrum from Hull stormed Gainsborough, taking 300 prisoners, including Lord Chaworth, the owner of Wiverton Hall, one of the smaller Royalist garrisons that formed a defensive ring around Newark.

The Newark Garrison to the End of the Year

On the same day as the Battle of Winceby, Newcastle lifted the siege of Hull and, by early November, had established himself with his army in Derbyshire. The next month, he moved to Nottinghamshire and quartered his army there over the Christmas period.[36] This mitigated the impact of the loss of Lincolnshire for the garrison at Newark and encouraged them to continue collecting provisions and subsidies from all around the region. According to the Royalist newsletter *Mercurius Aulicus*, on 27 November, the Newark Horse raided as far afield as Melton Mowbray in north Leicestershire and captured 'five companies of horse, one of foot and the entire parliamentarian committee for that county who were then gathered there'. It was claimed that the Royalists suffered no casualties.[37]

The year ended on a very unsavoury incident when the Marquis of Newcastle, raised in the peerage by the King in October, sought to bribe John and George Hutchinson to surrender the castle, town and bridges of Nottingham to the King. Whilst Newcastle's army was quartered in Nottinghamshire during December, Lucy Hutchinson claimed that 'the regiments [Royalist] that were quartered nearest to Nottingham were Sir Marmaduke Langdale's and Colonel Dacre's'.[38] Dacre was a close friend of George Hutchinson, and, through their friendship, he sought to convey from Newcastle a cash bribe to both brothers to change sides. They both declined the attempted bribe, and the correspondence was shared with Parliament, both to cover them and to blacken the character of Newcastle.[39]

35   'Siege of Bolingbroke Castle', <https://www.heritagelincolnshire.org/resources/the-siege-of-bolingbroke-castle>.

36   Wood, *Nottinghamshire in the Civil War*, p.59.

37   Early English Books Online (EEBO), *Mercurius Aulicus*, 1 December 1643.

38   Keeble (ed.), *Memoirs of Colonel Hutchinson*, pp.140–42.

39   Firth (ed.), *Memoirs of Colonel Hutchinson*, pp.409–15, Appendix VIV.

4

The Ebb and Flow of War, 1644

Start of a New Year

The garrison at Newark had been dangerously isolated by the fall of both Lincoln and Gainsborough to Parliamentarian forces following the defeat of Royalist forces at Winceby. The presence of the Marquis of Newcastle and his Northern Army overwintering in Nottinghamshire possibly mitigated the growing fears within the town. Early in January though, Newcastle had to leave the region and move northwards to confront the Scottish army, now siding with Parliament after the latter had passed the Solemn League and Covenant at Westminster in September 1643. Scottish forces subsequently crossed the River Tweed and entered England on 19 January 1644.

In spite of the deteriorating situation across the region, the year began with a number of attacks against Parliamentarian bases by forces sent out from Newark. Early in January, Newark cavalry raided the towns of Grantham and Sleaford, and, on 12 January, they surprised troops of Cromwell's regiment in their quarters at Harmston and Waddington.[1] On Tuesday, 16 January 1644, a rather audacious attempt was made upon the town of Nottingham by 1,500 troops from Newark under the command of Sir Charles Lucas. Lucy Hutchinson put their figure at around 3,000, but John Hutchinson's reported figure of 1,500 seems more accurate given the size of the garrison at Newark at this time. According to Lucy Hutchinson, scouts detected their approach and informed her husband. John Hutchinson sent two companies of foot along with the Nottinghamshire Horse to defend the unfinished outwork defences around the town. The Royalist force proved to be too large for the defences to be held, and so a successful strategic withdrawal back to the security of the castle was undertaken.[2] The forces of Lucas advanced right up to the walls of the castle and were just about to issue a summons to Hutchinson to surrender the castle and town when a Parliamentarian counterattack reversed the Royalist advances.

Whilst Lucy Hutchinson's account contains much information, as always, it has a tendency to downplay the actions of others whilst extolling

---

1   Holmes, *Seventeenth-Century Lincolnshire*, p.172.
2   Keeble (ed.), *Memoirs of Colonel Hutchinson*, pp.144–48.

Colonel John Hutchinson, Parliamentarian governor of Nottingham Castle. Engraver V. Focillon. (Author's collection)

the role of her husband, John Hutchinson. In a letter probably written to Gilbert Millington, the town's MP then sitting at Parliament, by Colonel John Hutchinson, he gave his own account of the actions of that day:

Sir – About six of the clock in the morning, Jan. 16th 1643, the enemy faced us on both sides of the town; and our horse with two foot companies went to the works, but they being a very great number, and the works not yet defensible in many places they (to give them their due) very bravely came on, and forced their way into the town, and our horse and foot were both forced to retreat to the castle, but we had not one man slain or wounded in the retreat. Our ordinance from the castle made a lane among them at their entry, and our musketeers killed many of them as they retreated into the castle. The enemy possessed themselves of St. Peter's Church, and those houses and street ends, which hindered our sallying out, but when our horse saw they were able to do no service (their body of horse being far greater), Colonel Thornhagh and all the other horse commanders encouraged their troopers to take muskets in their hands and serve as foot (which to their great glory they very cheerfully and courageously did), and with a foot company joined to part of them, sallied out and beat the Cavaliers out of the nearest houses to the castle and possessed them. When we saw our sally and retreat, both made indifferent safe, we drew our two other foot companies, and all the rest of the troopers with muskets, who went on with so great courage and valour, that they drove the enemy before them out of the town, with a great deal of dishonour and confusion. We have now eighty prisoners and all their arms, and a great many killed, the certain number whereof I cannot relate; divers of them were wounded and carried dead off from the field, some they had buried in the field before they had entered the town.[3]

The account of Colonel John Hutchinson goes on to recount that they followed a trail of blood in the snow for two miles as the Royalist made their way back to the garrison at Newark.

This setback did not discourage the garrison at Newark too much, for again, on 17 February 1644, they made another attempt at Nottingham. A force of soldiers under the command of Colonel Rowland Hacker attempted to gain entry into the town by capturing the fort at Trent Bridge. A small party of around 30 disguised as country folk attending the Saturday market led horses carrying sacks, in which they had hidden their weapons. Once they had gained control of the fort, they were to signal to the main party of Royalists outside the town to come on in. Unfortunately for them, Hutchinson had been forewarned about this plan, and he had additional security put in place for the market day. Of that small party, 12 were apprehended, and nine of them were forced into the River Trent, of whom five were drowned and the other four were apprehended on the other bank of the river. The bulk of the Royalist force outside the town, realising what had happened, retreated without any casualties back to Newark.[4] One of the most interesting things to note about the account is that, without any comment, the markets at Nottingham were continuing to be held throughout this period of conflict in the county town. In fact, the regularity of the event made it possible for the Royalists to plan an attempt on the town based on an anticipated market day.

Second Siege of Newark, 29 February–21 March 1644

The attempt by Colonel Hacker upon the town of Nottingham was to be the last venture before the Newark garrison was itself besieged. When Newcastle left Nottinghamshire to engage the Scottish army, he removed from Newark any troops that could be spared to strengthen his army and continued to do so at other Yorkshire garrisons. This weakening of Royalist garrisons left

---

3   The original letter can be found in the Tanner manuscripts at the Bodleian Library but is reproduced in full in Firth (ed.), *Memoirs of Colonel Hutchinson*, pp.418–20, Appendix XVIII.

4   Early English Books Online (EEBO), *Three Great Victories Obtained by the Parliaments Force, &c.*, TT: E34 (14); Wood, *Nottinghamshire in the Civil War*, pp.65–66.

Newark extremely vulnerable and open to attack. A Parliamentarian force under the command of Sir John Meldrum, though Lord Willoughby was present for some of the siege, marched towards Newark. Under Meldrum was a group of prominent county commanders. These included Colonel Rossiter with the Lincolnshire force, two Eastern Association regiments who were garrisoning the city of Lincoln, forces newly raised by Colonel King (then governor of Holland and Boston), Colonels Hutchinson and Thornhagh with the Nottinghamshire forces and Sir Edward Hartop with the Leicestershire and Derbyshire Horse.[5] According to Holmes, the diverse origins of the Parliamentarian commanders would prove beneficial to the defenders at Newark, for there were many 'dissentions and jealousies' amongst them.[6] A mixture of bad weather and poor discipline – Lucy Hutchinson bemoaned the fact that, once at Nottingham, Hartop was 'having more mind to drink than fight' – delayed the start of a close siege until the end of February.[7] The combined force of the Parliamentarians amounted to 2,000 horse, 5,000 foot, 11 guns and two mortars.[8] Unlike the first siege, this was a well-provisioned army sent to capture Newark, and the town was to experience life under considerable bombardment.

Sir John Meldrum, commander of the Parliamentarian forces at the second siege of Newark. Engraver unknown. (Author's collection)

Sir Richard Byron, then governor of Newark, was as prepared as he could be for a siege but, quite early on, had managed to get a message to the King explaining the dire circumstances that the town was in. Before the siege was complete, he had also managed to send away most of the Newark Horse to Royalist garrisons in Leicestershire and Derbyshire, retaining only six troops of horse at the town. This was essential, as large numbers of horse within the town would be a constant drain on the town's resources during a siege. Byron also had around 1,200 foot in the town, though some of the townspeople would have probably rallied to the defences over the duration of the siege, giving him on paper around 2,000 troops to face the might of the besieging force.

For the people of Newark, the siege was perceived as beginning on 29 February, for, in the minute book of the borough corporation, there is a note that reads, 'Particulars of such sums of money as were lent by the several persons under named unto his Majesty's commissioners here in the siege of this town begun 29 February 1643/4.'[9] The citizens of Newark clearly

---

5   Young and Holmes, *English Civil War*, pp.176–77.
6   Holmes, *Seventeenth-Century Lincolnshire*, p.172.
7   Keeble (ed.), *Memoirs of Colonel Hutchinson*, pp.154–55.
8   Young and Holmes, *English Civil War*, p.177.
9   NA: DC/NW/3/1/1: Borough Minutes, 29 February 1643/4.

responded to Byron's appeal for support, as the minute book goes on to record the sum of £75 5s was quickly raised for his use to strengthen the defences.

According to a report of the siege by the Parliamentarian Lieutenant Colonel Bury, submitted to the Council of State after the event, it was stated, 'When we first drew before Newarke, Colonell Kings Regiment marched to the Countesse of Exceters house, where a part of the Regiment had a sharp conflict, and after they had gained that place, the enemies horse gave them a hot & desperate charge, notwithstanding they remained masters of the place.'[10]

Not until 6 March was the Royalist fort at Muskham Bridge taken, thus securing the island opposite Newark for the Parliamentarians. The fort's importance to the defence of Newark was shown by the fact that Byron had placed a garrison there of 350 men. In the fight at the bridge, the Royalist regiment raised by Gervase Holles defending the fort was destroyed, and William Holles was killed fighting alongside his men.[11] This would have caused a deal of angst both in Newark and the surrounding area, not least because Gervase Holles had raised the regiment for the King in and around the town in 1642.

Now that the siege was complete, Meldrum could begin the bombardment of the town. Whilst the cannons fired upon the earthwork defences, it would have been the mortars, which were situated on Beacon Hill, that brought the greater destruction within the town and fear to the inhabitants. John Twentyman, who was in the town during the siege, recalled in his account, 'They shott after they had formed their League 13 peices of ordinance every night & 2 Bomballs about 12 and one of the clock'.

The mortar bombs fell indiscriminately on both the poor and the affluent civilians of the town. Their purpose was to create fear, and that they did. Fortunately, the wet weather leading up to the siege meant that the thatch roofs were sodden and not easy to set alight. Amongst the many buildings damaged or destroyed was that of the alderman, later mayor of Newark, Hercules Clay. After several disturbed nights of dreams, he moved his family out of their home in the marketplace into a different residence the day before his home was completely destroyed. In thankfulness, Clay noted in his will, 'that it pleased God of his infinite mercy wonderfully to p[re]serve me and my wife from a fearefull destruction by a terrible blowe of grenadoe'. He went on in his will to leave £100 to the poor and a further £100 for a sermon to be preached annually on 11 March – the anniversary of his deliverance.[12] Also during the siege, the homes of Alderman Baker (mayor, 1646) and Mr Christopher Martin (mayor, 1655) were hit by cannon shot, their social status ensuring that these events were remembered and recorded.[13]

10   Lieutenant Colonel Bury, *A Briefe Relation of the Siege at Newark* ... (London: Peter Cole, 1644), p.3.

11   Young and Holmes, *English Civil War*, p.177.

12   Newark Library, Will of Hercules Clay dated 11 December 1644. Typed Transcript, L98.3CLA.

13   Robert Thoroton, *The Antiquities of Nottinghamshire* (London: Robert White, 1677), pp.197–98.

It was the poor of Newark who probably suffered most during this bombardment. Their flimsy homes quickly disintegrated when struck and are rarely mentioned in the surviving records. Overcrowding became even worse as those made homeless had to be accommodated in the surviving buildings. A rare survival is a petition of one such poor family, which was fortunate to have been written on the reused parchment of the will of the influential Newark citizen Thomas Waite that was dated 20 July 1644. The quality of the handwriting suggests that it had been written by a third party after the siege had ended and when the corporation was then possibly in a position to respond to it. The petition states, 'Your poor peticioner hath in a verie large manner tasted of the miseries and affliccons of these tymes for at the last fight against Newarke he had his house blowne upp with a granado and all his goods burnt and broken to the utter undoeinge of your poore peticioner, his wife and seaven children.'[14] There survives no evidence as to if, or how, the corporation responded to this petition, and a number of the poor across the town may have possibly experienced similar hardships during the siege.

According to the Royalist newssheet *Mercurius Aulicus*, on 8 March, an attempt was made by the Parliamentarians to storm the defences of the town at three separate places simultaneously, but the defenders were able to drive them back, with a loss to the attackers of 500 men.[15] After this failure, the besiegers began an even more intensive bombardment of the town to soften up its defences. The Royalists within the town, whenever possible, sallied out to attack the besiegers. According to the report of Lieutenant Colonel Bury, 'When part of Sir Michael Hubbard Regiment were marching off the guard towards their quarters at Balderton, the Enemie sallied forth with nigh 100 Horse, finding them without light Matches fell upon them, tooke their Colours, and carried them prisoners into Newarke.'[16]

On this occasion, around 200 prisoners were brought into Newark, forcing the Parliamentarians to review their procedures for changing their watches at the siege works overnight. Extinguishing your matches as you returned to your barracks in the dark certainly made military sense prior to this attack, as the lighted match could have drawn the attention of Royalist snipers within the town.

After 10 March, the situation within Newark was becoming desperate, and even the besiegers felt that the town would soon fall. Royalist cavalry from Belvoir Castle, under the command of Gervase Lucas, made an attempt to break the siege, but they were easily driven back by the Parliamentarian forces. It was at this stage, realising the importance of Newark as a bridge between his forces in the north and south of the country, that the King stepped in. On 12 March, he gave a direct order to Prince Rupert, who at the time was at Chester, to march to Newark's relief. Rupert was hindered by a lack of troops, which meant that, on his march to Newark, he had to

---

14   Nottinghamshire Archives (NA): PR/NW 22 October 1645: Will of Thomas Waite. The petition is on the reverse of the will.

15   EEBO, *Mercurius Aulicus*, 16 March 1643/1644.

16   Bury, *Siege at Newark*, p.4.

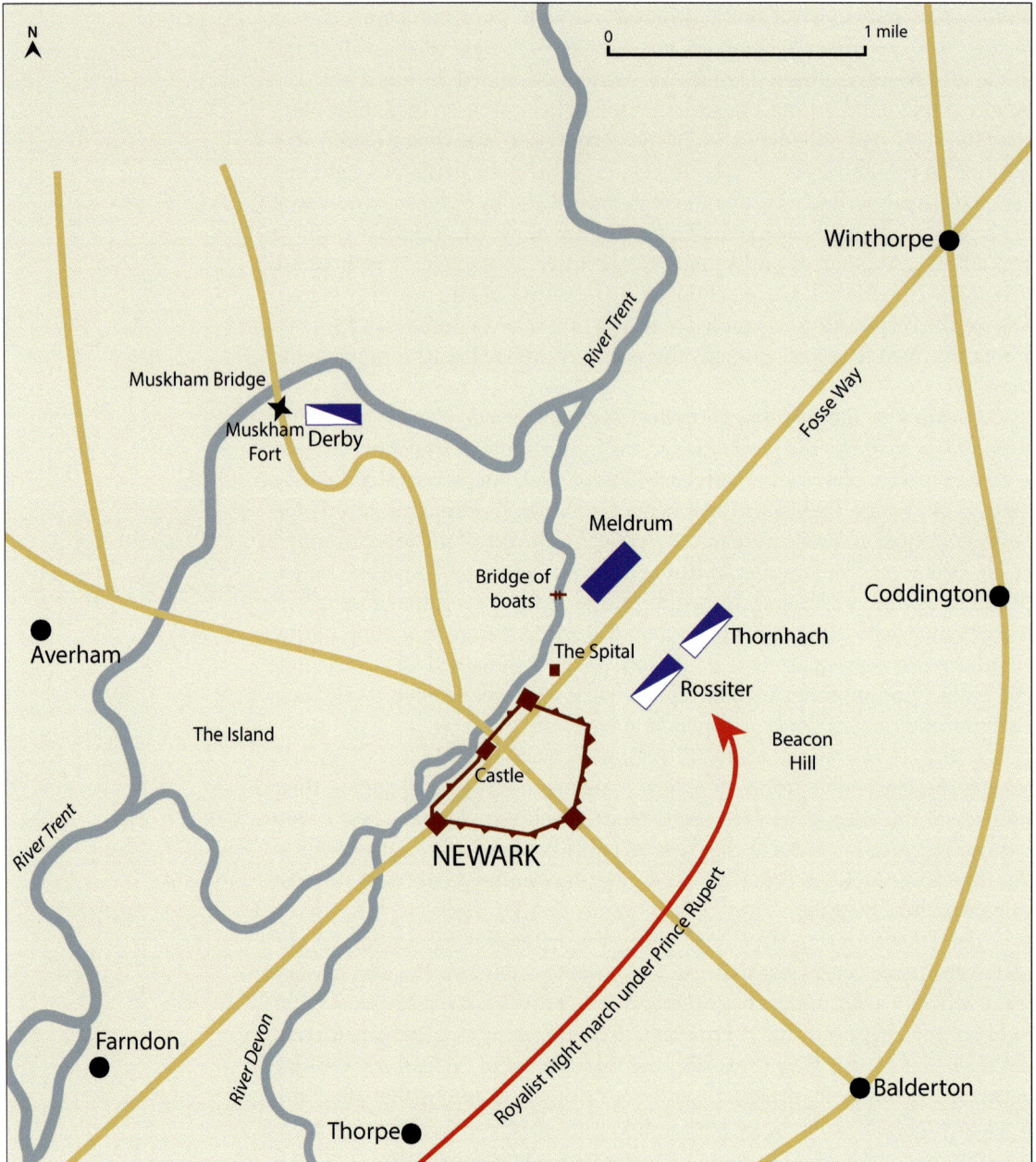

The second siege of Newark, 1644.

take a route via the Royalist garrisons at Chirk, Shrewsbury, Bridgnorth, Wolverhampton and Lichfield to collect additional soldiers from each of these places. He then made his way towards Ashby-de-la-Zouch, in north Leicestershire, where Lord Loughborough (Henry Hastings) was beginning to assemble a force of 2,700 men to join the prince. Meldrum was alerted to Loughborough's attempt to raise an army, but, as of then, he was unsure where Prince Rupert's forces were. On 16 March, Meldrum sent Sir Edward Hartop with 2,000 horse and dragoons from the siege to gather information about Royalist movements. Later in the morning, Hartop's forces skirmished with 600 Royalist musketeers under Major General Porter at Mountsorrel in Leicestershire who were making their way south to rendezvous with Loughborough's forces in anticipation of the arrival of Prince Rupert and his forces. A more extensive engagement ensued at Cotes Bridge, just north of Mountsorrel, the very next day as Hartop was returning back to Meldrum.[17]

Hartop returned to Newark with information about Prince Rupert's close presence at Ashby-de-la-Zouch, which gave Meldrum and his generals time, they believed, to hold a council of war. Sir Miles Hobart had advocated that they should lift the siege and retreat to Lincoln, but Meldrum felt they had time to prepare and so drew his foot into the Spittal and arranged his horse accordingly. The bridge of boats he had constructed across the river by the Spittal to the island, which they had earlier secured, provided them with an avenue of retreat if required. What Meldrum and his fellow commanders had not allowed for was a piece of innovative strategy on the part of Rupert. Realising that both speed and surprise were going to be essential for victory, Rupert did not tarry but forced his troops on, moving from Ashby to Rempstone on 19 March and arriving at Bingham, eight miles away from Newark, the next day. Here, he halted and sent spies ahead to observe Meldrum's forces. Travelling just over 42 miles in two days, with an army of not just horse but also foot, was quite an endurance achievement for the Royalist forces. Estimates about the exact size of Rupert's forces have been difficult to ascertain because of conflicting evidence from the time, but Wood's assessment of just less than 3,000 horse and 3,000 foot seems not unrealistic. It is also a figure that Lucy Hutchinson claimed in her *Memoirs*.[18] His force was not that much smaller than Meldrum's of 7,000, but, whereas the Parliamentarians had the benefit of fighting behind fortifications and earthworks, Rupert's had been on a forced march over two days. Also, Meldrum had sent the Derbyshire Horse over to the island to support the infantry there that were constructing a fort at Muskham Bridge, diminishing the total strength of his horse facing Rupert on Beacon Hill.[19] Rupert had one advantage that Meldrum appears to have underestimated though, and that was the Royalist forces within besieged Newark.

Rupert's scouts reported back to him at Bingham on the evening of 20 March, and their account of Meldrum's movement of troops across the

---

17 Jennings, *A Very Gallant Gentleman*, pp.50–52.
18 Wood, *Nottinghamshire in the Civil War*, p.76; Keeble (ed.), *Memoirs of Colonel Hutchinson*, p.156.
19 Young and Holmes, *English Civil War*, p.178.

bridge of boats, which he intended to use to strengthen the fort at Muskham Bridge, was interpreted by Rupert as a sign that he was going to withdraw. He acted quickly, calling a parade of his forces at 2:00 a.m. on 21 March, and led the van of his horse, interspersed with dragoons, as Rupert appears to have often favoured in his military tactics, leaving his foot and the rest of his forces to follow. The Royalists arrived at Beacon Hill on the morning of 21 March around 9:00 a.m., and Rupert immediately launched a holding attack on the Parliamentarian horse.

What unfolded over the next few hours was witnessed by John Twentyman from the church spire in Newark, and it is his eyewitness account that will introduce our analysis of one of Prince Rupert's greatest successes in the Civil War:

> Prince Rupert came & raised this seige. I saw the Engagement from the Pinacles or steeple. They of the Parliament drew up their horse into one main Body & 2 wings under the brow of Beacon Hill against that place where Spittle stood, & where all their Infantry were enskonsed & there they had a Bridge of Boats over the Trent. The Prince charged one wing coming with fury upon them from Codington ward, & after the charge both retired that wing to the main body & the Prince with his up the Hill, & presently he came down upon the other wing & they did as before on both sides. Upon the 3d assault the Prince coming with his whole Body upon theirs totally routed them & fell so in with them they made a length from the hill to Spittle; there the Horse would have broke into their own Foot, but they shott to keep them out. Many fled over the Bridge of Boates & all would have gone, but they were forced to stay some that they might make the better composition for themselves & they were & did leave all their armes behind them & march away. Thus the Lord delivered us this time also. This was the second siege.[20]

Twentyman had a panoramic view of the battle from the height of the steeple whilst those directly involved in the battle would have had a more limited view but a much more personal experience as it unfolded. As Wood himself pointed out, 'the details of the fight are lost in a maze of contradictory evidence', of which Twentyman's account is a part.[21] He claimed that the Royalist horse made three charges into the Parliamentarian horse, whilst other accounts speak only of two. What follows is an account that tries to create a general overview of the battle, incorporating the various accounts.

The battle began around 9:00 a.m., though which side initiated the first charge is unclear. Rupert had divided his horse and dragoons into two wings: his own regiment of around 500 horse on the right and his lifeguard, of which Rupert took command, on the left. Facing them, the Parliamentarian horse was also divided into two wings: the Lincolnshire Horse, under the command of Colonel Rossiter, and the Nottinghamshire Horse, supplemented by some troops of the Lincolnshire regiment, forming the other. The fighting was intense and hand to hand, and, at one point, Rossiter drove the right wing of the Royalists back up the hill on to their reserves, but they were able to

---

20   John Twentyman's full account of the Civil War at Newark is reproduced in Appendix I.
21   Wood, *Nottinghamshire in the Civil War*, p.78.

reform and charge the Lincolnshire Horse again, forcing them to retreat right back to the Spittal. On the other wing, the Nottinghamshire troops under Thornhagh's command also met the Royalist charge. The larger force under Rupert shattered the Nottinghamshire Horse, though not without a fierce fight in which Colonel Thornhagh was seriously wounded.[22] What was left of the Parliamentarian horse fled to the Spittal, where Meldrum began to send them across the river on the bridge made of boats.

This fierce cavalry action was followed by a lull in the fighting, during which time Rupert's infantry arrived from Bingham. An attempt was made upon Meldrum's fort by the Irish foot under the command of Henry Tiller, but they were repelled with considerable force by the Parliamentarian infantry. This may have been the third attack Twentyman saw and attributed to the Royalist horse. It was Royalist units from the town of Newark that eventually turned the battle in Rupert's favour. They crossed on to the island and made for the fort at Muskham Bridge to retake it. The Derbyshire Horse, covering the Parliamentarian infantry guarding the fort, fled at the approach of the Royalists. The remaining Parliamentarian horse at the Spittal tried to move on to the island, realising that, if the Royalist took the fort, they too might find their escape route blocked, and so many, but not all, were able to flee before the bridge fell. Once the Newark force took the fort, Meldrum and his infantry at the Spittal found themselves totally isolated and unable to escape.

An interrogation of a captured Parliamentarian soldier had revealed to Rupert that the soldiers at the Spittal had only two days of food left; he therefore decided that, rather than risk further casualties to his forces, he would wait and starve Meldrum out. He did not have long to wait. Around 9:00 p.m. in the evening, Meldrum sued for terms, and, after negotiations through the night and by 7:00 a.m. next morning, terms had been agreed. The Parliamentarian army was allowed to march out unmolested, but all their arms had to be left behind. In his report to the Council of State, Lieutenant Colonel Bury listed what this amounted to:

> Postscript
>
> The reporter judgeth the Enemy, being joined with the Newarkers, to be nigh 3,000 Foot and Dragoones and 4,000 horse, without artillery, and that we have lost two mortars, one Denay Cannon, one Sacre, Seven or eight Drakes, Armes for 3,000, and much Ammunition.[23]

The garrison at Newark may have been devoid of ordinance at the start of the siege, but they acquired plenty after the defeat of Meldrum, and this was to be incorporated into the extensive defences they were to build around the town over the next nine months.

This was to be one of Prince Rupert's most successful campaigns in the Civil War. It was certainly the bloodiest and largest battles fought within the county of Nottinghamshire. The Parliamentarians were estimated to have

---

22   Keeble (ed.), *Memoirs of Colonel Hutchinson*, pp.156–57.
23   Bury, *Siege at Newark*, p.8.

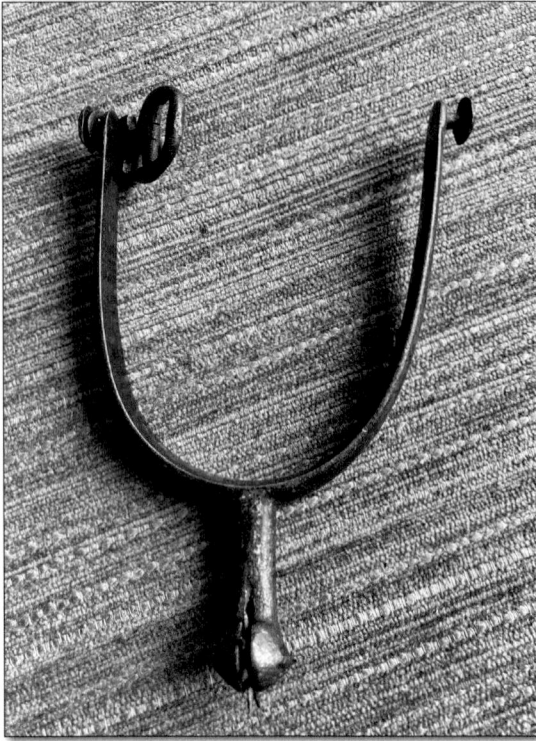

Broken seventeenth-century cavalry spur found outside of the town of Newark in the twentieth century. (Author's collection)

lost around 200 men, whilst the Royalist losses amounted to less than half that number.[24]

Immediate Aftermath of the Lifting of the Siege

The immediate aftermath for Parliamentarians across the region was devastating. Meldrum managed to march to Hull with 2,000 of his men, but the garrisons at Gainsborough, Lincoln and Sleaford were abandoned to the Royalists, who took control of most of Lincolnshire once again. Just as significant was the fact that the Nottingham and Derby Parliamentarians who managed to return to their towns now had to work with haste preparing their defences for an expected assault upon them by Rupert. Celebrations and bell ringing occurred within most Royalist centres, whilst the Newark Chamberlain's accounts for 1643/1644 record an additional financial outlay: 'Paide to Mr Hancke, maior, and by him disbursements to Prince Ruperts, Trumpeters and servants at the raising of the siege as Appears by Bill £5.10s'.[25]

Rupert's soldiers were exhausted, and the wounded needed to be cared for, so he remained at Newark until 27 March. His wounded soldiers appear to have been cared for in the homes of the town's citizens. There are two entries in the churchwarden's accounts immediately after the siege for 'winding sheets and inkles' for 'Prince Rupert's soldiers' who had succumbed to their wounds in the homes of townsfolk. It is interesting to note that the cost of their burials was paid by the parish by order of Mr Mayor and not those poor parishioners in whose homes they had died. Weeks later, the churchwardens again had to expend a further 3s 4d for two other of Rupert's men who had eventually succumbed to their wounds.[26]

On 25 March, whilst Rupert and his army was still recuperating in the town, the commissioners at Newark issued a summons to Colonel John Hutchinson to surrender Nottingham and its castle. Whether the commissioners believed the revitalised garrison troops at Newark were up to taking it, or if they believed Rupert would assist them, is unclear. The answer is probably irrelevant to the outcome, as, within two days, Rupert and his army were returning to Oxford, which he reached on 25 April. John Hutchinson delivered the following blunt reply to the summons:

---

24   Young and Holmes, *English Civil War*, p.179.
25   NCWC: NEKMS 2021.19.12–13: Newark Borough Miscellaneous Papers.
26   NA: PR/24810: Newark Churchwarden Accounts, 1643/1644.

To Sir John Digby and the rest of the gentlemen at Newark.

Gentlemen, – If the respect and care you express to this town and the country were directed the right way, it would be much happiness to both. As for your threats to this poor town, we have already had experience of your malicious endeavours to execute that mischief which you now threaten; but God restrained at that time both the rage of your cruel hearts, and the power of the devouring element, and I trust he will still do the same for us. I never engaged myself in this service with any respect to the success of other places. Though all the kingdom were quit by our forces, which I trust God will never permit, yet I would never forsake the trust and charge I have in my hand till the authority which honoured me with it shall command it from me. And if God suffer the place to perish I am resolved to perish with it, Being confidant that God at length will vindicate me to be a maintainer, and not a ruiner of my country.[27]

Two things are clear from the above response from the defenders at Nottingham. First, the Newark garrison were, by that time, already gaining a reputation for rapine and violence. Second, Hutchinson would not be intimidated, and he was totally committed to, what he believed, was the divine imperative of Parliament's cause.

The Road to Marston Moor and Its Subsequent Consequences

The Indian summer for Royalists at Newark, following Prince Rupert's success, was brief indeed. Newcastle, though having some initial success, was finding it increasingly difficult to hold back the Scottish army. He increasingly had to withdraw troops that could be spared from Royalist garrisons across Derbyshire, Nottinghamshire and Yorkshire to replenish his diminishing army, leaving Newark increasingly exposed. By 18 April 1643, Newcastle was hemmed in with his army in the city of York, and Parliament, realising that the opportunity to destroy Newcastle was at hand, ordered the army of the Eastern Association, under the command of the Earl of Manchester, to march through Lincolnshire to join the armies of Fairfax and the Scots in besieging York. On the morning of 6 May, the army of Manchester, amounting to around 6,000 men, stormed the city of Lincoln, taking an estimated 800 Royalist prisoners, most of whom had probably been recruited across the East Midlands. The Royalist hold on Lincolnshire, achieved after Rupert's success, was quickly broken, and their garrison at Gainsborough was also swiftly taken.[28]

Rupert was ordered by the King to go to Newcastle's help, but there was to be no repeat of his success at Newark. On 2 July, Rupert and Newcastle's armies were routed at the Battle of Marston Moor. Casualties were particularly high for the Royalists, with an estimated total of over 3,000 killed compared

---

27   Firth (ed.), *Memoirs of Colonel Hutchinson*, p.425, Appendix XXII.
28   Early English Books Online (EEBO), *True Relations of the Taking of the City of Lincoln*, E47;
       Anon., *HC Journal*, vol. III, p.486.

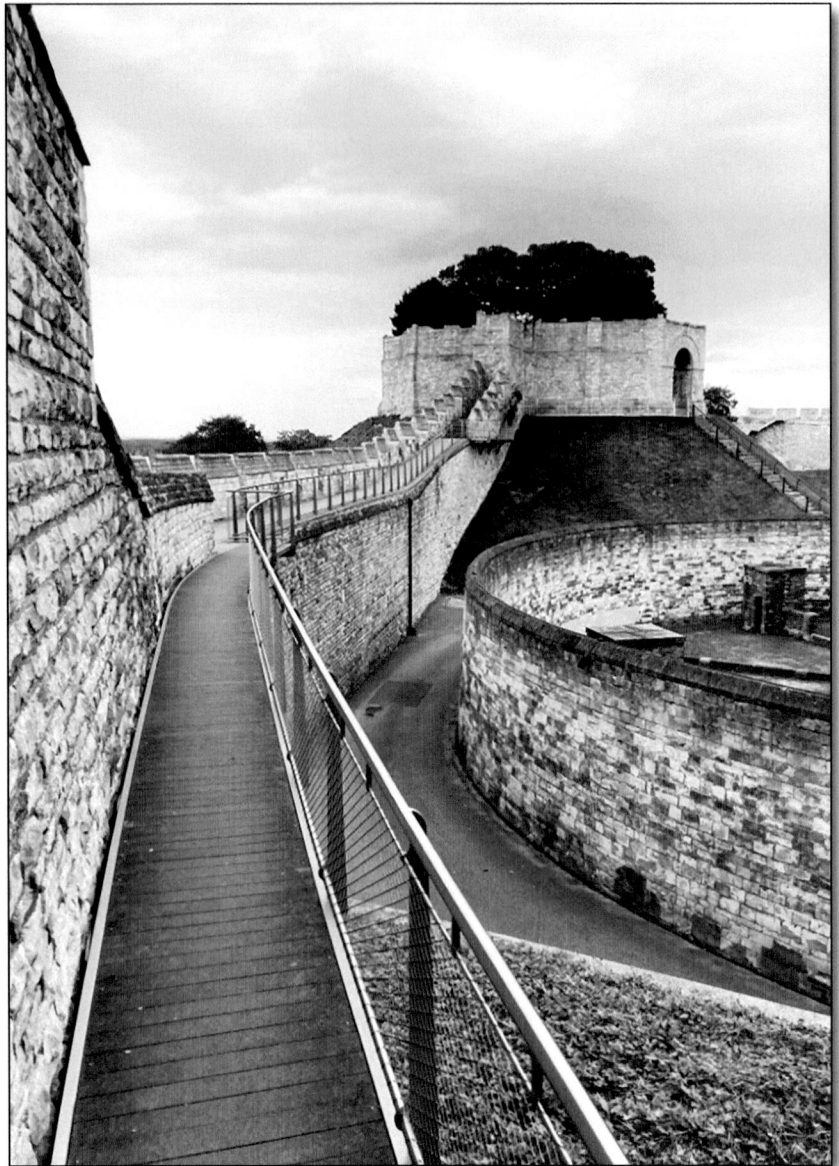

Lincoln Castle, stormed by the forces of the Earl of Manchester on their way to join General Fairfax and the Scottish army besieging the Royalist city of York, 1644. (Author's photograph)

to a figure of 300 given for the Parliamentarian forces.[29] Rupert did manage to get away with around 6,000 horse, but the majority of the Royalist foot had been either killed or captured. The whole of Newcastle's regiment, mainly recruited from the north-east but again probably replenished with troops from Nottinghamshire and Derbyshire at the start of the year, refused to surrender and continued fighting until the majority were killed. For the Royalists, control of the north had been lost, and the city of York eventually surrendered to Parliament on 16 July.

---

29 Peter Young, *Marston Moor 1644: The Campaign and the Battle* (Kineton: Roundwood Press, 1970), pp.217–18.

After their victory, the Parliamentarian forces broke up into their different parts, with the Eastern Association forces returning back to the East Midlands. On their return to Lincoln, they captured the Royalist garrisons at Sheffield, Stavely, Bolsover, Wingfield and Welbeck, the latter being the primary home of the Duke of Newcastle. The colonel of the Nottingham Horse, Francis Thornhagh, was appointed as the governor of that place.[30]

The forces at Newark were too weak to do anything about Manchester's movement across north Nottinghamshire, but, on 3 August, three troops of Manchester's horse were quartered at Tuxford. Over the night of 4 August, a surprise raid by the Newark Horse, under the command of Colonel Eyre, successfully attacked their quarters, capturing plunder and their colours.[31] Once Manchester reached Lincoln, he made little attempt to attack the Newark garrison, much to Oliver Cromwell's annoyance, and his hesitation was to create a division between the two commanders that was to eventually lead to the *Self-Denying Ordinance* of 1644. This stipulated that no member of the Houses of Commons or the Lords could hold command in the army. One of the consequences of this ordinance was the creation of the New Model Army in 1645, with the intention to achieve a complete victory over the King. Newark, though, had been spared in 1644 because of Manchester's failure to move against them.

On 2 September 1644, the Parliamentarian army under the control of the Earl of Essex was compelled to surrender to the Royalists at Lostwithiel in the county of Cornwall. This was in fact to be the last major success for the Royalists in the war, though, at the time, they hoped it would be the start of a revival in their cause. At Newark, the mayor of the town paid the sum of 2s 6d to the bell ringers 'ye 18th of Sept. upon the news of the routing of Essex his army'.[32] For a while, hope and bravado were restored to the Newark forces. The Earl of Manchester was ordered by Parliament to move his army south towards London from Lincoln, after the defeat of Earl of Essex, to help cover the capital from any potential Royalist attempt on it.

Throughout the autumn and early winter, Colonels Thornhagh and Rossiter, with the Nottinghamshire and Lincolnshire Horse respectively, were left alone to cover the movement of soldiers and goods into and out of Newark. Their forces, though, were totally inadequate to besiege the town, and, as the accounts of Colonel William Staunton's troop of horse show, troopers from Newark were still able to collect the contributions for their maintenance from villages across Nottinghamshire.[33]

There were inevitable clashes and minor skirmishes between the Parliamentarians and Royalist troopers of Newark over this period, as neither side could fully hinder the other from making raids. The largest action occurred at the end of October, as Royalist troops from Newark and its satellite garrisons gathered together to obey the King's order to relieve the besieged Royalist garrison at Crowland in Lincolnshire. Somewhere in the

---

30   Jennings, *A Very Gallant Gentleman*, p.57.
31   Wood, *Nottinghamshire in the Civil War*, p.85.
32   NA: PR/24810: Newark Churchwarden Accounts, 18 September 1644.
33   The functioning of Colonel William Staunton's regiment is explored further in Chapter 6.

vicinity of Belvoir, a Parliamentarian force, drawn from Nottinghamshire, Derbyshire and Lincolnshire, surprised them. The Royalists were routed, and Parliamentarian reports claim to have taken 800 prisoners whilst a number, including Sir John Girlington, were drowned in a milldam as they tried to escape. Crowland was not relieved and was eventually forced to surrender as a consequence.[34] On 18 November, Colonel Rossiter enjoyed success in a raid against Royalist forces quartered within a mile of Newark and took 80 prisoners.[35] Not to be outdone, Colonel Thornhagh, with the Nottinghamshire Horse, led a raiding party against what remained of Sir John Girlington's regiment of horse, quartered at Muskham Bridge, capturing some officers, horses and colours. In December, Thornhagh captured an outlying satellite garrison of Newark at Thurgarton, taking its commander, Sir Roger Cooper, and 40 men prisoners.[36]

The Newark Horse continued to be a problem though for both Parliamentarian commanders. At the very start of 1645, the Royalist newssheet *Mercurius Aulicus* reported:

> Colonel Eyre went out with some Newark Horse, fetched a compass round about the rebel's headquarter, and broke down a bridge, then gallantly charged the rebels, who instantly fled towards the bridge, which being broken, made four of them drown themselves for haste; the rest, two whole troops, both officers and soldiers, were taken to a man, who, with their colours, horses, and arms, were brought prisoners to Newark.[37]

Lucy Hutchinson supplies us with a little more detail about this event. She identified the two troops as being those of Captains Barrett and Sampson. The event happened at Southwell, less than seven miles away from Newark, and she blamed the defeat on the fact that Captain White's troop, being so near to their homes, 'presumed to be away one night when they should have been upon their guard'.[38]

The Royalist forces based at Newark probably hoped that this early successful start to the year was a harbinger of good things to come, but their hope proved to be ill placed.

---

34 Wood, *Nottinghamshire in the Civil War*, pp.86–88.
35 Bulstrode Whitelock, *Memorials of English Affairs from the Beginning of the Reign of Charles I to the Restoration of Charles II* (Oxford: Oxford University Press, 1853), vol. I, p.313.
36 Jennings, *A Very Gallant Gentleman*, p.58.
37 EEBO, *Mercurius Aulicus*, 6 January 1645.
38 Keeble (ed.), *Memoirs of Colonel Hutchinson*, p.191.

5

Construction of Newark's Final Defensive Fortifications, 1644–1645

The first two sieges of Newark had displayed to its governors just how vulnerable the town had been. Significant improvements had been made between the first and second sieges, as we have seen, and, although they had managed to keep Parliamentarian soldiers out of the town, they provided little protection against mortars and bombs being fired into it from strategic points in the surrounding landscape. The victory of Rupert at the end of the second siege had led to the capture of 11 cannons and two mortars, and these were left at Newark to be incorporated into a new network of earthwork defences around the town. The improvement of the defences continued from March 1644 right up to the end of the summer in 1645, which suggests a variety of individuals oversaw the construction work, as there were three different governors of the garrison over this period. The siege works of the Parliamentarian and Scottish forces will be explored in Chapter 8.

The final defensive works, as they existed in November 1645, appear to have been carefully laid out, with extensions beyond those put in place by Henderson and Byron. This has led to a theory that there was possibly an overall plan, or programme, that the two governors after Byron adhered to over the years 1644–1645. The architect or influencer of this overall plan of the defences is a matter of conjecture, assuming that there was only one, but plausible candidates have been suggested by a group of historians surveying the remaining siege works in the 1960s.[1] Certainly, the influence of the Dutch school of military engineering, and the technical skill displayed in the construction of the Royalist defences erected over the period of the Civil War, cannot be underestimated. Further research undertaken on the defensive remains (see below) since 1964 has in no way contradicted their findings, but they have broadened our understanding.

---

1   RCHM, *Newark Siegeworks*, pp.29–31.

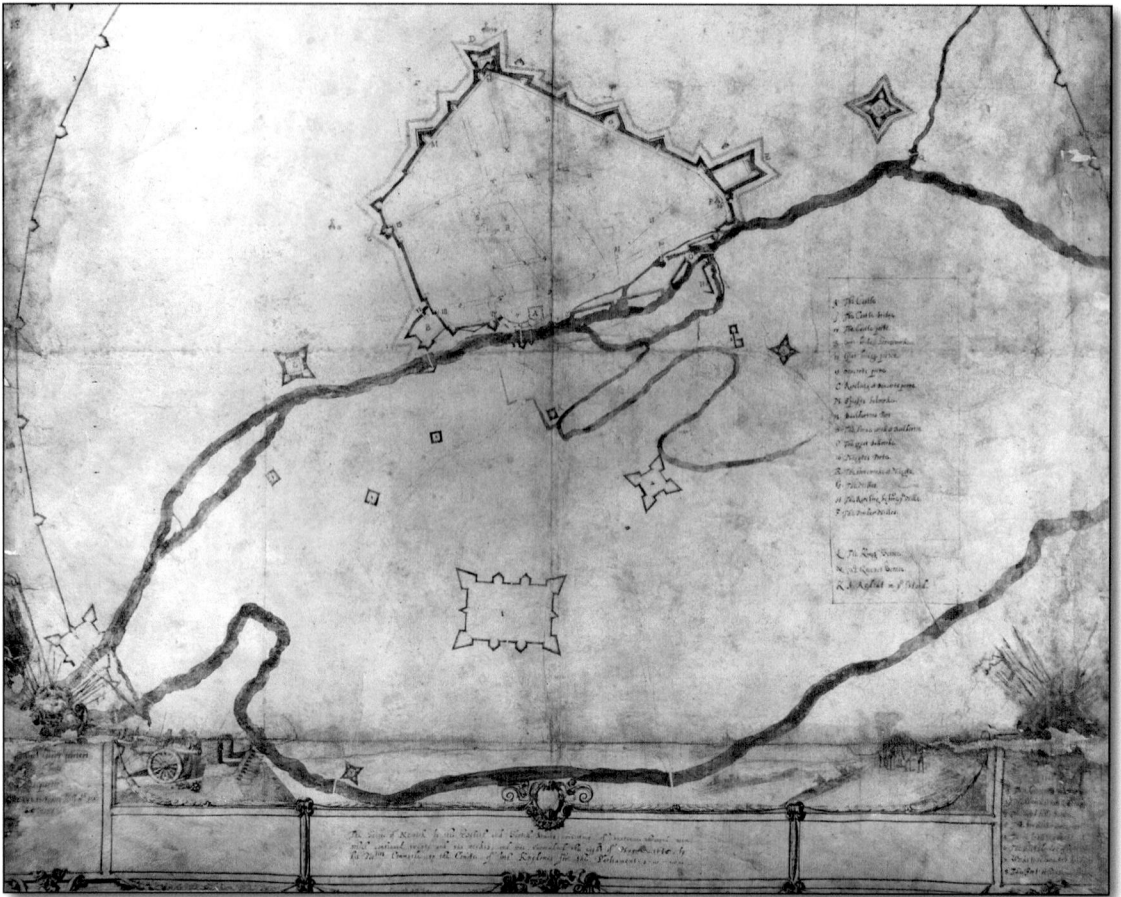

Newark Royalist siege map c. 1646, view from the west of the town looking over the two branches of the River Trent towards Newark. Unfinished drawing on Vellum. (National Civil War Centre, Newark, with permission)

Possible Influences upon the Construction of Newark's Defences

The name often associated with overseeing the design of many of the Royalist town defences across England is Bernard de Gomme.[2] At the National Civil War Centre – Newark Museum, there remains a contemporary map of the Royalist defensive works as they appeared around the end of the siege, which certainly is not adjudged to be in the style, or even the hand of de Gomme, but he may have possibly been with Rupert at Newark in 1644 and again in 1645.[3] The evidence for de Gomme's input is certainly circumstantial, but the argument is worth considering.

De Gomme was a Dutch engineer who, as a young man, served Frederick Henry, Prince of Orange, during a number of campaigns. He increasingly became recognised as an important contributor in the development of both constructing and destroying siege defences over the seventeenth century. Constant warfare across Europe over the sixteenth and seventeenth centuries,

---

2   RCHM, *Newark Siegeworks*, pp.30, 47, 65.
3   National Civil War Centre – Newark Museum (NCWC): *Original Plan on Vellum of the Siege of Newark* (Undated).

coupled with the development of ordinance utilising gunpowder, changed the nature of warfare over this period, and the technological advances achieved over at this time had a considerable impact upon the conduct of the British Civil Wars.[4] During this period, de Gomme became acquainted with Prince Rupert and, in 1642, accompanied him when he came to England to fight for his uncle Charles I. Such was his growing fame that, on his arrival, he was appointed as Engineer and Quartermaster General of the Royalist army, a post he held until May 1646.[5]

De Gomme often accompanied Rupert in his military campaigns during the Civil War, offering advice and technical expertise. The plans he drew up for the fortifications of Liverpool in 1644 still survive and are deposited in the British Museum.[6] By the time that Rupert was able to reach Newark to break the siege of 1644, the Parliamentarian besiegers of 7,000 men had been in place for three weeks. The prince would have had no warning of what sort of siege works and fortifications he might encounter on his arrival. It is not too large an assumption to make that this may have been just the sort of occasion when he would have brought de Gomme along with him. After the siege was lifted, Rupert remained in Newark for six days, giving de Gomme time to survey the defences and terrain around Newark and make suggestions about improvements to the town's military and civic authorities. He may have also returned to Newark at the end of 1645, when he came with Prince Rupert from Bristol (de Gomme was certainly in the city at its surrender), who rode to defend his actions at Bristol before the King. This, though, would have been too late for him to make any major changes to what was already in place, for a siege that was to begin in weeks.

Another significant contribution to the construction of Newark's town defences would have been Robert Ward's book *Animadversions of Warre*, which was published in 1639. For professional soldiers who had served overseas, such as Henderson and Willis, and other gentlemen interested in all things related to military expertise, Ward's book would have been well known and possibly even owned by them. The defenders at the garrison may also have consulted it, as they reviewed the town's defensive works to identify any shortcomings. A number of the illustrations included in this chapter are taken from the copy of the book that is on display at the National Civil War Centre in the town.

Newark's Final Defences

Before we begin to explore the town defences in the immediate vicinity of Newark, it is important to note that a series of smaller satellite garrisons had been established as an additional defensive ring within 15 miles of the

4   Christopher Duffy, *Siege Warfare: The Fortress in the Early Modern World, 1494–1660* (London: Routledge, 1996).

5   Anon., *CSPD*, 1660–1661, p.448.

6   British Museum: Add. MS 5027, A.3.69. See also Andrew Saunders, *Fortress Builder: Bernard de Gomme, Charles II's Military Engineer* (Liverpool: Liverpool University Press, 2004).

town. These included the fortification of gentry and aristocracy residences at Wiverton Hall (12 miles), Shelford Hall (13), Thurgarton Hall (16) and Belvoir Castle (15). The purpose of these outlying forts was to be an initial obstacle that had to be eliminated by an enemy approaching the town. The troops at these garrisons would also monitor movement along roads and routes in their area. They also provided additional accommodation for quartering troops and access to additional villages farther away from Newark, from which to collect contributions of goods and money as provisions. Often, these garrisons possessed only small numbers of soldiers and would be quickly abandoned and moved back to Newark if a large enemy force approached. Shelford proved to be the exception and attempted to resist the army of the Northern Association under the command of General Poyntz in November 1645. The garrison had to be stormed by the Parliamentarian forces, and, as a consequence, no 'quarter' was offered to its defenders, resulting in 140 of its garrison soldiers being killed alongside its governor, Colonel William Stanhope, a son of the Earl of Chesterfield, who was also slain. Only 40 of the garrison were spared. The garrison at Wiverton, after the example set at Shelford, promptly surrendered when summoned by Poyntz in November 1645. The small garrison left behind its provisions and arms but was allowed to march away, possibly back to Newark. Belvoir Castle was the last to be besieged and held out until the end of January 1646, when it surrendered before being stormed. By that time, both a Scottish and a Parliamentarian army were besieging Newark, and so the garrison soldiers at Belvoir, after surrendering on terms, were escorted to Lichfield so as not to strengthen Newark. These satellite garrisons, though, formed an important part of Newark's wider defences right up until the third siege in November 1645.[7]

We start our review of the final strengthened Newark defences, which were to protect the town for six months during the final siege, with comments made about them by John Twentyman:

> And there was built a very noble & strong worke which the Townsmen kept & built up an house of 3 or 4 Bay of Building in the middle of it, & called it the Royall Sconse or else changed this name with that in my close which in my time when it was made was called the king sconce but it seemes was altered to the Royall Sconse, this new one takeing the old name from it & because at Milngate End upon the south above Markhall Bridge there was another very noble work called the Queen's sconse. The loyall Townsmen kept the King's Skonce & were formed into a Regiment.

From both Twentyman's account and other accounts supplied from the time of the third siege (1645–1646), plus the substantial remains of the Queen's Sconce still visible today, it is clear that the most significant and observable additions to the town defences were two great sconces that were constructed beyond the outer works. To the north-west of the town was the King's Sconce, and to the south–east the Queen's Sconce.

---

7   Wood, *Nottinghamshire in the Civil War*, pp.102–06.

Richard Franck was an officer in the Parliamentarian forces besieging Newark and was probably the quartermaster of the Nottinghamshire Horse, under the command of Colonel Thornhagh.[8] Looking back from 1658, he recorded his impression of the Royalist defences at Newark during the height of the siege:

From the south-west end of this maiden garrison, stood the Queen's sconce facing the Trent, but the King's Sconce (or Sconce Royal) was to the eastward. So that the whole town seemed invincible (as it was defensible) because so well defended with men, arms, ammunition and artillery, besides such deep graffs [ditches], bastions, horns, half-moons, counter-scarps, redoubts, pitfalls, and an impregnable line of sadd [sod] and turff, palizadoed and stockaded, and every fort so furnished with great guns and cannon, that this bulky bulwark of Newark represented to the besiegers but one entire sconce: nor was there a tree to hinder her prospect.[9]

In 1904, Fred Crampton produced for Newark Borough Council a detailed map of Newark and its Civil War defences and siege works based on Richard Clampe's plan of 1646. Above are the legend and Newark coat of arms, as well as details of the defensive works around the town from Crampton's map. (National Civil War Centre, Newark, with permission)

Using these eyewitness accounts, plus the seventeenth-century map of the Royalist defences and a more recent reconstruction of these defences upon a map of Newark, the rest of this chapter will examine these final defences.

Before Newark's defences could be approached, attackers had to cross a large expanse of ground, cleared of trees and buildings, that gave the defenders a clear field of fire and offered no shelter at all for assailants. The whole town had been enclosed with a high earthen rampart and palisade, into which were set, at regular intervals, small bastions. These angular bastions projected out from the ramparts but remained connected to them, thus allowing both cannon and musket to provide sweeping enfilade fire against attackers of the defences. These Royalist defences, plus the two sconces (see

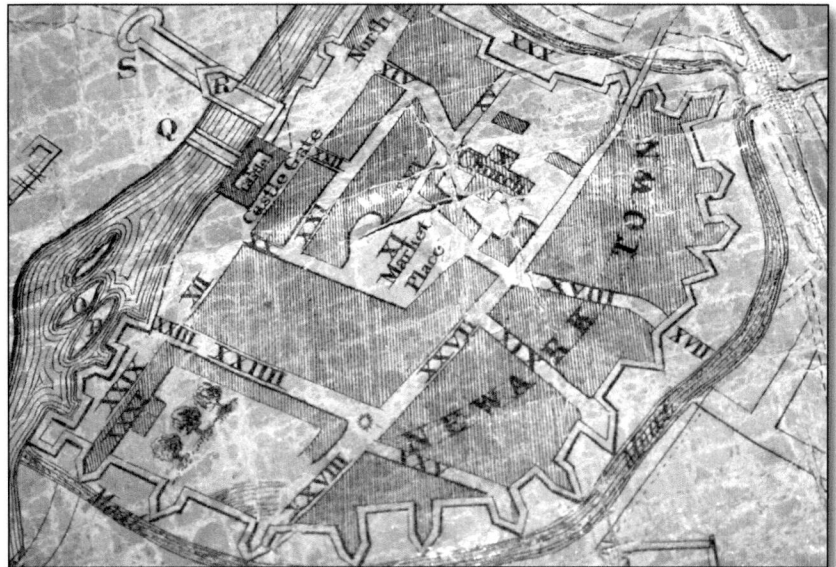

---

8   Jennings, *A Very Gallant Gentleman*, pp.119–20.
9   Richard Franck, *Northern Memoirs, Calculated for the Meridian of Scotland; To Which Is Added, the Contemplative and Practical Angler* (Edinburgh: Archibald Constable and Co., 1821), pp.269–70.

below), would have required extensive use of turf to face and strengthen them against artillery fire and the winter weather. This probably resulted in large areas of pasture around the town being dug up, ruining the pasture until long after the war had finished. The fact that the Scots had to forage as far afield as south Yorkshire and Derbyshire to obtain fodder for their horses (see Chapter 8) may possibly suggest that much of the island's pasture, to the west of the town, had been dug up before the Scots army occupied it.

In front of the town defences was dug a very deep dry ditch or moat. Recent maintenance work by Severn Trent Water in the north of the town has yielded archaeological evidence of just how large this ditch would have been. The county archaeologist of Nottinghamshire, Ursilla Spence, noted, 'The ditch is cut into heavy clay and is massive; it would have been hard work to dig. This is first-rate tangible evidence of what Newark and its people went through 370 years ago, right under our feet.'[10]

This ditch was very different to the earlier shallow one that could easily be leapt, according to John Twentyman, at the time of the first siege. This larger ditch would have taken considerable time and energy to complete, and construction would have probably begun after the defeat of the Royalist army in the north, at the Battle of Marston Moor, on 2 July 1644. It was from the north that Newark initially feared a hostile approach, either by the Earl of Manchester, with the army of the Eastern Association, or the Scottish army. Between this ditch and the ramparts was set a double row of holes, six feet deep and possibly with wooden stakes at the bottom to hinder any sudden assault by the enemy.[11] Sir Henry Slingsby, a civilian with Royalist sympathies, was in Newark for the duration of the third siege and present at the surrender of the town. In his diary, he noted:

> The garrison was well fortified & victual'd especial for bread & bear & had their fortifycations as well wth out ye town by two regular lines or sconces as about it wth a deep graft [ditch] & strong bulwarks; & on ye outside of ye graft they made two Rows of holes ye height of a man in depth, & so near yt it might hinder their sudden assaulting of ye works.[12]

Beyond the town's defences lay two sconces already mentioned, one to the north and the other to the south. The sconce was a detached fortress in its own right, not linked at all with the town ramparts. It had its own ditch, defences and four artillery bastions, and, as with the town defences, these, too, were surrounded by a large open expanse of ground, in effect a killing field. These were situated both to create additional protection to the main entrances into the town and to allow its defenders to fire on siege trenches being dug towards the main defences by any attackers. Parliamentarian

---

10   'Newark's Civil War History Uncovered Thanks to Severn Trent', *Severn Trent Water*, <https://www.stwater.co.uk/news/news-releases/newark/>, accessed 25 Oct. 2022.

11   Brown, *History of Newark*, vol. II, pp.92–95; Thoroton, *Antiquities of Nottinghamshire*, pp.197–98.

12   Sir Henry Slingsby, *The Diary of Sir Henry Slingsby of Scriven, Bart* (London: Longman Rees, 1836), p.175.

forces could not safely attack the main town defences without neutralising these outworks first. The fact that the town regiment is estimated to be around a company size (80–100 men) and, according to Twentyman, had the responsibility of defending the King's Sconce, it probably suggests that this was the usual number of soldiers at each sconce.[13] To these would be added artillery troops for the canons, ammunition and provisions, so they would have been somewhat crowded outworks. Soldiers from Colonel William Staunton's regiment of foot also spent periods of duty at the Queen's Sconce, as is shown in the surviving accounts of the regiment.[14] Protected by the sconce's impressive defences, a body of men of company strength, along with the cannons, could inflict considerable hurt upon any attacking force against the town.

Newark's Two Sconces

The King's Sconce, to the north of the town, had been raised on top of the ruins of the Spittal, alongside the river. These stone ruins were the remains of a fine house, built by the Countess of Exeter, and lay beyond the town's defences throughout the war. This stone shell had long created difficulties for the defenders at Newark. During the first siege of the town (1643), they had been used by Parliamentarian troops as a base from which to launch an attack on the town. During the second siege (1644), on the approach of Prince Rupert to break the siege, Meldrum had drawn the Parliamentarian foot behind its ruined walls to face the forces of the prince before finally surrendering. Over the period 1644–1645, earthworks had been laid on top of these ruins, possibly leaving the stones to strengthen the core, creating a substantial sconce that defended the northern approaches to the town. Nothing survives of this sconce today, but it is believed, from surviving plans, to have been slightly larger in size but similar in layout to the Queen's Sconce, whose impressive remains survive to this day.

The surviving sconce to the south of the town known as the 'Queen's Sconce', named after Queen Henrietta, was constructed on an elevated spur of gravel. Its height gave the defenders good views across the wide meadows that lay to the south of the town. It also enabled them to provide cover to the southern approaches to the town along the Fosse Way and the crossing over the River Devon as it entered the River Trent just south of the town. Constructed of river gravel and possibly strengthened by timber stakes, its design enabled it to absorb and deflect round shot. The full defences of the sconce cover a little over three acres, and its four angular bastions provided an excellent platform from which to enfilade attacking soldiers with both cannon and musket fire. A dry ditch enclosed these defensive works, which, in some places, may have been up to 70 feet wide and 15 feet deep. Its flat bottom and steep sides would make it a killing zone for any attackers caught

---

13 Jennings, *These Uncertaine Tymes*, p.48.
14 See Chapter 7 and Appendix II.

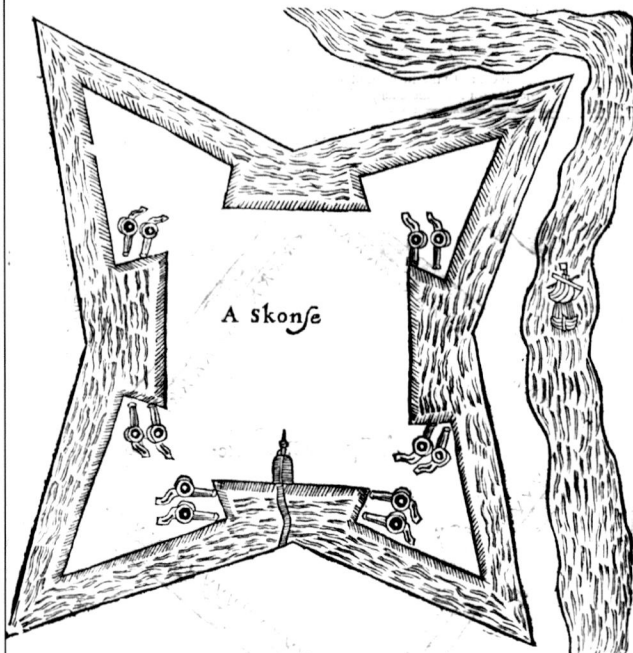

88   *The manner of Fortification.* SECT.3.

CHAP. XXXVI.

The manner of framing a Quadrangle Skonse.

His Foure-square Skonfe, is of greater ftrength than your Triangle, and if it be favoured with a ftrong Scituation, as great Rivers, or upon a Rocke, or where it may be flankered from the Bulworks of a Fort, it will ftand in great ftead ; otherwife it is not to be taken for a ftrength of any moment : The Bulworkes and Curtines are to be made very high, thicke, and ftrong, that it may endure the battering of the Enemies Ordnance.

A skonfe

CHAP. XXXVII.

Military instructions about the construction and use of sconces from Robert Ward's 1639 publication *Animàdversions of warre.* (National Civil War Centre, Newark, with permission)

Aerial view of the Queen's Sconce as it survives today. Photographer Ian Bracegirdle. (National Civil War Centre, Newark, with permission)

The Queen's Sconce as seen on the ground today. (Author's photograph)

in it. It appears that there was also a palisade on the outer lip of the ditch.[15] The two sconces alone provided a formidable defence even before the besiegers could ever reach the town's main defences.

Construction, the Island, Destruction of Property and Royalist Ordinance

The civilians living in the town undertook a lot of the construction of these final defences and, on occasions, even helped to protect the works. According to Richard Franck, a force of 1,000 fit and able citizens could be rallied to the works to help in their construction and protection.[16] The involvement of women and children in these works, on and around the defences, is referred to in a Parliamentarian newssheet of 1644: 'Yesterday the Governor of Newark commanded all shops in the town to be shut, and all the townsmen to guard the works, most whereof are very willing.'[17]

15 RCHM, *Newark Siegeworks*, pp.31–32.
16 Franck, *Northern Memoirs*, pp.269–70.
17 British Library (BL): *A Continuation of True Intelligence from the Army under the Command of the Earl of Manchester from July 27th to August 16th 1644* (London: Wood Street, 1644).

This civilian labour force was in addition to the town regiment, which had been raised to serve the garrison. There remains little evidence in the Newark Corporation records of the tensions and disaffections within the town, alleged in later Parliamentarian publications during the final siege.

Buildings within and around the defences of Newark were also dismantled or destroyed so as not to compromise the security of the town. A petition from the town to Charles II in 1661 claims that an expense of £40,000 was incurred 'by the burning of a sixth part of the town when it was made a garrison erection of works, moneys lent and never repaid, [and] quartering of soldiers'.[18]

As late as 27 September 1645, the military authorities were finalising the town's defences. The corporation minute book of Newark records an order being issued to the executors of the will of Thomas Waite:

> Whereas there is a small tenement consisting of two bayes of building lately erected upon the townes land at Milngate and nere the river of Trent by Thomas Waite deceased, w[hi]ch said tenem[en]t is by order of the Generall and commissioners appointed to be taken downe for the strengthening and better fortifieing of the Bulwarkes there … and the same to reedifie upon some part of the ground belonging to the Corporacion, so soone as the same may or can be done with convenience.[19]

The Newark branch of the River Trent separated the western side of the town from the island. Yet, even here, defences and bulwarks had to be further constructed in case the island was taken, as it was by the Scottish army in November 1645. The riverside alongside the Newark branch of the Trent was partly defended by the high castle curtain wall, which gave extensive fields of fire across the island. The 'Castle porte' (gate) gave access to the bridge over the river, with the latter being defended by an iron turnpike. On the other bank of the river, by the bridge, a bulwark guarded the bridge, with an additional small outwork beyond this providing additional protection.[20]

The island was far too large to defend against a sizeable enemy force, but it was a useful barrier for the town of Newark. To provide a degree of security for the town, a drawbridge was constructed on Muskham Bridge on the west side of the island, and a fort was constructed to the south-west of the bridge before the second siege of 1644. These were never designed to be part of Newark's continuous defences but rather as isolated outposts to delay the approach of an enemy.[21] A further Royalist earthwork was constructed at Crankley Lane, possibly a raised battery, which provided further cover for the crossing at Muskham.

The defeat of the second siege in 1644 had resulted in the Royalist garrison gaining 'two morter peeces, one Denny cannon, one sacre and eight drakes'

18   Anon., *CSPD*, 1661–1662, 27 July 1661, p.45.
19   NA: DC/NW/3/1/1: Borough Minutes, p.214a.
20   RCHM, *Newark Siegeworks*, p.31.
21   RCHM, *Newark Siegeworks*, pp.33–34.

A replica Civil War piece of ordinance facing out over the island from the west curtain wall of Newark Castle. (Author's photograph)

A depiction of a large cannon on the Newark siege plan. It may be an image of the one named 'Sweet Lips', captured from the Parliamentarians at the second siege of Newark. (National Civil War Centre, Newark, with permission)

left behind by the defeated Parliamentarian forces.[22] These were all to prove useful for the defence of Newark over the period of the third and final siege. Richard Clampe's map of the siege of Newark, though drawn up from a Parliamentarian perspective, clearly shows the position of the Royalist guns on the Newark defences. Five cannons were positioned on the Queen's Sconce, facing the main threat from the Parliamentarian forces approaching the town from the south. Two further cannons were placed on the King's Sconce, whilst a further five cannons were positioned along the town's defensive circuit, four of which were on the bulwarks between the hornworks at Balderton Gate and that at Mill Gate.

An illustration on the Newark Royalist siege plan depicts a large cannon behind an earthwork defence, reinforced with storm poles, but there appears to be no palisade. The size of the cannon depicted suggests this may in fact be the notorious 'Sweet Lips', and it has been suggested from this image that it may well have been on the Goat Bridge Hornwork. The Royalists had captured this piece of artillery at the end of the second siege of the town. It had originally been brought from the town of Hull by Meldrum and was a 32-pounder gun that was over 12 feet long. Tradition from the seventeenth century suggests that it was named after a notorious sixteenth-century prostitute who lived in Hull.[23]

Newark's Own Company of Soldiers

A circuit of defences as large as this required a good number of soldiers to guard them. As we have already seen, the townsfolk were not averse to coming to the works, but, just prior to the second siege of 1644, the borough minutes record the establishment of a small company of foot made up of men from the town. On 3 January 1644, an order was issued by the town mayor, Thomas Hancke, for the payment of £1 19s 6d 'for colours for the townsmen listed as soldiers for his Majesties service under ye command of Capt. Gervase Lee'.[24] This company was certainly active over the period of 1644–1645, for the chamberlain's accounts record that the sum of £4 8s 9d was 'paid to Mr Newton for ribbon and match to the town's soldiers as appears by Bill and warrant'.[25]

Gervase Lee, named as the first captain of this embryonic company, had accumulated a long and honorary record of service in the county's trained bands, and, in 1642, he had taken up arms for the King's cause. He was a frail

---

22 Bury, *Siege at Newark*, p.8.
23 RCHM, *Newark Siegeworks*, pp.19, 31, 53.
24 NCWC: NEKMS 2021.19.56: Miscellaneous Papers.
25 NCWC: NEKMS 2021.19.54: Miscellaneous Papers.

man by 1642, and, in his defence before the Committee of Compounding in June 1646, he claimed to have laid down his arms at the end of 1643 due to ill health and infirmity.[26]

Edward Twentyman, an uncle to John Twentyman, was clearly identified as the first active captain of the town company. He was to later develop gangrene in his foot, and his burial is recorded in the Newark registers on 2 March 1646, thus sparing him the ignominy of having to partake in the surrender of the town two months later. The absence of a list of soldiers, or any records of payment to them, which may have been part of the destroyed garrison papers, makes it difficult to be sure of the strength of the town company. John Twentyman, in his memoirs, told that the town's soldiers took on regular duties defending the King's Sconce. That it was able to undertake these duties probably suggests a permanent strength of around a company size (80–100 men). The livery of Newark Borough Corporation was blue, and this 'blew broad cloth' was also provided to the regiment to make sashes for the soldiers.[27] Before the third and final siege was in place, the governor of Newark had sent around a 1,000 of the Newark Horse to the Lichfield garrison to reduce the demands upon the town's provisions. This would have diminished the overall strength of the Royalist forces, and so the presence of the town's company of soldiers to supplement the garrison would have been of considerable benefit in the defence of the town.

By the time the final siege of the town began in November 1645, extensive defences and the gathering in of substantial provisions had well prepared Newark for the six-month siege that lay ahead.

---

26   Anon., *CCC*, part II, p.1319.
27   Jennings, *These Uncertaine Tymes*, pp.46–48, 93.

6

Collapse of the Royalist Cause, 1645

Fortunate Beginnings

Despite the defeat of Newcastle's Northern Army and the collapse of Royalist dominance across most of the north-east, a combination of factors all helped to reduce the pressure upon the Royalist garrison at Newark. In Nottingham, discord amongst the Parliamentarian authorities and lack of pay for its troops severely curtailed its operations against the county's Royalists. Serious disagreements about authority and jurisdiction between the Nottingham Committee and the governor of the castle, John Hutchinson, actually meant that both spent a considerable amount of time away from the town, appearing before the Committee of Both Kingdoms. Lack of pay for both Colonels Hutchinson's foot and Thornhagh's troopers made it difficult to encourage them to venture far from the town for military duties.[1] It was the latter issue that Hutchinson first addressed. Lucy Hutchinson wrote that 'he procured a month's pay for the foot and twenty shillings a man for the horse, as soon as he came home; and recruited all the stores, which the committee had purposely wasted in his absence'.[2]

Over this period of uncertainty, the Newark Horse appeared to have free range across much of north Nottinghamshire, but it, too, was not without an enforced change in its command structures. According to Lucy Hutchinson in early January 1645, 'The king's commissioners and the governor of Newark fell into such high discontents, that Sir Richard Byron, the governor was changed, and Sir Richard Willis put into his place.'[3]

In the opening weeks of February, a raiding party from Newark under the command of Colonel Roger Molyneux was able to operate as far away as Wirksworth in Derbyshire.[4] Likewise, William Staunton's troop of horse

---

1   Firth (ed.), *Memoirs of Colonel Hutchinson*, pp.219–20.
2   Firth (ed.), *Memoirs of Colonel Hutchinson*, p.220.
3   Firth (ed.), *Memoirs of Colonel Hutchinson*, pp.227–28.
4   Early English Books Online (EEBO), *Mercurius Rusticus*, 25 February 1645; Wood, *Nottinghamshire in the Civil War*, p.88.

was freely collecting their contributions from a circuit across the county from their base at Newark.[5] Around the turn of the year, the garrison at Newark had sent 60 soldiers to the home of Gervase Lee at Norwell, which lay seven miles to the north-east of the town. The intention was to make it another satellite garrison for the town, covering any approach from south Yorkshire. In response, a Parliamentarian force consisting of 200 foot and 'eight regiments [sic] of horse and dragoons' under the command of Colonel Francis Thornhagh, from Nottingham, besieged the garrison from the middle of February. After Thornhagh had summoned the garrison, an initial attempt was made upon it by the Parliamentarians, which failed, leaving 28 men dead in front of the house and many wounded. Events beyond the county, though, were to end this siege and bring additional succour to the Royalists at Newark.[6]

The garrison at Newark was, by the start of 1645, one of the most important garrisons for the King still operational in the north-east of England. It covered the rear of the King's army at Oxford from Parliamentarian intrusion from Yorkshire now that Newcastle's army had ceased to exist. It was also an important staging post for aid to the two remaining Royalist garrisons in the region, Pontefract and Scarborough, both of which were being closely besieged. The situation at Pontefract was becoming critical, and, on 22 February, the King ordered Sir Marmaduke Langdale to take 1,500 horse, break the siege and get fresh provisions into the garrison. Thornhagh and the Nottinghamshire Horse were tied up before Norwell, so Colonel Edward Rossiter, with the Lincolnshire Horse, rode to intercept Langdale on his journey north. Just outside Melton Mowbray, on 25 February, a ferocious cavalry action occurred between the two forces, resulting in the rout of Rossiter's forces and 50 of his men being killed. Langdale then rode on to Newark and picked up there a further 900 horse and foot as reinforcements.[7] That such numbers of additional troops could be collected from Newark is itself a testimony to the growing strength of the garrison as more and more Royalists began to make their way there from Yorkshire, as their garrisons fell. For Thornhagh, though, Rossiter's defeat meant that he had to lift the siege of Norwell and return to Nottingham. It was too dangerous to remain in the field, with no support from Rossiter and Newark and Langdale's forces so close to his position. At the beginning of March, Langdale, and his Northern Horse, finally reached Pontefract, broke the siege and forced the Parliamentarians to withdraw.

In the town of Nottingham, the tensions between the county committee and John Hutchinson continued to be fractious, and, in April, both parties were again summoned down to London to attempt to achieve reconciliation. Whilst John was away, his brother George Hutchinson was appointed to take charge of the garrison. According to Lucy Hutchinson:

---

5   See Chapter 7.
6   Jennings, *A Very Gallant Gentleman*, p.63.
7   Early English Books Online (EEBO), *Perfect Diurnall*, 3–10 March 1644/1645. See also Wood, *Nottinghamshire in the Civil War*, p.89.

As the Governor's absence was the occasion of many neglects in the government, not by his brother's fault but the soldiers', who were discontent and through that careless of their duty, and of wanting their pay (which, while the Committee should have been providing, they were spending it in vexatious prosecutions of the Governor), so, on the other side, the Cavaliers, who were not ignorant of the dissensions in the garrison, took the advantage.[8]

On 20 April 1645, a raiding party from Newark surprised the small garrison of 33 men at the Trent Fort on the way into Nottingham. According to John Hutchinson, 20 of the men were slain, whilst the rest escaped by swimming across the river and going into the town. Hutchinson claimed that the attackers were estimated to be 1,600 strong; this figure was most certainly inflated in an attempt to justify the failure.[9] The capture of the fort quickly focused the minds of both the county committee and Hutchinson about their common foe, and a swift return by both parties to Nottingham followed. On his return, Hutchinson 'in a month's space God restored to the Governor the fort that was lost in his absence'.

Storming of Leicester, 30 May 1645

Whilst all these military activities were underway within Nottinghamshire, peace negotiations between the King and his Parliament had been underway at Uxbridge through most of February. These centred on three key areas: reform of the church, control of the army and the future of Ireland. No agreement could be reached on any of these issues, and, on 22 February, these talks broke down completely. Parliament responded to this breakdown by passing the *Self-Denying Ordinance* and the formation of the New Model Army. For Charles I, the successes of the Earl of Montrose in Scotland encouraged him to march north with most of his forces to join him and create a large field army. He called upon Prince Rupert and Lord Goring to join him with their forces, although Goring was to return back to his siege of Taunton before the Battle of Naseby. Charles left Oxford on 7 May with 11,000 men, but, almost immediately, Parliamentarian forces under the command of Sir Thomas Fairfax besieged his capital. This persuaded the King to remain in the midlands area so as to draw Fairfax away from his capital city.[10]

After a council of war, Charles decided 'that the best way to draw him [Fairfax] from thence, would be to fall upon some place possessed by the Parliament', and the place chosen was Leicester.[11] The garrison at Leicester was judged as being far too small to adequately defend the length of its medieval walls. By 28 May, the King was at Cotes, just outside Loughborough, and here his force was joined by a further 1,200 horse from Newark under

8   Keeble (ed.), *Memoirs of Colonel Hutchinson*, pp.195–96.
9   Anon., *HC Journal*, vol. IV, p.118.
10   Young and Holmes, *English Civil War*, pp.236–38.
11   Edward Hyde, *The History of the Rebellion and Civil Wars in England* (Oxford: Oxford University Press, 1828), vol. V, p.175.

The surrender of Leicester to Prince Rupert, 1645. Plate from John Throsby, *The History and Antiquities of the Ancient Town of Leicester* (1791). Engravers W. and J. Walker. (Author's collection)

the command of their governor, Sir Richard Willis. Over the night of 30–31 May, Leicester was stormed, and, after fierce fighting, which saw a number of civilian deaths, the town was captured and then sacked. The Newark Horse formed part of 'the army of horse' that 'faced in bodyes all night in several places', seeking to cut off either escape from the town or new resources coming in to strengthen the town defenders.[12]

The plunder taken from the town filled 140 carts, and this was taken back to Newark accompanied by Willis and 400 of the Newark Horse.[13] On the return of the governor and some of the Newark Horse with the plunder, the mayor of the town ordered that the bell ringers were to be paid the sum of 2s 6d 'for ringing at ye taking of Leicester'.[14] The remaining 800 Newark Horse remained with the King, and an examination of their use at the Battle of Naseby (see below) possibly suggests that they were nominally under the command of Prince Rupert. Large amounts of silver plate appear to have been taken at Leicester, and it is possible that some of this was to be used later at Newark to make the town's siege coins during the third siege. The Mace, town seals and archives were also 'taken away by unruly souldiers', and, although

---

12   C. E. Long (ed.), *Richard Symond's Diary of the Marches of the Royal Army* (Cambridge: Cambridge University Press, 1998), p.181.

13   Wood, *Nottinghamshire in the Civil War*, p.92.

14   NA: PR/24810: Newark Churchwarden Accounts, 1645.

the archives were later retrieved, the Mace had to be replaced at a cost of £24 6s 6d. Also taken away by the Royalists were 50 barrels of gunpowder, 1,000 muskets and nine cannons. Whether all of this stayed with the King's army as it moved on, or if some of it was taken back to Newark for safety, is unclear. The Royalists are estimated to have had 200 killed in the storming, of which 28–30 were officers, and, based on subsequent burials recorded in Leicester immediately after the siege, the total loss of both sides is estimated to be 709.[15]

After taking Leicester, Charles left a garrison of 1,200 to repair the fortifications and control the town, thus diminishing the overall size of his field army further. He moved on to Daventry, where he halted to allow his soldiers to rest and gather in provisions for the town of Oxford once the siege had lifted. When news reached Parliament of the sacking of Leicester, it urgently pleaded that 'the army of the parliament should be ordered forthwith to march against the enemy, as well for the regaining of Leicester, if it were possible, before it should be made impregnable by fortifications, as also for prevention of the enemy's further surprising of other places of strength, and destroying the rest who had appeared in defence of the parliament'.[16]

Naseby, 14 June 1645

As a consequence of the King's success at Leicester, Fairfax lifted the siege of Oxford and marched towards Newport Pagnall, where troops of Vermuyden's brigade joined his forces. Its commander, Colonel Vermuyden, had recently resigned his commission, leading Fairfax to ask Parliament to release Oliver Cromwell from duties at Parliament and appoint him as his lieutenant general. Fairfax was keen to engage the King's army, whilst Charles was also in an optimistic mood after hearing that the siege at Oxford had been lifted. On 14 June 1645, the two armies were to clash in battle just outside the village of Naseby in Northamptonshire.

According to Clarendon, the King's army had been greatly diminished in size because of the actions around Leicester. His infantry, in particular, had been reduced by a combination of casualties and men deserting with the plunder that they had gathered. He put the Royalist army at only 3,300 foot and 4,100 horse.[17] Whilst this may be an underestimation, what can be ascertained is that the King's army was considerably smaller than Fairfax's forces. Even so, and contrary to Prince Rupert's advice, Charles opted to stand and fight. As the Royalist army was drawn up for battle, the 800 Newark Horse were assigned to the Royalist reserve, split into two bodies, with Rupert's regiment of Bluecoats on either wing, whilst the lifeguard of horse, under the command of Lord Bernard Stuart, occupied the centre of the reserve.[18]

---

15   Jonathan Wilshere and Susan Green, *The Siege of Leicester–1645* (Leicester: Leicester Research Department, 1984), pp.22–24.

16   Wilshere and Green, *Siege of Leicester*, p.25.

17   Hyde, *History of the Rebellion*, vol. V, pp.181–82.

18   Young and Holmes, *English Civil War*, p.240.

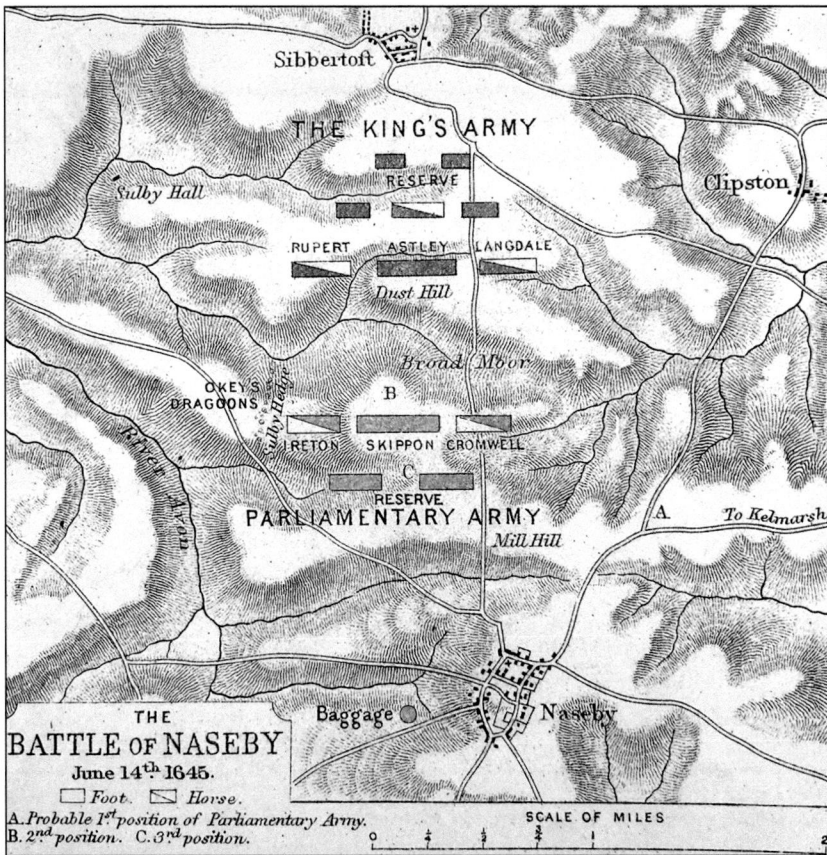

Map of the Battle of Naseby, 1645. Plate from S. R. Gardiner (ed.), *A School Atlas of English History* (1907). Engraver unknown. (Author's collection)

It remains unclear as to which side initiated the battle, but, almost immediately, Fairfax's superior numbers took their toll. On the Royalist right wing, a charge by the Royalist horse led by Princes Rupert and Maurice defeated the Parliamentarian horse under the command of Henry Ireton. Unfortunately, the Royalist horse fell upon the enemy's baggage train and was distracted, for a period, by the potential of plunder instead of returning to the battle. On the left wing, the Royalist horse under the command of Sir Marmaduke Langdale were so under strength that they were quickly overwhelmed by the charge of a body of Oliver Cromwell's regiment. The Royalist foot, under the command of Sir Jacob Astley, at first made some gains against their New Model opponents. Over time though, the larger numbers of their opponents, and the fact that the Parliamentarian horse under the command of Cromwell were disciplined enough to turn around after scattering Langdale's horse and attack the Royalist foot from the rear, helped turn the tide of the battle. The King's desire to use his reserve, which included sections of the Newark Horse, to redress the balance was halted by his advisors, fearing for the King's safety, and so they fled the battlefield.

According to some historians, the most remarkable thing about Naseby was not that the Royalists lost but that they came very close to winning in spite of a failure in strategy and the absence of Goring's horse.[19] According to the diary of the Royalist Richard Symonds, who was present at the battle, 'The horse escaped to Leicester, this afternoone, and were persued by a body of the enemye's horse and loose scowters to Great Glyn [Glen], and there the Earle of Lichfield charged their loose men with halfe a score horse and beate them back'.[20]

At Leicester, Charles was joined by Rupert, Maurice and other troopers who had been able to flee on their mounts, and, after seeing the wounded were tended to, he 'left two regiments of horse there, viz the Queenes and Colonel Caryes' and left that same night with the rest of his horse for the safety of Ashby-de-la-Zouch.[21] From here the next day, the King rode to Lichfield, but it is probable that the survivors of the Newark Horse were allowed to return to their own garrison. The defeat at Naseby was catastrophic for the King's cause, with as many as 4,500 of his soldiers being taken prisoner, the majority of whom were his foot who were proving so difficult to get replacements for. It is estimated that the Royalists had around 1,000 men slain, whilst the Parliamentarians lost only an estimated 200 men.[22]

Situation at Newark, May–November 1645

Although a large number of the Newark Horse were away with the King for the Leicester and Naseby campaigns, the rest of the garrison within the town were far from inactive. The accounts for William Staunton's forces based at Newark continue to record disbursements right to the start of July 1645. Interestingly though, receipts for the contributions levied upon parishes, previously recorded by the treasurer, Lieutenant Gervase Hewet, came to an abrupt end in April. This may possibly reflect the fact that the troop of horse, raised by Staunton to support his foot, were no longer available to ride around the parishes allocated to them to collect it. They may well have gone as part of the Newark Horse to join the King at the storming of Leicester.[23]

When Fairfax lifted the siege of Oxford and marched into the South Midlands to confront the army of the King after it had stormed Leicester, he wrote on 8 June to Colonel Rossiter, urging him to march south with the Lincolnshire Horse to join him in anticipation of an engagement with the army of the King. The garrison at Newark, possibly through a network of spies, gained information about this summons and, believing that Rossiter had already left Lincolnshire to join Fairfax, sent out a party of horse on 9 June to seize Hougham House, near Grantham. They successfully captured the house early in the morning, taking its small garrison as prisoners. Unfortunately for them, Rossiter had not yet left Lincolnshire, and, by the early afternoon, he had arrived before the house with the Lincolnshire Horse

19   Young and Holmes, *English Civil War*, p.249.
20   Long (ed.), *Symond's Dairy*, p.193.
21   Long (ed.), *Symond's Dairy*, p.195.
22   Young and Holmes, *English Civil War*, p.249.
23   Bennett, Jennings, and Whyld, 'Two Military Account Books', pp.116–21.

Monument to the fallen at the battlefield of Naseby. (Author's photograph)

and quickly retook the garrison with his superior numbers. All the Royalists in the house were taken prisoner.[24]

The defeat of the King's field army at Naseby, rather than weakening the garrison at Newark, gave it a new impetus. Lucy Hutchinson wrote, 'By reason of the rout at Naseby, and the surrender of Carlisle and several other garrisons to the Scots, the broken forces of the Cavaliers had all repaired to Newark, and that was now become the strongest and best fortified garrison the king had'.[25] This was to cause some friction within the garrison at Newark itself, which Charles had to later address. The majority of those who opted to continue to fight for the King at the surrender of their garrisons across the north were usually officers; the majority of ordinary soldiers chose to return to their homes. Officers were paid more, when money was available, and generally expected better conditions. This was to place a considerable strain on the resources of the garrison and its neighbouring parishes.

Amongst those new arrivals to Newark over the late spring was a soldier of African descent who was described in the surviving records as a 'blackamore'. An entry in the baptismal records of the parish church, dated 30 March 1645, records that 'a John Americanus, a blackamore' was christened.[26] The fact that no parent, owner or master is recorded in the entry, as they usually were for most minors baptised in the church at this time, probably suggests that this was an adult rather than a child baptism. He may have been a slave or servant to one of the Royalist officers. Certainly, the Earl of Newcastle had black stable boys working at his estate at Welbeck. It is possible that they were brought over to Newark to help take care of the garrison's horses. In the diary of Abraham de la Pryme, he recorded a tale told to him by an old soldier from Newark. A raiding party set out from Newark to try and capture some Scottish soldiers for interrogation, and amongst the party was a 'blackamore'. When he attempted to capture a Scottish soldier alive, who had never seen a black man before, the Scottish soldier exclaimed, 'O God! O God! O God! Have mercy on my sowl, the de'ils got my body'. He absolutely refused to be taken captive and was therefore killed so as not to alert others nearby.[27]

Newark was also fortunate in that, initially, it did not figure prominently in the plans of Parliament after its victory at Naseby. Fairfax and the New Model Army were ordered to march to the south-west of the country to confront the King's remaining army under the command of Lord George Goring, who was then besieging Taunton. On 20 June 1645, Parliament issued an ordinance 'for associating the counties of York, Lancaster, Nottingham, Bishopric of Durham, Northumberland, Cumberland, and Westmoreland into a Northern Association'.[28] Sydenham Poyntz was appointed the commander-in-chief of this association and given the rank of colonel general. Colonel Thornhagh and the Nottinghamshire Horse fell under the command of Poyntz, and,

24   Wood, *Nottinghamshire in the Civil War*, p.92.
25   Keeble (ed.), *Memoirs of Colonel Hutchinson*, p.200.
26   NA: PR/27256–257: Newark Parish Registers, 30 March 1645.
27   Abraham de la Pryme, *The Diary of Abraham de la Pryme, the Yorkshire Antiquary* (Durham: Andrews & Co., 1870), pp.108–10, entry for 13 August 1695.
28   C. H. Firth and R. S. Rait (eds), *Acts and Ordinances of the Interregnum, 1642-1660* (London: HMSO, 1911), vol. I, pp.703–14, 20 June 1645.

from 22 August, they were part of the army that was instructed to follow the King's remaining forces on its travels, culminating in their defeat at the Battle of Rowton Heath on 24 September 1645. This left Colonel Rossiter and the Lincolnshire Horse alone to attempt to limit the activities of the Newark garrison as best as they could.[29]

With only limited resources available to local Parliamentarians, the Royalists at Newark were still able to raid across both Nottinghamshire and Lincolnshire with a degree of freedom. Only four days after the defeat of the King at Naseby, a raiding party from Newark under the command of Captain Wright defeated a force of 200 Parliamentarians at Riby in Lincolnshire. They took 50 prisoners with their arms and horses and killed their commander-in-chief, Lieutenant Colonel Harrington.[30] On 16 July, they were able to retake Welbeck, the home of the Earl of Newcastle, and took a further 200 prisoners, three cannons and over 300 arms. In his diary, Richard Symonds provided a detailed account of the event:

> Welbeck was surprised by Newarke Horse under the command of Sir Richard Willys, about three weeks since. In a wood neare the port stood his horse in ambush, and when the trevall was beate, and [they] lett downe the bridge for their scouts, our horse under the command of Major Jarnot, a Frenchman, rid hard, and though they pulld up the bridge a foot high, yet they gott in and took it. They disputed every yard, and our men alighted, and with their pistols scald [scaled] and gott in.[31]

On 1 August 1645, Newark forces destroyed Torksey House in Lincolnshire, taking 140 prisoners and killing eight of that garrison. Later that month, a raiding party from Newark advanced as far as Barton on Humber in Lincolnshire (53 miles from their base) and captured a number of affluent individuals, including Sir Alexander Hope, a Scot with two brethren as well as 'a good booty in money and jewels'.[32]

It was against the backcloth of this persistent Royalist activity from Newark and the strengthening of that garrison that the Committee of Both Kingdoms wrote to the Committee at York on 16 July 1645. They stated:

> We are informed that the garrison of Newark is grown very numerous and strong, and that if there be not present course taken to prevent it, they will be able to take the field, and be very dangerous to those parts. We therefore, recommend it to you that some of your forces be appointed to block up Skipton, Bolton, and Sandall, while the rest may be sent to Newark, to join with the forces of those parts in straitening that garrison, and so disabling them from bringing in provisions during the harvest time.[33]

29   Jennings, *A Very Gallant Gentleman*, pp.64–68.
30   Brown, *History of Newark*, vol. II, p.80.
31   Long (ed.), *Symond's Dairy*, p.224.
32   Brown, *History of Newark*, vol. II, pp.81–82.
33   Anon., *CSPD*, 1645–1647, p.13.

Events nationally were to delay this instruction being implemented quickly, and the garrison at Newark was able to successfully gather in provisions from parishes across the immediate region and continue to strengthen their defences. As a result of these constant raids from the town, Parliament was beginning to create the formation of a plan to block up Newark. This was ultimately to come to fruition in the autumn and will be explored fully in Chapter 8.

The King at Newark, 27 August and 4 October–3 November 1645

Following the King's defeat at the Battle of Naseby and Lord Goring's rout at Langport (10 July 1645), the Royalist cause across England was plunged into terminal decline. North of the border in Scotland, things were looking considerably better for the Royalists, with the Marquis of Montrose, James Graham, together with his ally Alasdair MacColla, enjoying a series of successes against the Scottish Covenanter forces. This situation persuaded Charles to attempt a march north with what forces he could muster and join up with Montrose in Scotland. He arrived at Welbeck, in north Nottinghamshire, on 15 August 1645 with 2,000 horse and a small number of foot, having been advised by Lord George Digby to avoid Ashby-de-la-Zouch because of plague there as well as Newark 'so as to avoid the prejudice that our horse might do to the Newark quarters'.[34] At Welbeck, he was joined by reinforcements from the Newark garrison under the command of its governor, Sir Richard Willis. According to the Royalist *Perfect Diurnall*, Willis brought with him 1,500 horse and 500 dragoons, plus part of the surplus arms that they had accumulated at Newark.[35] Digby claimed that, by the time they had reached Doncaster, the King had around 3,000 horse and 2,000 foot. There is, though, a degree of confusion regarding the contribution of the Newark garrison.

According to a later history of the Staunton family, the author, confusing the King's stay in Newark in August with that in October, claimed that 'in October 1646 [sic] King Charles departed from Newark with Lord Digby, on his way to join the gallant Montrose in Scotland, and Colonel Staunton accompanied him with his regiment'.[36]

Charles I, plate from c. 1880. Engraver W. Holl, after Anthony van Vandyke. (Author's collection)

---

34   Brown, *History of Newark*, vol. II, p.82.

35   EEBO, *Perfect Diurnall*, 18–25 August.

36   George W. Staunton and Frank M. Stenton, *The Family of Staunton of Staunton, Nottinghamshire: An Essay* (Newark: S. Whiles, 1911), Chapter IV, <http://www.nottshistory.org.uk/books/

At Rotherham, it is claimed, the King received news that Montrose had been badly defeated, and so he returned back to Newark. In reality, by October 1646, Charles was a prisoner of the Scots, and the garrison of Newark had surrendered. The event referred to clearly relates to events in August, when Charles advanced as far as Doncaster, but, hearing that the Northern Horse were blocking his way and that 4,000 Scots under the command of David Leslie were at Rotherham, the King fell back to Newark, where he arrived on 21 August. To greet the King's arrival, the mayor paid the bell ringers at Newark the sum of 5s.[37] According to Clarendon, the Scottish forces were 'in a very ill posture' to defend themselves, a fact underlined by their condition when they arrived at Newark in November 1645 to join the siege of the town.[38] The King and his advisors were completely unaware of this fact, thus withdrawal appeared the wisest option. The presence of William Staunton's regiment of foot from Newark at the August advance would explain why a 'small body of foot' had become around 3,000 by the time it reached Doncaster. Charles remained at Newark for only one day before moving southwards towards Huntingdon with his original force, but Staunton's regiment and the foot from Welbeck remained at their original garrisons.

Over the month of September 1645, the King's cause in both England and Scotland was to witness complete devastation. On 10 September, Prince Rupert surrendered the city of Bristol to Sir Thomas Fairfax, and, three days later, the forces of Montrose in Scotland were routed at the Battle of Philliphaugh, leaving the Marquis a fugitive fleeing for his life. Finally, on 24 September, King Charles witnessed from the walls of Chester the defeat of his remaining cavalry on Rowton Heath, with Parliamentarian cavalry from the town of Nottingham playing an important role.[39] At this stage, Lord Digby made a suggestion to the King that he might consider concentrating all his remaining forces by abandoning all his remaining small garrisons and gathering all the soldiers into a single last army.[40] Charles arrived at Newark with 1,500 men on 4 October, but his hopes of forming a single new army were quickly extinguished, as it became clear that local Royalists were unwilling to leave their homes and estates vulnerable to Parliamentarian raids. Newark itself was in the process of preparing for a prolonged siege, and so the forces that came with the King had to be quartered not just in the town but also across parishes in the vicinity of Newark. According to Symonds:

> The court, horseguards and Sir Marmaduke Langdale's horse at Newarke, and Newarke horse, now about 300, there too. General Gerard's horseguards at Belvoir, his regiment gone to Wales. Earle of Northampton's regiment at Wirton [Wiverton], a garrison of ours commanded by Major Honywood. Sir William Blakeston's, Prince Rupert's remainder, Lucas 50 & c. at Welbeck. Toto 120

---

staunton1911/staunton5.htm>, accessed 22 Nov. 2022.

37   NA: PR/24810: Newark Churchwarden Accounts, 21 August 1645.
38   Wood, *Nottinghamshire in the Civil War*, p.96. See also Chapter 8.
39   Jennings, *A Very Gallant Gentleman*, pp.66–68.
40   Brown, *History of Newark*, vol. II, pp.84–85.

Queene's regiment at Shelford, tsken by the enemy and all put to the sword, refusing quarter when the king was at Newark.[41]

The Newark Horse had been greatly reduced in size because 1,000 of them had been sent to the Royalist garrison at Lichfield in preparation for the forthcoming siege. Keeping large numbers of horse at Newark would have put considerable pressure on the limited resources of the garrison in the midst of a siege. Only 800 of the Newark Horse were kept on duty in the town for foraging and raiding duties.[42] The disaster at Shelford will be explored in Chapter 8, as part of the preparation for the third and final siege of Newark.

The increasingly straitened situation at Newark necessitated the King to quarter his remaining troops across a wide area of the county, but this left some of them exposed to attacks by the resurgent local Parliamentarians. These were recorded and probably exaggerated with glee by Parliamentarian newssheets. A party of 50 of the Queen's regiment at East Bridgford were charged by a party of 20 Parliamentarian cavalry from Thornhagh's regiment, resulting in 16 of them being taken prisoner. At Langar, a party of 30-plus Parliamentarian cavalry attacked 50 of Northampton's horse, killing 20 and taking 14 prisoners, without experiencing any casualties of their own.[43] Such defeats probably testify to the growing disillusion amongst some of the King's troops. The Newark forces appear to have been as active as ever, though they, too, suffered a number of setbacks. The French officer Major Jammot led a party of Newark Horse out from Welbeck towards Worksop. His vanguard of around 60 men encountered a party of around 200 Parliamentarians under the command of a Captain Rhodes on Thorpe Moor. The Parliamentarians attacked the smaller Royalist force and routed them, killing five of their number and taking 40 prisoners, many of whom, it was claimed, were killed after their surrender.[44] The bulk of Jammot's force managed to return back to Welbeck safely.

In the midst of all this military activity, Charles decided again to attempt to join up with Montrose in Scotland, devoid of news about the situation north of the border. He arrived at Welbeck on 13 October, where he began to make plans for an immediate advance. On 14 October, he received news of the Marquis' defeat at Philliphaugh and the destruction of most of his army. Charles had no choice but to return back to the defences of Newark, but he did allow Lord Digby, along with Marmaduke Langdale, with his remaining 1,500 Northern Horse, to attempt to reach Scotland and reverse the situation there.

It was not only the military situation that was to tax Charles during his time at Newark; there were also growing problems within the garrison itself. According to Wood, there were over two dozen generals and colonels in the town, which was garrisoned by only around 2,000 horse and foot by the autumn of 1645. Their pay and provisions meant that little, if any, of the

---

41 Long (ed.), *Symond's Dairy*, p.249.
42 Wood, *Nottinghamshire in the Civil War*, p.107.
43 Wood, *Nottinghamshire in the Civil War*, p.97.
44 John Holland, *The History, Antiquities, and Description of the Town and Parish of Worksop, in the County of Nottingham* (Sheffield: P. Sissons and Son, 1826), p.139.

contributions extracted from a decreasingly number of parishes they were able to visit eventually made its way down to the ordinary soldiers, causing considerable resentment amongst both them and the town people, many of whom they were quartered with. An additional acrimonious disagreement had also arisen between the governor of the garrison, Sir Richard Willis, and the county commissioners of array based at Newark. The King first set about removing some of these superfluous senior officers and reducing the pay and provisions of others in order to get Newark's finances into some sort of order before the siege began.

Prince Rupert and the King at Newark

The surrender of the city of Bristol by Rupert on 10 September 1645 came as a devastating blow to his uncle the King. Its loss left the Royalists with possession of only one single port in England, that at Chester. Rupert had generated a number of opponents within the royal court, and their whispering campaign to the King, coupled with the loss of Bristol, led to Charles dismissing Rupert from all his offices and ordering him to leave England. The reality of the situation at Bristol was that a much larger Parliamentarian army, under the command of Fairfax, had already breached the town defences on 9 September and Rupert was seeking to spare further bloodshed on a cause already lost.[45] A man of honour and pride, Rupert was devastated by his uncle's reactions and took the decision, once he had reached Oxford, to present his case in person before the King.

It came as a considerable shock, and displeasure, to Charles to be informed that his nephew had arrived at one of Newark's satellite garrisons, Belvoir Castle, on 15 October, and, although Charles ordered the prince to remain there to await further instructions, Rupert rode into Newark the next day. The governor of the town, Sir Richard Willis, Lord Gerard and other Royalist officers rode out of Newark to greet the prince. Willis had served under Rupert in the west of the country in 1645, prior to his appointment to Newark.[46] His entry into Newark was a completely different affair to that of his last visit in 1644, when the bells had rung out and crowds cheered. Now, there was probably an awkward silence as both civilian and soldier realised the difficult encounter that lay ahead. Rupert was able, perhaps with assistance from supporters within the garrison, to force his way into the royal presence, in breach of protocol, and demand that he be allowed to make a defence of his actions before a council of war. The building long associated with this dramatic encounter is the Governor's House on Stodman Street, facing the marketplace that still stands in the town to this day.[47] The

45 John Lynch, *For King and Parliament: Bristol and the Civil War* (Stroud: Sutton Press, 1999), pp.138–62.

46 'Sir Richard Willys', *Civil War Petitions*, <https://www.civilwarpetitions.ac.uk/?s=sir+richard +willys>, accessed 12 Oct. 2022.

47 Sharon Ingham (ed.), *Discovering the Civil War in Nottinghamshire* (Nottingham: Nottinghamshire County Council, 1992), p.19.

The house where Prince Rupert came before Charles to defend his surrender of Bristol. (Author's photograph)

King begrudgingly agreed to this request from Rupert, and the hearing, probably held in the same building, went on to absolve the prince from any accusations made against his actions, courage or loyalty to the King. Though Rupert was cleared, the ill will created between uncle and nephew was less easy to dissipate and was to flare up again a few days later.

After the distraction of Rupert's arrival, Charles continued to address the pressing issue of preparing the town in anticipation of the siege that now seemed inevitable. The disharmony between the commissioners of array and the governor was not the best way to prepare for a siege, and, on 26 October, Charles made the decision that the only way to resolve this would be to replace the governor. He tried to make his decision as palatable as possible for Sir Richard Willis, granting him a public audience where Charles would personally thank him for his service, and offered him command of the royal horse guards. Willis, though, saw the decision as a personal affront, with the King siding with the commissioners. Later, early in the evening, as Charles was at dinner, Willis came before the King, accompanied by Prince Rupert, Lord Gerard and a number of other Royalist officers, to protest about the public shaming he felt at being publicly dismissed from his post. Rupert, as impetuous as ever, leaped in to defend his friend, claiming that Charles was punishing Willis for his friendship and support of the prince. The discussion got very heated, with a number of other grievances being aired in anger. Charles, being both angry and hurt, ordered the party to leave his presence.

Whilst tempers were still hot, Rupert, Willis and Gerard petitioned for passes granting them permission to leave Newark. This the King, with great sadness, issued, and, on the afternoon of 27 October, Rupert, Willis, Gerard and Prince Maurice left Newark with around 200 supporters. It was claimed that Charles watched their departure from a window and wept as they passed. Rupert and his party rode to Wiverton, where they petitioned Parliament for passes to go overseas. This was refused unless they would first pledge never again to take up arms against Parliament. By now, tempers had calmed down, and they realised that their sense of honour would not allow them to do this. They made their way back to Oxford, where, at a later date, they were able to make their peace with the King.[48]

Departure of the King and Final Preparations for the Siege

The man appointed to replace Willis as military governor was John Lord Bellasis, a man who possessed a local estate at Holme and was known and respected within the town. He was also a man who Charles trusted completely to work with the commissioners in defending the town for him. The disruption created by Rupert's arrival had delayed the King's departure from Newark, and, with the Parliamentarian forces drawing ever closer to the town, it was imperative for the King to make his escape. Whilst Poyntz was occupied with the taking of Shelford (see Chapter 8), Charles slipped out of Newark on the morning of 3 November with a bodyguard of 400–500 troopers.

Final preparations for the anticipated siege had begun at Newark by the end of the summer. As early as 22 August 1645, Charles had issued a warrant to Sir Richard Willis, then the garrison governor, to bring in corn from the surrounding parishes and store it within the town. The purpose of this instruction, it was claimed, was to protect its owners from theft, and they were to 'receive eyther satisfaction or have liberty to dispose of it'.[49] In effect, Newark became a grain storage centre for many of the local parishes, which also had the added benefit of denying any potential besieging Parliamentarian force having access to such resources.

By the autumn of 1645, the availability of coinage had become extremely scarce, both within Newark and across much of north Nottinghamshire. The Royalist Sir Henry Slingsby recorded in his diary a visit that he made to his home in order to remedy his own lack of cash. This clearly shows that, although Newark was by now being closely blockaded by Parliamentarian forces, there was not at that stage a close siege around the town. Slingsby wrote:

---

48   Wood, *Nottinghamshire in the Civil War*, pp.99–100.
49   NCWC: NEKMS 2021.19.86: Military Document.

[going] in disguise from Newark to my own household with intention to supply my want with money, whereof a long time I had had great scarcity … I went to my own house … after I had satisfy'd myself with one day's stay, and taken £40 in gold, I resolved to go back to Newark … and as I came so I went, in disguise … and by good fortune return'd to Newark.[50]

By the end of the year, the availability of coinage in Newark had become critical, and a temporary mint had to be established within the now besieged town. Using silver plate, dishes and trenchers, either deposited in the town by Royalist supporters for safe keeping or possibly even plate removed from Leicester and taken to Newark after the town had been stormed, were broken up and cut into lozenge-shaped coins. These came in values of 2s 6d, 1s, 9d and 6d. Each siege coin had a specified weight of silver for its particular value. The silver 2s 6d weighed 14.15g, silver 1s weighed 5.17g, silver 9d weighed 3.98g, and the silver 6d weighed 2.76g. The first siege coin issued was probably the 1s, for it carries the date '1645', though, under the old calendar, the new year began on 25 March (1646). The earliest coins styled the name of the town as 'Newarke', but later coins used the spelling 'Newark'. On the reverse of the coins were stamped the initials 'OBS', which is an abbreviation of the Latin *obsessum*, meaning 'under siege'.[51]

One of the final preparations required for the expected siege involved

Selection of Newark siege coins. (National Civil War Centre, Newark, with permission)

the allocation of soldiers to duties around the town's defensive works, and, according to John Twentyman, it was the town regiment who were given the responsibility of defending the King's Sconce, which lay to the north of the town.

The contribution of the town's citizens to the defence of the town over the years 1644–1646 cannot be underestimated. A Parliamentarian pamphlet of 1644 notes, 'Yesterday, the Governor of Newark commanded all shops in the town to be shut, and all the townsmen to guard the works, most whereof are very willing.'[52]

With the King departed, both the garrison and the town authorities braced themselves for the inevitable siege that threatened as Parliamentarian and Scottish forces closed in around Newark.

---

50 Brown, *History of Newark*, vol. II, pp.125–26.
51 Jennings, *These Uncertaine Tymes*, p.50.
52 BL: *Continuation of True Intelligence*.

7

Funding the Soldiers: Royalist 'Contribution' and the Regiment of Colonel William Staunton

At the Restoration of Charles II in 1660, the widow of Colonel William Staunton submitted a petition to the King seeking support for her son. This was due to the impoverishment of the family's estate because of her husband's faithful service to his late father, Charles I. Staunton's regiment, as this chapter will show, served for much of the Civil War after 1642 in and around Newark, and the majority of its soldiers had been recruited from the counties of Nottinghamshire and Lincolnshire. Anne Staunton wrote:

> That her deceased Husband did faithfully serve yo[u]r Ma[jest]ie's Royal Father from the time of his setting up the standard at Nottm during all the times of the war, and at his owne charges, and raysed a Regiment of Foot and a Troop of Horse and served at Edgehill, Branford [Brentford] and in the Garrison at Newark til the place [sur] rendered, and by this meanes was enforced to expose his house, estate & family to the cruelty of the enemy & to contract great debts by composition & other pressures wch chiefly occasioned the sale of most of his Ancient paternal fortunes, and yo'r petitioner's jointure, so that she and her children are left in a deplorable condition.[1]

The Regiment of Foot and Troop of Horse of William Staunton

When Charles I raised his standard at Nottingham, on 22 August 1642, William Staunton rushed to the side of his sovereign with a body of men drawn from his servants, tenants and their sons.[2] Everyone who came with

---

1 The National Archives (TNA): SP 29/9/159: Petition of Anne Staunton, July 1660. See also Appendix III.
2 Wood, *Nottinghamshire in the Civil War*, p.24.

Life portrait of Colonel William Staunton. (Image and permission to use granted by Mr W. Staunton)

him had been armed and equipped at Staunton's own expense. This group rode with the King to Shrewsbury and fought for him at both the Battle of Edgehill and later at Brentford. After these two engagements, the King sent him back to Nottinghamshire with instructions to raise a regiment of foot for the Royalist cause. The petition of his widow, Anne, in 1661 clearly shows that he raised not only a regiment of foot but also a troop of horse, or, as the commissions issued to its officers stated, 'harquebusiers'. From 1643 to the King's surrender in May 1646, Staunton and his regiment were based at the garrison at Newark, with only occasional ventures beyond the county.

Within the Staunton family papers, there survives a number of rare and informative documents relating to the period of the Civil War.[3] The commission appointing Staunton as a colonel, signed by William, Earl of Newcastle, survives as well as a separate commission appointing Gervase Huett, or Hewit, as the lieutenant of a troop of harquebusiers attached to Colonel Staunton. The Earl of Newcastle also issued Staunton with a blank commission to appoint a captain of his horse, but no name is entered, suggesting that it may not have been used. According to the Staunton family history, Sir Gervase Eyre took charge of the troop of horse, though Staunton would have remained the senior officer of both the foot and horse. A regiment of foot in the seventeenth century usually consisted of between 800 and 1,000 men. If Staunton had raised 1,200 men over the war as per the family history, it would suggest that the regiment of foot was kept at nearly full strength throughout the course of the war, as well as his troop of horse, recruiting replacements as casualties were inflicted.

It is possible that the troops of horse might have functioned as a very small regiment within the Newark garrison, with its own compliment of officers. It could have served alongside other troops or regiments as part of the Newark Horse, under the overall command of Anthony Eyre, the son of Sir Gervase Eyre, after the death of Charles Cavendish at Gainsborough in 1643. Gervase Eyre died at Newark on 5 May 1644, which may explain the family's warm description of him as 'the gallant Sir Gervase'. According to military manuals of the time, a regiment of horse should be 600 strong and divided into six troops. In reality, the cost of raising and equipping such a regiment meant that a number of those raised across the localities, such as at Newark, were considerably smaller than the ideal. Troops of

---

3   The following three paragraphs arose out of conversations with Professor Martyn Bennett and the contribution we both made to Bennett, Jennings, and Whyld, 'Two Military Account Books', pp.116–21. See also Appendix II.

horse could be as small as 40 troopers, and, as the war progressed and the Royalist cause declined, recruitment became even more difficult, resulting in some regional Royalist regiments being as small as 100 troopers by the summer of 1645.[4] As appears to have been the case in a number of Royalist Civil War regiments, lieutenants would often serve as the regimental treasurers, and Lieutenant Hewit was no exception. Each troop of horse had a quartermaster and usually two trumpeters, and their presence is testified in Hewit's accounts. There were usually three corporals to a troop of horse as well, but the accounts only identify by name one individual, a Corporal Wright.[5] The accounts survive for the period of 10 December 1644–April 1645 and appear to have been written in Hewit's hand. Such documents are a very rare survival, as usually Royalist accounts were deliberately destroyed as the war drew to a close since they contained too much incriminating evidence, naming both individuals and parishes who contributed to the King's cause. The unused commission for a captain of horse possibly suggests that there may have originally been an intention to expand the troop considerably, but, for some undocumented reason, this failed to materialise. With all the papers of the Newark garrison apparently destroyed before its surrender, it proves to be extremely difficult to be sure about both structures of command and company finances of those serving at the garrison. The survival of Staunton's accounts, albeit only for a short period, provides us with a glimpse of how the Royalist tax, known as 'contribution', worked for one Royalist troop.

Over the period of the First Civil War, the important garrison at Newark appears to have enjoyed a large degree of independence from either Henry Hastings (Lord Loughborough), who was the Royalist colonel general of Leicestershire, Derbyshire, Nottinghamshire, Rutland and Staffordshire, and William Cavendish (Earl of Newcastle), the overall commander of all Royalist forces north of the River Trent. Placing Staunton's regiment of foot and troop of horse within the region's Royalist command structures is therefore difficult to ascertain. He would have been directly answerable to the military governor at Newark, but, at times, when the King was at Newark, Staunton appears to have taken direct instructions from Charles. There remains in the family papers a written order signed by the King instructing Staunton to withdraw his regiment from Newark to join him in a march to the north, which in the event failed to happen.[6]

4   Martyn Bennett, *The English Civil War: A Historical Companion* (London: W. H. Smith, 1992), pp.14–16.
5   Mark Cartwright, 'Cavalry in the English Civil Wars', *World History Encyclopedia* (2022), <https://www.worldhistory.org/article/1930/cavalry-in-the-english-civil-wars/>, accessed 5 Nov. 2022.
6   Details about the Staunton papers from the Civil War can be found in Staunton and Stenton, *The Family of Staunton*. I would like to echo the thanks given to the Staunton family by Professor Bennett for allowing us both to have access to these documents.

The Royalist Levy or Contribution

According to the historian Jens Engberg, it came as a surprise to both protagonists in the Civil War 'that the king was able to maintain an army in the field against Parliament'.[7] Having control of London and its finances, Westminster and the navy certainly made it easier for Parliament to raise cash through levies, loans and excise. Whilst it is beyond the scope of this book to explore the national scene, the surviving accounts of Gervase Hewit provide us with a brief snapshot of how the collection and expenditure of resources for a troop of horse based at Newark were achieved. The levy raised by Royalists was to fund both their garrisons and their field armies, and it was widely referred to as 'contribution', rather than the Parliamentarian levy that was known as 'assessment'. In 1642, the King had issued commissions of array to each county, initially to raise troops for his army, but later they took on responsibility for allocating the levy across parishes in their county via meetings with the local constables. According to Professor Bennett, 'traditional county divisions such as hundreds and wapentakes were used in the process of allocation'.[8] It was left to troops stationed in the various Royalist garrisons to collect the levies being raised by the constables. Surviving constables' accounts show that the contributions were made in both cash and goods, with the latter usually amounting to less than a third of the total collected. Hewit's brief accounts only record payments of cash as contribution, again suggesting that they were far from complete. The contribution levy for Nottinghamshire appears to have been set by the commissioners on the basis of property tax rates. Research undertaken on the Coddington constable's accounts, within the orbit of the Newark garrison but not part of Staunton's circuit, provides us with details of the Royalist levies laid upon the parish. In 1643, the sums collected were 2d for an acre of land, 2d for a score of sheep, 1d for a pastured beast and 1d for a dwelling. By 1644, the rates had nearly doubled, except for a pastured beast, which had risen to 1s.[9] It was left to the parish constables to divide the sum set amongst their parishioners. The accounts for Staunton's horse suggest that they collected, when possible, the contribution on a monthly basis. The Nottinghamshire commissioners were based at Newark throughout the war, and William Staunton was one of them, but his military commitments meant that he was less active in this role. The commissioners of array had begun meeting with parish constables from February 1643.[10] Additional levies, often of goods, were made from the various parishes when the armies of Charles, Henrietta Maria and Prince Rupert were staying at Newark, as is testified by the rare survival of a complete set of constable's accounts for the nearby parish of Upton.[11]

7   Jans Engberg, 'Royalist Finances during the English Civil War, 1642-1646', *Scandinavian Economic History Review*, 14:2 (1966), pp.73–96.

8   Bennett, *English Civil War*, Contributions, p.68.

9   Nottinghamshire Archives (NA): PR/1531: Coddington Constable Accounts. I am indebted to Professor Martyn Bennett for drawing my attention to these details.

10   Martyn Bennett, 'Contribution and Assessment: Financial Exactions in the English Civil War, 1642-1646', *War and Society*, 5:1 (1986), p.3.

11   Bennett (ed.), *Accounts of the Constables of Upton*.

The Accounts of Gervase Hewit, Treasurer to Colonel Staunton's Troop of Horse

These accounts that survive amongst the family papers relate only to the troop of horse – the accounts for the regiment of foot failed to survive. The regiment of foot appears to have been an integral part of the garrison and may have been funded by a garrison-wide levy, but, as the garrison papers have not survived, it is now not possible to prove this. It is probable that, as Colonel Staunton was primarily involved with the command of the foot, the troop of horse had a greater degree of autonomy but had to keep their colonel fully informed of their financial circumstances, and this may explain why they survived.

The accounts of Gervase Hewit consist of eight folios, with the first two folios recording sums received over the period 10 December 1644–11 April 1645. Folios three to six record disbursements over the same period. Folio six list sums of cash received on 25 April 1645, whilst the last folio records a single sum of cash received on 16 July 1645 (see Appendix II). The total income calculated by Hewit from the sums recorded on the first two folios amounted to £306 17s 3d. The total expenditure for the same period amounted to £231 11s 6d. This gave an on-paper balance of £75 5s 6d. The accounts for the later period (folios six to seven) record an income of £108 6s 3d, whilst disbursements listed total to £54 18s 6s, resulting in another credit balance of £53 7s 9d. The final two folios of accounts are badly faded with age, and, in places, some entries are no longer legible, but payments amounting to £17 3s 6d were recorded as being paid to the soldiers in two payments 'by weekly list'. This amounted to around 31 percent of the total disbursements made for the period. It is difficult to come to any certain conclusions about regimental finances, as these details may well be incomplete and only cover a short period of around six months. The accounts end after April 1645, as the troop of horse attached to Staunton's regiment, which collected from the circuit of parishes, were probably part of the Newark Horse that accompanied the King's field army first to the storming of Leicester and that afterwards either escorted the plunder taken back to Newark or fought at the Battle of Naseby.

The troopers attached to Staunton's regiment collected contributions from a list of specified parishes that were scattered around the county as a whole. According to a separate docket, the parishes listed were Upton '*cum membris*' (probably including Hockerton and Morton), which lay 6.5 miles from Newark, Basford (24 miles), Selston (30 miles), Bunny and Bradmore (23 miles), Thrumpton (27 miles), Keyworth (23 miles), Plumtree (19 miles) and Edwalton (19 miles).[12] The accounts list contributions from four of these parishes, plus two other parishes, Underwood (30 miles) and Bagthorpe (31 miles).[13] It appears most likely that parishes were allocated to a regiment, not by geography but rather on a financial basis. The commissioners estimated the running cost of a regiment, and then a number of parishes were grouped

---

12   These distances are given for travel by known lanes or track, not 'as the crow flies'.
13   Royal Commission on Historical Manuscripts, *Report on Manuscripts in Various Collections* (London: HMSO, 1914), vol. VII, pp.373–74.

together, their total contributions adding up to the sum required to meet its need. The interesting point about these accounts was that, despite the order from Parliament to the Nottinghamshire and Lincolnshire Horse to closely restrict the activities of the Newark garrison over the period of the accounts, they were, in fact, able to continue collecting. The parish of Bunny and Bradmore is an interesting case. Lying only six miles south of Nottingham, with a strong Parliamentarian garrison based at the castle there, Bunny was also the home to one of Nottinghamshire's notorious Royalists, Sir Isham Parkyns, who was then serving as governor of the garrison at Ashby-de-la-Zouch. Parliament had ordered Parkyns' estate to be sequestrated and movements in and out of the parish to be closely monitored, yet Staunton's troopers were able to continue to collect cash amounting to £21 1s 11d from it over the period of Hewit's accounts.[14]

The first three sums collected for the troop in the accounts are all from Colonel Staunton himself and amounted to £31 4s, yet he only received payments of £20 16s 6d and a further expense of £4 for 'ye cornet'. After two years of war, the colonel appears to still have been subsidising his own soldiers. Amongst the list of parishes that paid the contribution, several individuals are also named. For the majority, it is unclear whether they were parish constables, acting as their representatives, or if they were paying the levy on their own estates. The exception is a Mr Draper, who, from 11 February to 11 April 1645, handed over to the treasurer the large sum of £137 10s, with £59 16s of the total coming into the account via Mr Draper's payment to the quartermaster. On 11 February, Draper was paid from the regiment's accounts the sum of £15 'for Colonel Hollis at Oxford'. In the same month, Draper was also paid £4 15s 6d 'for his allowance for ye receipts'. This individual was almost certainly Richard Draper, a gentleman of Flintham, in Nottinghamshire. For 25 September 1648, the House of Commons Journal records the receipt of £284 from Richard Draper for the offence 'that he was in Arms against the Parliament: He rendered upon the Articles of Newark: His estate in Fee, Possessions per Annum, Ninety-five pounds thirteen shillings; out of which issues for quit Rents, per Annum, Fifteen shillings which leaves the fine, at a sixth, Two hundred and Eighty-four pounds'.[15] The payment of his fine resulted in his pardon and the complete lifting of the sequestration upon his estate. As a gentleman, he would, if in arms, probably have been an officer, but the regiment, if any, he served with is unclear from the surviving evidence. He might have served as a civilian administrator though, as no military rank is assigned to him in any of the surviving documents. His frequent appearance in the Staunton accounts might suggest that it was this regiment he was serving in a civilian capacity.

---

14   Stuart B. Jennings, *Bunny and Bradmore, 1640–1690: Change and Continuity in an Age of Revolutions*, 1991, Unpublished, University of Nottingham, MA, pp.28–31.
15   Anon., *HC Journal*, vol. VI, p.31, 25 September 1649.

Everyday Life for Soldiers in the Garrison, as Evidenced in the Accounts

For soldiers serving either in a field army or based at a garrison, one of the pressing issues would have been pay. The accounts record that, from 10 December 1644 to 2 April 1645, the soldiers were paid on six occasions. The total amount paid out from the accounts was £178 3s 9d, and this amounted to just over 58 percent of the total expenditure for the period. Payments were made at irregular periods and for various amounts, with the longest gap being between the fifth and sixth payments, which were separated by approximately eight weeks. It is therefore extremely difficult to come to any certainty about what the weekly pay to soldiers amounted to. It has been estimated that a cavalry trooper cost around 2s 6d per day to maintain. The sums being outlaid for pay to the troopers in Hewit's accounts suggest that either the troop was relatively small or, more likely, that it was generally in arrears of pay.[16] Yet, even in those straightened military circumstances, some pay continued to reach the troopers.

The cost of fodder for the horses was to take up over 12 percent of the total expenditure for the period 10 December 1644–11 April 1645. With the winter falling over the period of the accounts, this was possibly one of the most expensive times to feed the horses, as grazing would have been extremely difficult on the meadows in the flood plain. The sum of £10 6d was spent on hay, with an additional outlay of £1 2s 6d for its collection and carriage. The amount of £12 6s was spent on oats, and an additional £15 15s on pease, with the overall total for the three commodities coming to £39 4s. In order to purchase eight horses, possibly as replacements for those injured or maimed, the troop had to pay out a further £11. The sum of 19s was recuperated by Hewit as he sold one horse that was no longer deemed fit for military use. Finally, the sum of 2s was paid out 'to by things for use of 2 horses'. The cost of feeding, replacing and shoeing mounts for the cavalry would have been a constant drain on the troop's accounts.

The troop of horse, as well as probably the regiment of foot, all appear to have been quartered either in or around Newark. The main base for most of the horse appears to have been the Angel Inn, which lay on the west side of the marketplace. An expenditure of 18s 5d was required in 1645 for 'repaireing of ye stables at ye Angell'. In that same year, 4s was paid to the soldiers for 'clenging ye yeard at ye Angell and 'clenging ye street against wid Teylers', which probably was adjacent to the inn. Colonel Staunton and many of his officers were meanwhile staying at 'Ye [White] Hart' on the opposite side of the marketplace.

Military duties often took their toll upon the troop, with men being taken prisoner, wounded or even killed. For 20 February 1645, an entry in the accounts records a payment of 10s 'to John Clarke and Mr Wright in ye time of their imprisonment at Nottingham'. Mr Wright may well be the

---

16   Cartwright, 'Cavalry in the English Civil Wars', <https://www.worldhistory.org/article/1930/cavalry-in-the-english civil wars/>.

John Wright identified as a corporal later in the accounts.[17] An additional, or replacement, trumpeter was recruited in April, with an individual identified as 'Porter' being paid £1 for 'teaching ye trumpeter to sound'. This Porter may well have been the other trumpeter to the troop. An additional horse also had to be purchased from John Gamble for the sum of £1 'for ye trumpet'. Further expenditure, details illegible, was also provided for the trumpeter at the end of the month. In the same month, a cornet was commissioned to the troop, and, on 22 May, he received his first payment of £1. An additional payment, dated 2 April, was made 'for ye burial of Edw Kitchen'. This may have been a local trooper, possibly from Upton, whose death had occurred whilst in service (see Appendix II for these details).

The Cost of Loyalty

At the start of 1645, Parliamentarian forces attacked Staunton Hall, the family home of William Staunton. The only inhabitants of the Hall at the time were Staunton's wife and a few elderly retainers, too frail to serve in Staunton's regiment. The house was quickly taken, and its possessions plundered, with the whole of the family estate subsequently being sequestrated and administered by the Nottingham Parliamentarian committee. Anne Staunton managed to escape from the house with her servants and was to spend the remainder of the war lodging in London.[18] Lying just over six miles from the town of Newark, from the end of 1645, it appears that the Staunton estate, being under sequestration, was extensively utilised by Parliamentarian forces to supply materials to help construct the siege works around Newark.

After the surrender of Newark, Colonel Staunton would have returned to a damaged house, probably unoccupied for over 12 months, and an estate greatly exploited. On 6 July 1646, the Committee for Compounding identified Staunton as a delinquent who 'was a colonel in arms against Parliament at Newark when it surrendered'. For these actions on 12 August, he was fined the large sum of £1,520 to reclaim his home and estate from sequestration.[19] Usually, up to half of the fine had to be paid upfront, to lift off the sequestration, and the remainder usually had to be paid off within a specified period of time.[20]

By 1649, Staunton's finances were in so desperate a state that he still had not paid off the remainder of his fine, and so he petitioned the commissioners to have his fine reduced in size. He claimed:

> That your petitioner submittinge to the fine imposed on him for his delinquency did according to order pay one moyty unto the treasurie of this committee and

---

17   See also RCHM, *Newark Siegeworks*, p.89.

18   Staunton and Stenton, *Staunton of Staunton*, Chapter IV, <http://www.nottshistory.org.uk/books/staunton1911/staunton5.htm>.

19   Anon., *CCC*, part II, p.1382.

20   For details of sequestration, see Charlotte Young, *A Study of English Civil War Sequestration*, 2019, Unpublished, Royal Holloway, PhD.

although he hath used his utmost endeavours by all means possible for payment of the remainder either by mortgage sale or otherwise, yet by reason of his greate sufferinge in his goods, felling of his woods at the seidge of Newarke for the use of the state, with which he should have raised money, the many judgments and extents upon his estate not allowed him, and being through mistake much over fined, he comeing in upon the articles of Newarke, but not allowed him as to others comprised within the said Articles by reason of all which petition[er] is utterly disabled to raise money for his second payment unlesse you shall afford him the like mercy as others have received in his condition.

Staunton went on to list some of his losses 'to the state' during the Civil War. These included £300 for loss of household goods, £300 for woods cut down and £2,000 for spoils and waste committed on his house.[21] His petition was received and accepted, resulting in the original fine being reduced to £828 3s 6d.[22]

William Staunton died at his home on 1 March 1656 and was buried in the family vault at Staunton in the Vale parish church. He did not live to see the Restoration of the monarchy and left to his eldest son a much-diminished estate. The petition of Anne Staunton, mentioned at the start of this chapter, proved to enjoy a degree of success, as the family was to get a degree of recognition and support as requested by Charles II.

Memorial to Colonel William Staunton at the Staunton Estate. (Photographer Richard Croft)

The Widow and the Future Archbishop of Canterbury

At the Restoration of the monarchy, many Royalist families who had been impoverished because of their support for Charles I petitioned the new king for help and redress. Anne Staunton, the widow of Colonel William Staunton, was just one such petitioner. To add weight and validity to their appeals, the petitioner usually attached a statement of verification for their claim, from either a local dignitary with a known Royalist past or, if they were fortunate enough, from a person with close links to the new court. At the bottom of the Staunton petition was added, 'I know all this to be most true, Gilb Sheldon'.

If this was the Gilbert Sheldon, who had been a chaplain to Charles I prior to the Civil War and was to go on to become Bishop of London in 1660 and Archbishop of Canterbury on the death of William Juxon in 1663,

---

21 The National Archives (TNA): SP 23/185/386: Committee for Compounding with Delinquents, Royalists Composition Papers: 'Petition of William Staunton, 4 May 1649'.
22 Anon., *CCC*, part II, 16 July 1649, p.1382.

which seems the most probable identification, how did he come to know about the activities of a rural gentleman in remote Nottinghamshire? The link between the two individuals appears to have been through the Hacker family of East Bridgford in Nottinghamshire. Francis Hacker's eldest son, also called Francis, is known for his support of Parliament in the Civil War and his role in the execution of Charles I in 1649, for which he was later to be executed for in 1660. Two other sons, Thomas and Rowland, fought for the King, with Thomas being killed at Colston Bassett in 1643 and Rowland ending the war serving as a colonel at the Newark garrison alongside William Staunton. Hacker and Staunton had most likely known each other prior to the Civil War, and their service together at Newark during the final siege probably helped them deepen their friendship. The father of the three brothers, Francis, never bore arms during the conflict but is claimed to have financially supported the Royalist cause.[23]

The issue that then must be resolved is how did Gilbert Sheldon come to be involved with this Nottinghamshire network. Sheldon had been stripped of all his ecclesial duties after the execution of Charles I in 1649 and was initially imprisoned at Wallingford Castle for his Royalist connections. He was later released but with strict conditions limiting his freedom of movement. He was to spend the rest of the interregnum staying with friends in Derbyshire, Staffordshire and, more importantly, with the Hacker family in Nottinghamshire. The father of the three brothers, Francis Hacker, had died in 1646, and so it was with Rowland and his family that he most likely stayed.[24] It was the Hacker family, therefore, who provided the link between the Staunton family and Gilbert Sheldon, and, as William Staunton lived until 1 March 1656, it is also possible that the two men had met. This would be in addition to the conversations Sheldon would have had with Rowland Hacker during his stay at his house. However the contact was made, Sheldon was impressed enough by Staunton's Royalist service to verify Anne Staunton's petition, and this greatly helped in getting Anne's request fully met.

---

23   Cornelius Brown, *A History of Nottinghamshire* (London: Elliot Stock, 1891), p.56.
24   The National Archives (TNA): PROB 11/200/390: Will of Francis Hacker of Colston Bassett, dated 20 May 1647.

8

Third and Final Siege of Newark

Plans for a Siege

Following his defeat at Rowton Moor in September, Charles made his way back south and arrived at Newark with 1,500 men on 4 October. Following him, under orders from Parliament, was Colonel General Poyntz with the army of the Northern Association, which included Colonel Thornhagh's regiment of Nottinghamshire Horse. Over the summer, the Newark forces had been the cause of numerous complaints to the Commons from parishes across the region. During this period, the Committee of Both Kingdoms had been trying to persuade neighbouring Parliamentarian committees to send troops to help straiten the Newark garrison. On 25 September, a day after the Parliamentarian success at Rowton Moor, both houses of Parliament issued a request to the Scottish army in England to march to Newark and besiege it.[1] Nothing initially came of these requests, but, with the arrival of Poyntz and the Northern Association in north Nottinghamshire and the King established at Newark, Parliament began once again to establish a siege. A thousand horse were sent from London, and the committees of Yorkshire, Nottinghamshire, Derbyshire and Leicestershire were urged to release as many troops as they could spare so that a force of 4,500 might be formed to assist Poyntz.[2] Until these forces finally arrived in Nottinghamshire, Poyntz had not got sufficient troops to initiate a close siege of Newark, so instead the decision was made to take out some of the town's satellite garrisons so that, when the siege began, there would be no chance of his forces being attacked in the rear from Royalists at these places.

---

1   Anon., *HC Journal*, vol. IV, p.283.
2   Anon., *HC Journal*, vol. IV, p.297; Anon., *CSPD*, 1645 1647, pp.185, 213.

Shelford, Wiverton and Belvoir Castle

The garrison that was identified as offering the most immediate danger to any potential Parliamentarian siege line around Newark was that established at Shelford, which lay 13 miles to the south-west of Newark, adjacent to the Fosse Way. Here in the manor house was based a garrison of around 200 men, including the remnants of the Queen's regiment, all under the command of Colonel Philip Stanhope, a son of Lord Chesterfield. Over the summer, they had constructed extensive defences, which included a deep ditch and palisade around the house. Poyntz arrived in the county with his army, which had been temporarily quartered around Nottingham, and rendezvoused with Colonel Rossiter outside Shelford on 1 November 1645. Lucy Hutchinson wrote that the Parliamentarians had to fight their way into the village because a small group of Royalist soldiers had shut themselves up in the church tower and were firing down at them. Colonel Hutchinson smoked them down out of the tower by setting fires within the church, which caused some damage to the parish church but succeeded in dislodging them.[3]

On 3 November, Poyntz was prepared to storm the manor, but, before doing so, he issued a formal summons to Stanhope to surrender the garrison or suffer the consequences. The Royalists at Shelford wrongly believed that they were both well protected by their defences and that a relief force from Newark would come to their assistance. The Parliamentarians were well aware of the potential of a relief force arriving, and so Poyntz kept the Nottinghamshire and Lincolnshire Horse outside the village to intercept any such attempt at relief. With great bravado, Stanhope responded to the Parliamentarian summons:

> I keep this garrison for the king and in defence of it I will live and dye, and your number is not so great nor you so much master of the field but that I am confident soone to lessen your number and see you abroad; and for relief we need none. Therefore desire you to be satisfied with this answer.[4]

Around 4:00 p.m., the assault on the house began, with Poyntz having issued an order of 'no quarter' being offered to the defenders. After around 45 minutes of hand-to-hand fighting at the outer defences, the Parliamentarians broke into the manor house and set about slaughtering its defenders and destroying the property. Of the defenders, 140 were killed, with the Royalist governor dying of his wounds a few hours after the Parliamentarian victory. Around 40 of the Royalists were spared and taken prisoner, but the majority of those killed were of the Queen's regiment, whom the attackers presumed to be Catholics. Poyntz had a stunning victory and had issued a warning to the other satellite garrisons of their potential fate.[5] Yet, in his moment of triumph, an even greater prize eluded him, for, on the day of the assault at

---

3   Keeble (ed.), *Memoirs of Colonel Hutchinson*, pp.201–04.
4   Quoted in Wood, *Nottinghamshire in the Civil War*, p.102.
5   David J. Appleby, 'Fleshing Out a Massacre: The Storming of Shelford House and Social Forgetting in Restoration England', *Historical Research*, 93:260 (2020), pp.286–308.

Shelford, Charles left Newark with a bodyguard of around 450 horse, reaching Belvoir Castle around 3:00 p.m. and travelling on to Oxford, arriving there on 5 November.

Within 48 hours of his victory at Shelford, Poyntz drew up his army at the smaller Royalist satellite garrison at Wiverton and once again issued a summons for its surrender. Bad news appears to have travelled quickly, for the garrison had been made aware of what had happened at Shelford and, having obtained favourable terms, surrendered the garrison on 9 November. Leaving all their weapons behind, they were allowed to march back to Newark. The Parliamentarians took possession of 150 firearms, 40 pikes, three barrels of powder, bullets, match, beer and provisions at Wiverton, replenishing their supplies used at Shelford.[6] From here, they went to the most impressively fortified and defended of all the satellite garrisons, that at Belvoir Castle. The Nottinghamshire foot and horse, under the command of Hutchinson and Thornhagh respectively, went from Wiverton to Newark to prepare works for the siege and limit, as far as possible, the movement of troops and goods into and out of the town.

By 17 November, Poyntz and Rossiter had established a headquarters at Bottesford, in anticipation of storming Belvoir Castle. Whilst surveying the defensive works, a party of 60 Royalists from the castle attacked the two commanders and their bodyguards, and they had a very narrow escape from capture or worse.[7] The garrison at Belvoir was summoned to surrender, but, unlike at Wiverton, the events at Shelford strengthened the governor's resolve to defend the castle. On 22 November, the Parliamentarians attempted to storm the defences at Belvoir, and, although the stables and outworks were captured, after heavy fighting, large numbers of casualties were inflicted upon Poyntz's forces. The defenders had been offered no quarter, but the majority of the Royalists were able to withdraw back into the castle and refused to surrender. With additional forces now arriving at Newark to begin a siege, including the Scottish army, Poyntz left six troops of horse and 500 foot to blockade Belvoir and marched the rest of his forces back to Newark to begin coordinating the siege.[8]

Local historian Malcolm Fox uncovered an attempt, in November 1645, by at least one Newark individual to betray the town so as to avoid a bloody assault and the destruction of property.[9] There survives in the State Papers two letters dated 1 November 1645, both sent by the Committee of Both Kingdoms. The first went to a Major White, informing him of a contact, a Mr Thompson, who might be willing to deliver the town of Newark, thus avoiding bloodshed and destruction. He was instructed to '… make what use of him he shall think fit for gaining of that place'. A further letter was forwarded to Colonel General Poyntz, both informing him of Thompson and advising

---

6   Wood, *Nottinghamshire in the Civil War*, p.104.

7   EEBO, *Kingdomes Weekly Intelligencer*, Nov. 11'19, and *Kingdomes Weekly Post*, Nov. 17, E309 (22).

8   Jennings, *A Very Gallant Gentleman*, pp.71–72.

9   Malcolm Fox, *Urban Elite and Town Government: Newark on Trent in the Mid-Seventeenth Century*, 1985, Unpublished, Nottingham University, MA, p.28.

him that 'if you shall proceed with those of the town you may promise them security for their persons and estates'.[10] Mr Thompson was identified by Fox as Alderman Lancelot Thompson, who had served as an alderman of the town for 15 years and was later, after the war had ended, identified by Parliament as a Royalist delinquent. Major White was probably Charles White, an officer of horse and dragoons in the Nottingham-based force, under the command of Colonel John Hutchinson. White was an individual viewed very negatively in the *Memoirs* of Lucy Hutchinson, described as 'the greatest dissembler, flatterer, traitor and hypocrite that ever was'.[11]

There survives no other evidence, within both the Newark archives or that of Parliament, about this plan. At the time that it was allegedly being devised, the King was still at Newark, and the impression gained from surviving sources is that the majority of Newark's authorities remained loyal to the Royalist cause, with the mayor suggesting to the military governor of Newark that he should ignore the instruction of the King to surrender the garrison in May 1646 and 'trust God and sally forth' against the besieging foe.[12]

Beginning of the Third Siege

Although both the Nottinghamshire and Lincolnshire Horse had been limiting the activities of the Newark garrison for most of November, the third and final siege is generally said to have begun with the arrival of the Scottish army on the west bank of the River Trent, opposite Newark, on 26 November. The commander of the Scottish forces was the Earl of Leven, and, after only a few days, he had secured Muskham Bridge, which crossed onto the island from the west bank of the second branch of the river. Here, the Scots also captured the Royalist earthworks covering the bridge and created additional defences. In the early months of 1646, they were also able to take control of the island, right up to the Trent Bridge on the other side of the island, opposite Newark Castle, and occupy the defences there, which the Royalists had withdrawn from. The island was now completely under the control of the Scots, and the two branches of the river proved to be an additional line of defences to protect the Scottish forces.[13] So important was the arrival of the Scots and their establishment on the island that Sir Henry Slingsby, who was a resident in Newark at this time, made extensive comments about them in his diary:

> About ye latter end of November, ye Scots came to Muscome [Muskham] a little off Newark, where at ye bridge we had a guard; but being not able to maintain it, we fired ye bridge & retreated not so directly [discreetly] as we ought: for leaving

10   Anon., *CSPD, 1645–1647*, 1 November 1645.
11   Keeble (ed.), *Memoirs of Colonel Hutchinson*, pp.93–94. For Major White's relationship with Colonel Thornhagh, commander of the Nottinghamshire Horse, see Jennings, *A Very Gallant Gentleman*.
12   Warner, *Civil War and Siegeworks*, p.55.
13   Anon., *Journal of the House of Lords, 1645–1647* [*HL Journal*] (London: HMSO, 1767–1830), vol. VIII, pp.29–30.

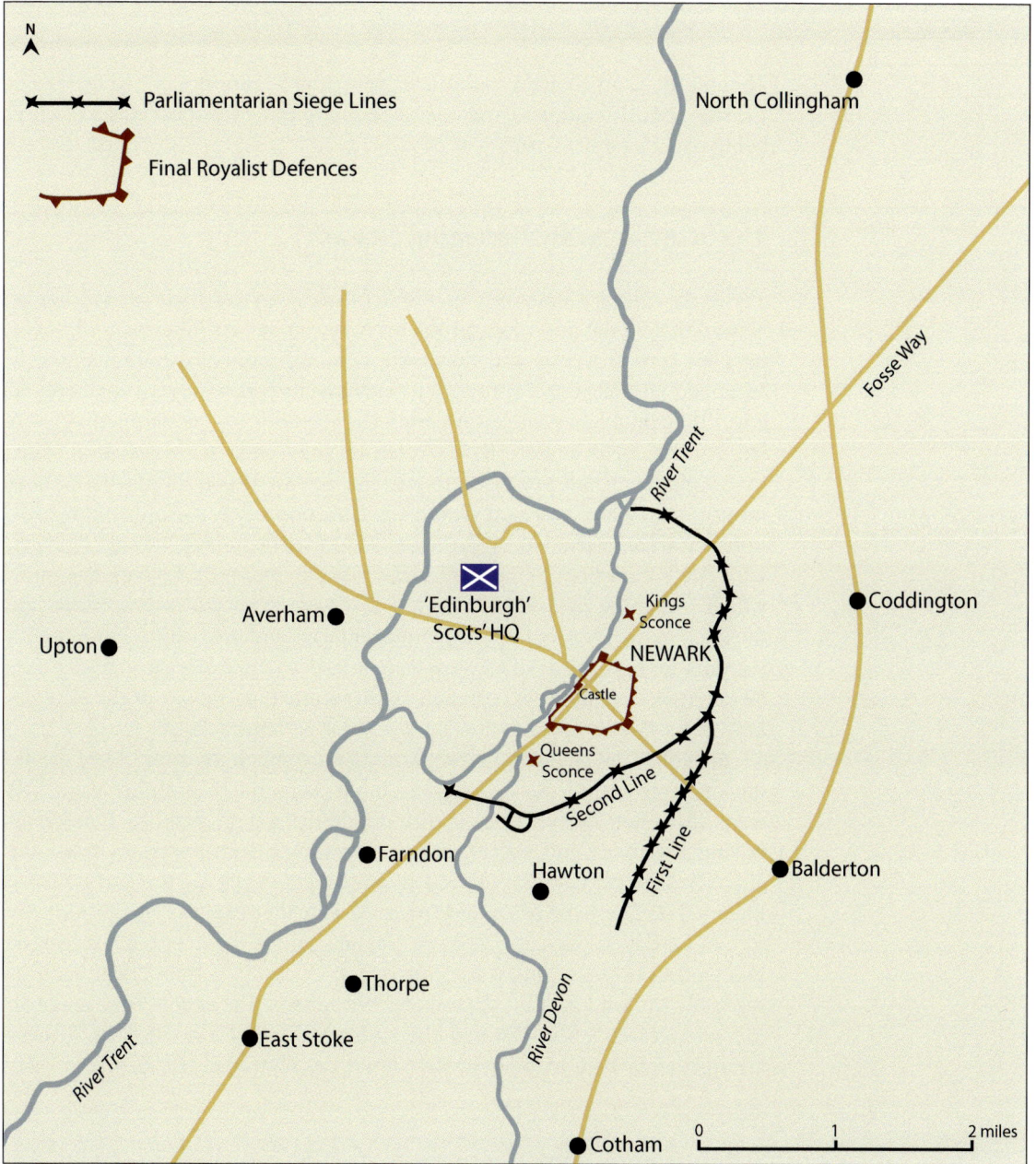

N

Parliamentarian Siege Lines

Final Royalist Defences

North Collingham

Fosse Way

River Trent

Kings Sconce

'Edinburgh' Scots' HQ

Averham

Upton

NEWARK

Coddington

Castle

Queens Sconce

Second Line

First Line

Farndon

Hawton

Balderton

River Devon

Thorpe

East Stoke

River Trent

0   1   2 miles

Cotham

The Third and Final Siege of Newark.

it before ye fire had well taken hold ye Scots came and quench'd it: this gave ye advantage without interruption to encamp their foot upon ye meadows within ye Isle, & so falls to work making their approaches nearer by two redoubts they cast upon either hand. From these they sent us some drake shott, wch might hinder our men from working at ye bridge [Trent Bridge], where we made a spurwork & also where we made a damm across ye Water to keep it high.[14]

Though the Scottish army had made promising beginnings, it had arrived at the siege poorly equipped and consisted predominantly of cavalry, as well as being considerably in arrears of pay.

The Scottish Army Besieging Newark[15]

The early military successes of the Scottish army on their arrival before Newark belied the numerous problems besetting it. Its soldiers had not been paid for several weeks, and they were running short of munitions, poorly equipped and lacking in provisions. Parliament had requested the Scots to cover the approaches to Newark from the west during the planned siege. A letter dated 2 November 1645, written by the Venetian ambassador, states that Parliament had promised to pay the Scots £31,000 'by the 10 of next month if they had besieged Newark'.[16] The committee at Goldsmiths' Hall, London, were instructed by Parliament to raise the money 'by way of loans', with the subscribers being paid eight percent interest.[17] Out of this sum, which was to be paid monthly, the Scots were expected to reimburse any financial demands owed upon them for quarter and provisions. Parliament's commissioners outside of Newark were instructed 'to take care that accounts be taken of provisions, & corn and all discounted on the pay of the army, as also all provisions taken by the Scots with or without ticket'.[18]

Although the Scots had arrived on 22 November, the promised £31,000 did not arrive until the end of December. Subsequent monthly payments were also often delayed due to the difficulties experienced in London of raising the loans and the logistics of arranging transportation from the city. The first convoy that arrived in Nottinghamshire, at the end of 1645, included 23 chests of coins and incurred a further expense of £240 for the hire of carriages, oxen and drivers. Captain John Beech, with 60 dragoons, was paid £116 17s to guard the convoy for 19 days: the time taken from its assembly in London to its arrival at Nottingham. The agents who made all the arrangements also claimed the additional fee of £16 10s 11d.[19] These arrangements had to be repeated monthly, with the last being in May

14   Slingsby, *Diary*, p.174.

15   Some of this research first appeared in Stuart B. Jennings, 'The Third and Final Siege of Newark (1645-1646) and the Impact of the Scottish Army upon Nottinghamshire and Adjacent Counties', *Midland History*, 37:2 (2012), pp.142–62.

16   Anon., *Calendar of State Papers Venetian, 1643–1647* (London: HMSO, 1864), p.221.

17   Anon., *CSPD*, 1645–1647, 3 December 1645, p.221.

18   Anon., *CSPD*, 1645–1647, 16 December 1645, p.264.

19   Anon., *CCC*, part VI, 6 December 1645–6 January 1646, p.789.

1646, but they were often in arrears. The April convoy included six chests containing £6,000 in coins and that, in May, included five chests of £5,000 in coins.[20] By the time that the May convoy had reached Nottingham, the Scots had withdrawn to Newcastle, with the King as their prisoner. Colonel Hutchinson was able to use this money, now safely at Nottingham, to pay his soldiers at the Nottingham garrison at their disbandment when the war was ended.[21]

Logistics and delays meant that many of the Scottish soldiers began the siege near destitute and poorly equipped, and things were only to gradually improve over the next six months. A full muster of the Scottish forces on 6 January 1646 showed that their 'horse was above 4,000, the foot 3,000 and a small train'.[22] The Parliamentarian commissioners at Newark complained about the cost of sustaining so many cavalry at a siege, asserting, 'We cannot think of any way (for subsistence) for so many horse on the north side of the Trent: neither doth the service of these parts require the forth part.'[23]

As a result of this muster, the Scottish monthly payment was reduced to £21,000, causing further hardship for the Scottish soldiers. With little cash, poor provisions and the hardship of a winter siege, a number of the Scots took to requisitioning what they needed from parishioners both across north Nottinghamshire and south Yorkshire. This led to a plethora of petitions being sent up to Westminster from both counties, complaining about the behaviour of the Scots. Colonel Hugh Fraser's Dragoons was one that was mentioned frequently in the complaints received by Parliament.[24]

It was not only money that was in short supply for the Scottish soldiers; there was also a shortage of munitions, and the majority of the army were poorly clothed for a winter siege. The first convoy of provisions and money from London to reach the Scots in December included 2,100 suits of clothes, 5,000 pairs of shoes, 2,000 stockings and 1,000 shirts.[25] A second convoy, in January 1646, delivered an additional 2,900 suits of clothes, 300 pairs of boots, 3,000 stockings, 4,000 shirts and 1,000 pistols and holders.[26] Over one of the coldest winters so far experienced in the seventeenth century, a number of Scottish soldiers would have been poorly shod and clothed, thus vulnerable to the effects of the elements.

As a result of the extensive military clashes on arriving outside Newark, the Scottish arsenal was seriously depleted. In March 1646, 200 barrels of gunpowder with match was supplied to them from London.[27] The following month, a further '100 barrells of powder with match and bullet', along with

---

20 Anon., *CCC*, part IV, 4 April 1646 and 2 May 1646, pp.36–37.

21 Keeble (ed.), *Memoirs of Colonel Hutchinson*, p.215.

22 Anon., *HL Journal*, vol. VIII, 23 January 1646, Letter from the Committee with the Army before Newark.

23 G. F. T. Jones, 'The Payment of Arrears to the Army of the Covenant', *English Historical Review*, 73 (1958), p.463.

24 These are explored in more detail in Jennings, 'Third and Final Siege', pp.155–57. Also see Alisdair McRae, *How the Scots Won the English Civil War: The Triumph of Fraser's Dragoons* (Stroud: Spellmount, 2011), Chapter 9.

25 Anon., *CCC*, part IV, 18 December 1645, p.30.

26 Anon., *CCC*, part VI, 15 January 1646, p.31.

27 Anon., *CSPD*, 1645–1647, 23 March 1646, p.386.

200 hand grenades, were added to the Scottish arsenal.[28] Feeding the Scottish army could not be adequately done from the local resources available. In anticipation of the coming siege, the Royalists at Newark had gathered in most of the available produce from the countryside. Being far from home, and regarded with deep suspicion by many of the local inhabitants, the Scottish troops struggled to obtain much fodder or food and were having to go farther afield to gather in small amounts of provisions. At this point, the Parliamentarian commissioners had to step in and order monthly provisions of pease, oats, meat, bread, butter and cheese, to specified values, from counties and hundreds farther afield from Nottinghamshire. Those issued with instructions included Cambridge and Ely (£900 per month), Norfolk (£1,000), Huntingdonshire (£400), Lincoln (£800), Kesteven (£300), Holland (£500), Bedfordshire (£200), Leicestershire (£1,000), Northamptonshire (£800), Rutland (£300), Derbyshire (£1,000) and Lancashire (£600). The scale of these levies testifies to the depth of the problem in providing provisions for the Scottish army, and one should also bear in mind that many of these counties were already supplying money and provisions to their own forces serving under Poyntz, with the Parliamentarian army on the east bank of the river before Newark (see below).[29] Each county was responsible for delivering its monthly provisions directly to the Scottish quartermasters, but they met their quotas with differing degrees of success.

Although the Scottish army was only slightly the smaller of the two armies besieging Newark, the problem of logistics affected the Scots much more, which often impaired their impact upon the siege. To the defenders at Newark, as the siege progressed, it was the Scots who were considered the most vulnerable to raids and attacks, and they undertook several on to the island against them.

Parliamentarian Forces before Newark

The town of Newark sits on the east bank of the river, and the challenge facing the commander of the English forces was how to cover both the northern, eastern and southern approaches to the town. With two-and-a-quarter miles of siege defences, it was to prove to be a monumental task for the Parliamentarian forces to block up Newark. The task was further complicated by the slow arrival of troops to join Poyntz's Northern Association and the fact that the area immediately in front of Newark's outer defences had been cleared of all cover such as trees, hedges and buildings, leaving the besieging forces exposed to fire from the town.

On 1 November 1645, as Poyntz was preparing to storm the garrison at Shelford, the Committee of Both Kingdoms made the decision to besiege Newark. They issued an instruction that 4,500 foot should be raised from the garrisons of the former Eastern Association to rendezvous with Poyntz

---

28   Anon., *CCC*, part VI, p.36.
29   Anon., *HL Journal*, vol. VIII, 23 January 1646, Assessments on Several Counties for Provisions for the Scots Army.

before Newark as soon as was possible. The allocation of soldiers across England was as follows: Bedford (100), Derby (500), Cambridge (200), Rutland (100), Lincolnshire (1,500), Lynn (500), Newport Pagnall (200), Nottingham (500), Isle of Ely (300), Leicester (500), and Huntingdon was to supply foot and dragoons (100).[30] Cavalry were not required because both the Nottinghamshire and Lincolnshire regiments were already available to Poyntz and their use at a siege was somewhat limited. Although Poyntz, with the majority of his forces, was able to join Thornhagh and Rossiter before the town at the end of November, leaving a small force behind at Belvoir Castle to continue the siege, the majority of the other forces set aside by Parliament did not arrive until the new year. A trickle of soldiers from Yorkshire and Ely were able to join up with those Parliamentarian forces before Newark around the end of December, but the forces due from the Eastern Association and a mortar from Reading had still not arrived by the end of January.[31] This meant that siege works around Newark were slow to be constructed, let alone manned, until the early part of 1646 and were only completed by the start of April. This allowed the Royalists in the garrison to continue to break out for supplies, as well as to attack the besieging forces (see below).

The Parliamentarian forces that were finally assembled before Newark in 1646 were financially better provided for than their Scottish allies on the other side of the River Trent. All of southern Nottinghamshire was by then under Parliamentarian control, enabling money and provisions to be collected by the forces before Newark. A series of ordinances passed over 1645 had empowered county commissioners to raise monies for the maintenance of their forces in local garrisons. This was expected to continue for those forces, even though, by 1646, they were far from home, encamped before Newark supporting the siege. On 26 December 1645, the county committee at Cambridge petitioned Parliament to be released of their weekly assessment of £14, to maintain their garrison at the castle, because it was now on duty beyond the county at the siege of Newark. Their appeal was rejected by Parliament, ensuring that there were to be no further challenges by other county committees.[32] Although money and provisions were often in arrears, they continued to trickle into the various company quartermasters over the course of the siege. Finances for Poyntz's forces were further enhanced in February 1646, when £20,000 was paid out of the excise to the impoverished Eastern Association 'for the forces raised for the siege of Newark'.[33] The Parliamentarian soldiers at the siege were spared the extremes of hardship that their Scottish counterparts periodically endured. They were further cushioned by the fact that many of the villages around Newark were turned into forts, serving the circumvallation of siege works, constructed in 1646 (see below). This meant that, for periods, when not on duty, soldiers could be rested under cover and sheltered from the extreme weather of winter. This was not without its dangers, for a Parliamentarian newspaper dated 9–16

---

30   Anon., *CSPD, 1645–1647*, 1 November 1645, p.213.
31   Wood, *Nottinghamshire in the Civil War*, p.109.
32   Anon., *CSPD, 1645–1647*, 26 December 1645, p.280.
33   Firth and Rait (eds), *Acts and Ordinances*, vol. I, 24 February 1646.

January 1646 reports, 'The Nottinghamshire forces do keep their court in the church [East Stoke] where unfortunately happened so great a fire, which took hold of the straw, that they could not quench it until it had devoured all that was combustible by the fire, and nothing on the next morning but the walls remaining, a sad spectacle to the beholders.'[34]

Newark's Riposte to the Approaching Siege

The garrison at Newark was far from passive as the Scottish and Parliamentarian forces gathered around the town to begin the siege. Over the harsh winter of 1645/1646, there were numerous raids by the Newark Royalists against both armies to cause both disruption and fear. There were also sorties to gather in further provisions from parishes around the town. Not until the end of March 1646, when the siege works around the town were completed (see below) and Newark was completely blocked up, did these cease.

In December 1645, 300 soldiers from Newark attacked the quarters of Colonel Rossiter and, after ferocious fighting, were eventually driven back into the town. Amongst the Royalist casualties of this raid was Colonel Leake, whose subsequent burial was recorded in the parish registers of the town on 21 December 1645.[35] According to Parliamentarian newspaper of 9–16 January 1646:

> From Newark were this day letters intimating that the enemy had sallied forth and fallen upon Col. Gen. Poyntz his quarters, thinking to surprise the Major Gen., but being at the same time abroad with a party, and having notice of the enemy's object upon his quarters, came in person, and encountered with them, slew one with his own hand, which example of his did much encourage his soldiers that they behaved themselves with much gallantry, slew many of the enemy, and took some prisoners, and forced the rest to make what haste they could to Newark, which they performed with much dexterity that they carried away some few of ours prisoners, and a few other things which they plundered out of the Major General's quarters.[36]

The above account fails to stress the real danger that both the commander and the Parliamentarian forces could have faced from this action launched from the town. The Royalist raiding party consisted of 800 horse and 300 foot, a significant part of the garrison in fact. The *Moderate Intelligencer* claimed that he (Poyntz) had to run away, without putting on his boots, and that he lost his money and had his chamber ransacked. Meanwhile, the Royalist *Mercurius Rusticus* asserted that the soldiers from Newark killed or took about 200 of the enemy without serious loss to themselves.[37] Whatever

---

34   Brown, *History of Newark*, vol. II, p.99.
35   Early English Books Online (EEBO), *Perfect Occurrences*, 19–26 December.
36   Brown, *History of Newark*, vol. II, p.99.
37   Wood, *Nottinghamshire in the Civil War*, p.109.

the truth behind the respective claims, it is clear that this was a major skirmish and that the raiders from Newark came close to inflicting serious damage upon the Parliamentarian forces and their commander. This event was to focus the minds of those besieging the town upon swiftly completing the extensive siege works they were constructing around the town over the spring of 1646.

The Scottish forces encamped upon the island were not spared either from raids across the River Trent by the Royalists in Newark. On 5 March 1646, it was reported that 1,000 horse and 400 foot:

> … fell upon the Scots guard in the island with an intention to take from them a work which the Scots were making to keep them [the Royalists] from grazing any cattell on the Island. Muscomb Bridge being down, the Scots could not get any reliefe over to their men but verie slowly in boats, so that the enemy overpowered their horse, being but four small troops, and made them retreat towards Muscomb Bridge with some loss, though not much. Then the enemy attempted the work, but were beat off with some loss. As soon as the Lieu. General received the alarme, he and the rest of the company with him hasted with all speed over the river, where he commanded the horse to rally, and led them himselfe to the work.[38]

The harsh winter had almost cost the Scots the loss of their base on the island because large chunks of ice carried down by the river had 'broken down' the wooden bridge at Muskham. Even so, the Scots claimed to have endured casualties with a captain, two lieutenants and eight soldiers killed and 15–20 soldiers wounded. Only the quick action of David Leslie, then acting commander of the Scots in the absence of the Earl of Leven, saved the day and drove the Royalists back into Newark.

The Parliamentarian Siege Works around Newark, 1646

The attack on Poyntz's quarters in January 1646 had clearly shown to Parliamentarian commanders on the east bank of the river that Newark had to be 'closed up' and a stricter siege imposed upon the town. It was deemed by Poyntz and his fellow commanders that the town was too strongly defended to be taken by storm; therefore, they decided to starve it into surrender. The work began by creating a means of better communication and cooperation between the two armies on either side of the two branches of the River Trent. Two bridges, constructed of boats, were built to facilitate this – one at Winthorpe, north of Newark, and the other to replace the one destroyed by ice at Muskham – thus facilitating the main body of the Scottish army quicker access to its forward defences on the island at the Edinburgh Sconce. The Winthorpe Bridge was completed by 11 March, and it was defended by a fort constructed of earthen works on the right side of the river, opposite Crankley Point. Faint remains of this work can still be seen on the ground

---

38 Brown, *History of Newark*, vol. II, p.103. See also British Library (BL): E327 (18): 'A Great Fight at Newark', *Moderate Intelligencer*, 5–12 March 1646.

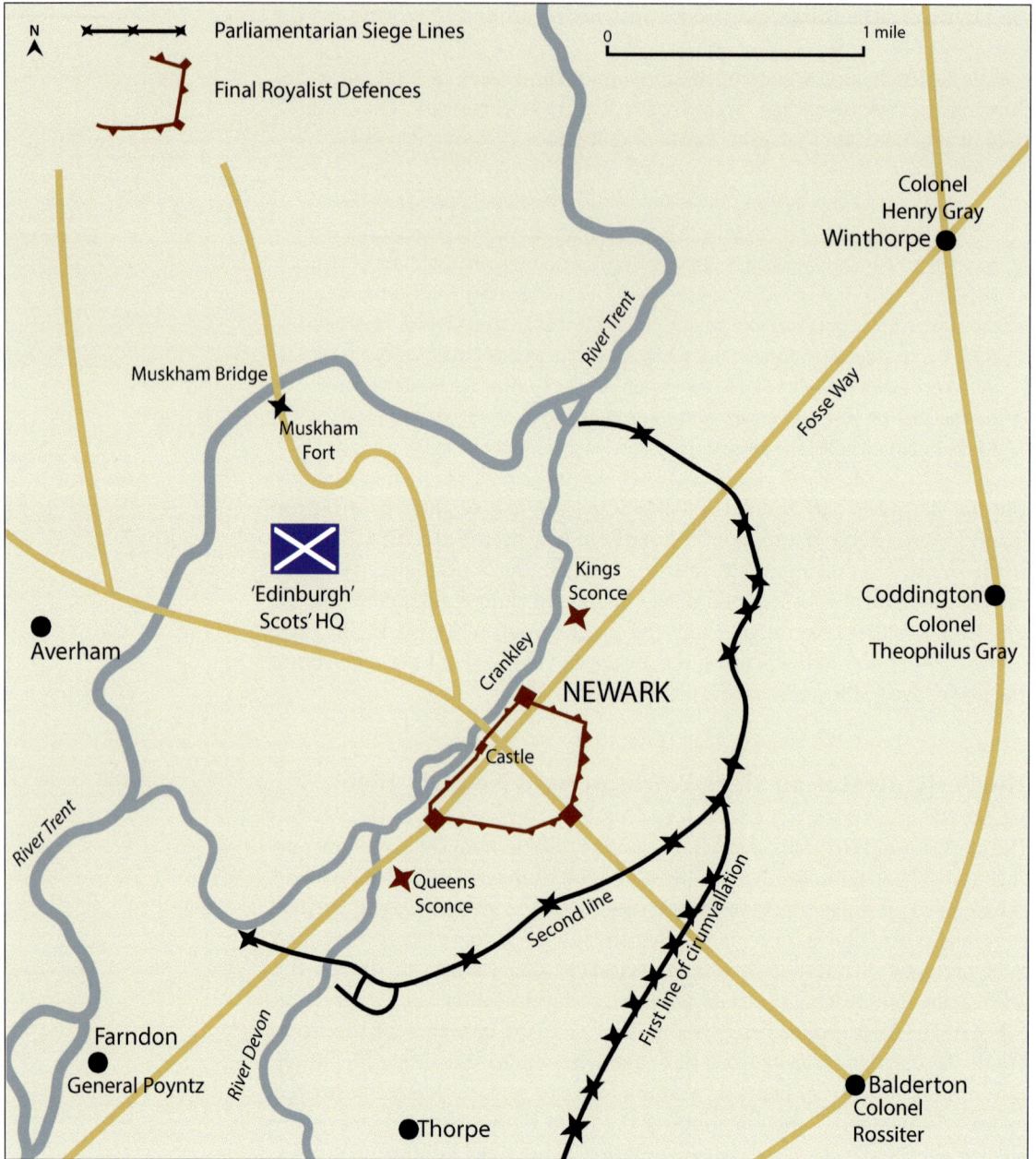

Parliamentarian siege works around Newark.

to this day.[39] The bridge at Muskham was completed and in use just over a week later.

As more soldiers arrived to join Poyntz at the siege during the first two months of 1646, the issue of where they could be quartered, so as to secure the siege, became more pressing. To give them clear lines of fire, the Royalists had cleared the area immediately in front of Newark's defences of all cover. The answer to this quandary lay in linking a circuit of villages that lay around two miles away from the centre of the town. Over a period of time, as the Parliamentarians advanced ever closer to Newark, these were fortified by a surrounding rampart and deep ditch, with demi-bastions and projecting bastions on the ramparts. The latter two features were around 200–250 yards apart along the ramparts, which allowed them to provide musket cover for one another. The first village to be reached and fortified appears to have been Farndon in December 1645. The Nottinghamshire Horse were quartered at East Stoke, where a large fire destroyed their base at the parish church in January 1646, suggesting that this village was fortified by then.[40] The village of Coddington was secured early in February 1646, and, by the start of March, the circumvallation of Newark was completed.[41]

According to Professor Wood, another fort was constructed 'nearer to the enemy's great sconce [the King's Sconce]' to provide fire onto that defensive work.[42] Correspondence dated 18 March 1646 records that 'the cannon from York to Winthorpe … [and] culverins and mortar pieces are come to Balderton and Farndon'.[43] It was to take time for the Parliamentarian gunners to get their ranging correct, for, as one contemporary account reports, 'The enemy within doe begin to be much distracted, and the rather because our mortar piece doth already begin to play upon them, although at first with greater fright than execution, because it is said that firemen could not finde the ground.'[44]

By the end of the siege, Richard Clampe's map of the Parliamentarian siege works (1646) depicts the presence of at least 23 cannons around the circumvallation. To keep the siege works adequately defended, a number of tent barracks were also constructed alongside the ramparts surrounding Newark, and these are also clearly depicted on Clampe's map. These existed alongside the fortified villages and probably reduced the necessity of 'free quartering' of soldiers in the homes of the local population.

Once the worst of the winter had passed and the extensive slabs of ice upon the rivers were gone, Poyntz attempted to construct dams across the River Smite, known today as the 'River Devon', and the arm of the River Trent that ran beneath Newark Castle. This was an attempt to put the town's gunpowder and corn mills out of action. It proved to be a larger task than first envisaged, and it was not until the middle of April that they managed

39   RCHM, *Newark Siegeworks*, pp.37–39.
40   Jennings, *A Very Gallant Gentleman*, p.58.
41   RCHM, *Newark Siegeworks*, p.35.
42   Wood, *Nottinghamshire in the Civil War*, p.110.
43   Brown, *History of Newark*, vol. II, p.104.
44   Early English Books Online (EEBO), *Mercurius Circus, London Intelligencer*, Thursday, 16 April–Thursday, 23 April 1646.

Note fome Granadoes are made of Canvafle with divers Piftoll-barrels charged with powder and bullets, and covered over.

A

B

C

Details about the use of mortars from Robert Ward's 1639 publication *Animàdversions of warre*. (National Civil War Centre, Newark, with permission)

to successfully change the course of the Trent and the Smite/Devon away from Newark. Around the same time, the Parliamentarians had managed to dig siege trenches and throw up forts against the Queen's Sconce as well as by Balderton Gate. The Scots had also managed to capture the Royalist earthwork on the island, known as 'Sandy Fort', and from here were able to fire cannons against Newark Castle. All three forts were also within musket range of Newark, and there would have been constant firing into the town and at its outer defences.[45]

Life within Newark was becoming increasingly difficult for both its soldiers and civilians. Plague was raging within the town, cutting a swathe through the civilian population and probably through the garrison troops. It is difficult to be sure about the mortality rate amongst soldiers because the surviving evidence suggests that they were not buried in the churchyard. Over the course of the war, only 28 soldiers' names are recorded in the burial register, and these were either gentlemen of note or local men. The same registers, though, are very detailed in their recording of the burials of numerous of the town's civilians.[46] Over the course of the war, demographic research for Newark has suggested that between 12 and 15 percent of the civilian population died from typhus, whilst up to a further 15 percent succumbed to plague. There is no reason to believe that the soldiers were in any way spared from catching these infections, especially as many of them were quartered in the homes of the town's people.[47]

By March 1646, provisions were beginning to run low within Newark, bringing to the defenders further hardship and difficulty. According to a Parliamentarian newssheet of that same month, it was reported:

There hath lately been in Newark, great contestation between Bellasis, the Governor, and the king's commissioners there, and the officers and soldiers

---

45 Wood, *Nottinghamshire in the Civil War*, p.116.

46 Stuart B. Jennings, "'A Miserable, Stinking, Infected Town": Pestilence, Plague and Death in a Civil War Garrison, Newark, 1640-1649', *Midland History*, 28:1 (2003), pp.51–70.

47 See Jennings, *These Uncertaine Tymes*, especially Chapters 4 and 5.

for pay and provisions. The Governor told the commissioners that his soldiers wanted money, but they professed that there was none for them to be had; but they told him that for provisions he might dispose unto them what quantities he pleased. Bellasis replied that soldiers must and should have monies whilst any of them had a farthing, and that for the provisions in the magazine he told the commissioners that the greatest part thereof was such as no dogge would eat, and therefore charged them to bring forth, or else he and his soldiers would rifle their houses and take their provisions they had stored up for themselves, and leave them the rotton stuff in the magazine to feed upon; and he further told them that they were not to expect that he and his soldiers would fight to preserve them and their town without those things should presently be remedied, and that for his part he said he did know well how to make honourable and good conditions for himself, his officers, and soldiers, and would leave them and the townsmen to shift for themselves if they took not care for them.[48]

Whilst conditions were certainly getting very harsh by March 1646, there survives no evidence within the borough minutes, which are fairly comprehensive for this period, to suggest that things were as bad within the town between the various authorities as this piece of Parliamentarian propaganda might imply. The destruction of the garrison papers before the surrender now makes it difficult to be definitive about this episode though, and there may well have been growing friction as the siege progressed. The response of the town authorities to the instruction of Charles I to surrender the town in May hardly suggests a beaten town (see Chapter 9). What is clear is that, by the middle of March, it would only be a matter of time before the garrison succumbed to the siege, as there was no chance of any external relief arriving at this late stage of the war. Even so, defiance continued right to the end. Cannon, mortar and musket fire continued to be directed from the town defences at the Parliamentarian and Scottish forces besieging Newark, and even the church bell ringers played their part by ringing on 'the King's coronation day', for which they were paid the sum of 10s by order of the mayor.[49]

---

48   Anon., *A Great Fight at Newarke* (London: Matthew Walbancke, 1646).
49   NA: Newark Churchwarden Accounts, 27 March 1646.

9

The Fall of Newark, 1646

Spies, Informers and Turncoats

As the various forces assembled around Newark to begin the siege, the governor of the town was kept abreast of events, both locally and at the Royalist headquarters at Oxford, by a group of informants and spies who were able to smuggle themselves into and out of the town. The elderly and the very poor were willing to earn rewards for doing so, in spite of the risk should they be caught, and, during the initial stages of the siege, their movement appears to have raised few alarms for the besiegers. Certainly, by the time the circumvallation of the town was completed by the start of March, Bellasis would have been well aware that the King's military cause was in terminal decline and that there was little chance of a relief force being raised to come to the town's assistance. He probably also would have been acquainted with the rumour of the growing tensions between the English and Scottish commissioners in London and outside Newark. As the ultimate success of the Parliamentarians became increasingly obvious following the

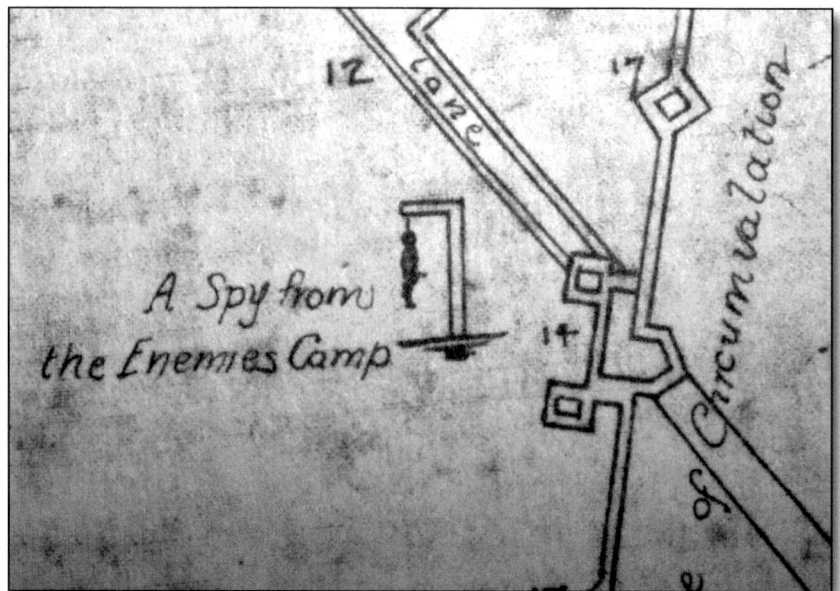

Details from the Crampton siege map of the hanging of a Royalist spy by the Parliamentarian besiegers. (National Civil War Centre, Newark, with permission)

defeat of the King's main field army at Naseby, their Scottish allies became more and more concerned about the English Parliament's willingness to honour the terms agreed in the Solemn League and Covenant (1643). In particular, they were concerned that the post-war settlement of the English Church would not be, as they believed it had been promised, structured along the model of Presbyterianism then settled in Scotland. In fact, John Pym (1584–1643), the English architect of the treaty, had worded the proposed reform carefully, saying it would be shaped 'according to the Word of God'. It was not his fault that the Scots interpreted this as meaning solely in the form of Presbyterianism.[1]

Bellasis may have also been alerted to the King's new political strategy of attempting to exploit this growing tension between the two allies to shatter their alliance. The Newark governor later claimed that 'he had advertisement from Oxforde by a ragged man whome he employed as his agent to be civil to the Scots there [at Newark] … but at first he sallied equally against them and was as willing to beat them as the English'.[2]

The Parliamentarian commanders besieging Newark also had a growing unease about the commitment of their Scottish allies across the river. Colonel Francis Thornhagh, the commander of the Nottinghamshire Horse, had established within and around Newark a number of agents and informers over the course of the war. On 6 October 1645, even before the arrival of the Scots at Newark, he reported to Parliament:

> George Biggin, of Eakin [Eakring] informed Mr Hawden, of Tuxford, Minister, that a Trumpet belonging to Col. Eyre, of Newarke, passed through Tuxford on Sunday, the 5th of this instant October, did in the presence of the said Mr Hawden, say and affirm that he was going with letters from his Majesty and from Sir Richard Willis [then] Governor of Newark, to General Leven, with hopes to bring him back with his army to Newark for the king, with as much joy as ever he did come from the Parliament: and Mr Hawden did see the two letters in the hand of the Trumpeter. And two Scottish gentlemen being at Tuxford with Mr Hawden the same day, he did affirm to them that the King and General Leven had long been in treaty, and he did not doubt but it was affected, and that this letter would bring him back. Taken at Nottingham in the presence of us …[3]

The slowness of money, provisions and munitions reaching the Scottish army after it arrived before Newark in November at the request of the Parliament did little to diminish the hopes of the Royalists or allay the anxieties of the Parliamentarians over the course of the siege. As the developing siege increasingly 'closed up' the town, the Parliamentarian newssheet *Moderate Intelligencer* claimed in March that the Royalists in Newark were increasingly aware of their desperate plight and had sent to Oxford to learn about the King's instruction about their future conduct, should they receive a summons

---

1   J. P. Kenyon, *The Stuart Constitution, 1603–1688* (Cambridge: Cambridge University Press, 1986), pp.239–42.

2   Royal Commission on Historical Manuscripts, *Manuscripts of the Duke of Portland*, vol. I, p.378.

3   Jennings, *A Very Gallant Gentleman*, p.69.

to surrender.[4] This may not in itself have been an admittance of defeat but rather an attempt to ascertain the King's next political move. At this stage, both provisions and munitions within the town were still in good supply, and Bellasis was willing to keep on defending the garrison in spite of the appearance of plague in the town.

Parliamentarians also had a network of informers both within and around the town from the end of 1644, at least. In the previous chapter, we referred to a private and informal contact that they had claimed to have made with one of the town's aldermen, Mr Thompson, about yielding up the town. Although the Parliamentarian newssheets for this period were primarily vehicles of propaganda for their cause, those references to Newark strongly suggest that they had some contacts within the town, supplying them with information about what was going on behind the town's defences.

Far more distressing for many civilians across the North Midlands would have been the experience of witnessing Royalist turncoats visiting their parishes, guiding or commanding troops of Scots to extract provisions. The Commons moved quickly to address this concern and, on 8 October 1645, had passed an order that 'no Englishman ought to take any commission from the General of the Scottish army'. In spite of this instruction, by the end of April 1646, the House of Lords were able to hand over to the Scottish commissioners a list of 100 English soldiers they had identified as serving with the Scots in their army, many of whom had been formerly in arms for the King.[5] Particularly relevant for those in the Nottinghamshire area was that 12 of those named had previously served in the Royalist garrison at Newark. It is possible that some of these were mercenaries who had initially been hired by the Royalists but had deserted to the Scots as the siege began. These hired soldiers, unlike locally raised soldiers, were less sympathetically attached to the region they were serving in and collecting levies from. Soldiers who had previously extracted provisions for Newark in anticipation of the siege were now returning to the same parishes to do the same again but this time for the more desperate Scots. Named individuals included a Corporal Sympson, who 'fled for a rape at Thorne', possibly whilst serving in a Royalist force, and a Mr Thomas Bullinger, 'hereunto an Intelligencer between Newark and Skipton'.[6]

It is probably because of cases like this that Article Ten of the final surrender document, regarding the release of all prisoners taken by either side, included an exclusion clause 'unless they be detained for criminall offences charged upon them, not as soldiers' (see Appendix IV).

The First Summons to Newark to Surrender, 28 March 1646

By mid-March, the town was closely besieged, and, on 18 March 1645, a letter was forwarded to the House of Lords signed by John, Earl of Rutland, and Edward, Earl of Sandwich, commissioners with the army before Newark. In it, they reported to the Lords:

---

4   Early English Books Online (EEBO), *Moderate Intelligencer*, 19–26 June.
5   Anon., *HL Journal*, vol. VIII, 11 May 1646.
6   See Jennings, *These Uncertaine Tymes*, pp.158–59.

… we have brought a Pinnace Musket within half a mile of Newark, wherein are two guns, and which will hold forty muskets. The cannon from York has come to Winthorpe. One strong fort is made to secure the bridge and another is preparing near the enemy's great [King's] sconce. Culverins and mortar pieces are come to Balderton and Faringdon. The great mortar piece is to run on Wednesday at Nottingham. We shall not lose any time or omit any opportunity of reducing Newark.[7]

The Parliamentarian forces besieging the town were clearly preparing for an attempt to storm the garrison. On Friday, 27 March, a day of prayer and preaching was held 'throughout the English and Scottish armies before Newark, to seek a blessing from Heaven upon the proceedings of the said forces in the present siege of that garrison'. Two of the appointed preachers on that day, Edward Reyner and Robert Ram, chaplain to Colonel Rossiter, both of Lincoln, subsequently published their sermons.[8]

On Saturday, 28 March, in an attempt to avoid the unnecessary shedding of blood, the Parliamentarian commissioners sent a summons to Bellasis to surrender the town of Newark. They assured the defenders of the town honourable and fair conditions. The summons continued, 'that they were able by force to attain what they rather desired by treaty having 16,000 horse and foot at present before Newark, who were soldiers of experience, united in health and courage'. As an additional warning to Newark's civic authorities, the summons mentioned that this would avoid 'that wealthy town be[ing] sacked'.[9]

Helmet as worn by Parliamentarian sappers digging trenches up to the outer defences of Newark. (National Civil War Centre, Newark, with permission)

Bellasis did not rush to respond to the summons, waiting until 31 March to send the response below. It appears that the governor of Newark had some awareness of the talks going on between his King and Parliament. His response included the following:

I shall in answer thereof, desire you to reflect upon the King's letter on 23 of March, sent to the two Houses of Parliament (which I received from your own Quarters) where, in a full compliance with all their desires, upon the most Gracious Conditions that ever Prince propounded, He offers to disband His Forces, and to dismantle His Garrisons: To what end do you demand that of the steward, whereof the Lord and Master makes a voluntary tender.

7   Anon., *HL Journal*, vol. VIII, 18 March 1646, p.220.
8   Brown, *History of Newark*, vol. II, pp.104–05.
9   Early English Books Online (EEBO), *A Letter to the Honourable William Lenthall, Esq …* (London: Edw. Husband, 1646), pp.5–6.

Although he concluded his response with a rejection, he declared a willingness to negotiate further with the following provision:

> If you will grant a passe to some Gentleman to go to the king and return, I may know His Majesties pleasure, whether according to His Letter, He will winde up the business in general, or leave me to steer my owne course: then I shall know what to determine: otherwise I desire you to take notice, that when I received my Commission for the Government of this place, I annexed my life as a Label to my Trust.
>
> Newark March 31
> J. Bellasyse[10]

The governor of Newark was not willing to make a response without the direct authorisation of his King. It seems most likely that his request went unanswered, for there was no armistice and the encroachment upon the town came ever closer.

The situation for the defenders within Newark was quickly deteriorating: plague was now raging amongst both the civilians and soldiers in the town, and the town defences were increasingly vulnerable. In April, the Parliamentarian newssheet *Mercurius Civicus* reported:

> Col. Generall Poyntz and Col. Rossiter had made their approaches meete before the garrison at Newark, and they have turned the river since another way; it is wonderfully perplexed the besieged to find the course of the two Rivers Trent and Smite [Devon] turned. In regard to the turning of the Trent, they made no works or moment to defend themselves on that side of the town. As we make more neer our approaches, we do raise forts to make good the place. We have raised a fort to cut off all correspondence betwixt Queen's fort [sconce] and the towne; another fort is raised at Balderton, another upon Beacon Hill. The Scots also have raised a fort to defend themselves from any more sallies of the enemy, and to secure them in their more neere approaches.[11]

The end for the garrison at Newark was drawing ever nearer, but it was to be events beyond its immediate control that were to hasten its final surrender.

Machinations of the King and the Road to Surrender

With the surrender of Sir Ralph Hopton and the Royalist army in the west on 14 March 1646, and the defeat of the last Royalist force in the field at Stow-on-the-Wold seven days later, all military options for Charles had come to an end. He now sought a political success against his foes by attempting to divide the English Parliamentarians from their Scottish allies. He wrote to the English Parliament on 23 March 1646, stating that he was willing to disband what remained of his forces, order the surrender of his garrisons

---

10   EEBO, *Letter to William Lenthall*, pp.7–8.
11   Early English Books Online (EEBO), *Mercurius Civicus*, 16 April–25 April 1646.

and return to Westminster for further discussions, providing that an act of oblivion was passed for his supporters and that sequestrations upon their estates were removed. The same day, he also wrote separately to the Scottish commissioners in London, saying that he was willing to give them 'full contentment' in church governance, providing it was not contrary to his conscience.[12] If Parliament rejected his proposals, the King promised to hand himself over to the Scottish army at Newark. He also assured them that, if they received him, he would order the garrison at Newark to surrender to the Scottish army. The Royalists in the town were beginning to lose control of their own future in this developing scenario.

The French government decided at this point to give additional support to Charles. A divided England and support for their long-term allies, the Scots, was deemed to be beneficial for their own foreign policy. In August 1645, they sent Jean de Montreuil to London, as an agent to both the Scots and the English. He initially opened a dialogue with English Presbyterians in the Parliament but failed to persuade the Independents in the House to engage with him. At the same time, he engaged in facilitating communications between Charles and the Scottish commissioners in London. On 1 April, fearing that Charles' return to Westminster might stimulate growing unrest in the capital against the war, Parliament rejected the King's proposals, but, at the same time, Montreuil, on behalf of Charles, was able to reach an agreement with the Scottish commissioners. On 5 April, Montreuil went to the Scottish army before Newark but disappointingly found the Scottish generals cautious about agreeing the terms accepted by their commissioners in London.

As all this was developing, it remains unclear as to what extent Bellasis at Newark was either informed or aware of what was going on between his King and the Scots. On April 27, as the besieging forces drew up to within musket range of Newark's defences, a second summons to surrender was issued to the town, with the caveat 'we shall give you conditions for the surrender thereof which you must not expect to be such as you might have formerly obtained'.[13] On this occasion, the governor of Newark, for reasons that remain uncertain, agreed to negotiate. On 29 April 1646, he announced the names of the 10 commissioners who were to represent the garrison of Newark at the negotiations, and, around the same time, the commissioners for the two armies besieging Newark were also named. The meeting between these Royalist and Parliamentarian commissioners to agree on terms of surrender began on 3 May at Poyntz's quarters on the siege works.

Negotiations were brought to an abrupt halt on the morning of 5 May 1646, as all parties involved were caught by surprise by events unfolding at the Scots quarters. At 7:00 a.m. that morning, the King, accompanied by two companions, arrived at Montreuil's apartment at the King's Arms in Southwell to hand himself over to the Scottish army.[14] Charles had completely misread the situation involving negotiations between

---

12   Wood, *Nottinghamshire in the Civil War*, p.114.
13   Wood, *Nottinghamshire in the Civil War*, p.116.
14   The inn still remains at Southwell but today is called the Saracens Head.

Montreuil and the Scottish army officers and found himself not as a guest, as he imagined, but rather their prisoner. Lord Lothian rode to Southwell from the Scottish headquarters on the island and immediately demanded of the King that he should order the surrender of the garrison at Newark, sign the Solemn League and Covenant and agree to the establishment of Presbyterianism across England.[15] The Scots then moved the King to Kelham so that he might be better accommodated, they claimed, but in reality it made for a more secure detention centre for the King. Meanwhile, the Scottish commissioners at Newark met with their Parliamentarian counterparts there to try and diffuse any further potential schism between both parties. Each was already suspicious of the other's motives and plans prior to this unexpected turn of events.

On 6 May, Charles wrote to the governor of Newark from Kelham, instructing him:

> Such is the condition of affaires att this present that I can give you no hope att all of reliefe nor off better condisions than what I sent you last night; wherefore the best for my service will be that you conclude upon them with all expedition, the cheefe reason being that according to my designe I am necessitated to march with the Scotch [sic] army this day northwards but cannot move till the agreement be consented to by you. I am heartily sorry that my business stands so that I must impose such condisions upon you.[16]

Writing to the Speaker of the House of Commons on 5 May, Poyntz informed the House of the King's presence with the Scots at Kelham but went on to claim that 'our process in the Treaty [with Newark] was in great forwardness, but we now rather expect his Majesty's command for a surrender than the prosecution of a parley'.[17] Going back to the account of Robert Thoroton in 1677, it has been a long tradition that Bellasis wept upon receiving these instructions from the King and that the mayor of the town at that time, Mr Thomas Smith, urged the governor to 'trust God and sally forth'.[18] Although Bellasis could not disobey his King, he still managed to obtain favourable conditions for both his men and the town. At midnight on 6 May, the governor signed the articles of surrender, and Newark's role as a Royalist garrison came to an end.

Articles of Surrender and Dismantling the Royalist Defences

At the time of the surrender, plague was raging within the town of Newark, causing considerable fear and many deaths. A contemporary witness wrote of the town, 'and truely it is become a miserable, stinking, infected towne. I pray God they do not infect the counties and townes adjacent, which is the care

---

15   Wood, *Nottinghamshire in the Civil War*, pp.118–19.
16   Royal Commission on Historical Manuscripts, *Manuscripts of the Duke of Portland*, vol. I, p.358.
17   Brown, *History of Newark*, vol. II, p.114.
18   Brown, *History of Newark*, vol. II, p.115.

of the commissioners to prevent'.[19] As a result, not only were the terms carefully observed, but the garrison's Royalist troops also marched out on 8 May, a day earlier than agreed to in the articles of surrender, in an to attempt to flee the infection. The Royalists left behind them in the town a 'great gun known as "Sweet Lips", eleven other great pieces of ordnance, two mortar pieces, divers drakes and small pieces, 4,000 arms, forty barrels of gunpowder, and a great store of bullets, match and other ammunition'. The store of provisions left behind were much reduced and included 'little fresh meat, of salt meat "some plenty", but much of it tainted; some store of butter and cheese, many barrels of beer and wine, a good store of corn, but "fewel for fire very little"'.[20]

As soon as the garrison had surrendered, the Scottish army, with the King, broke the siege and marched north towards Newcastle. The Scots still hoped that the King might be persuaded to accept their conditions, but, if that failed, he could be used as a bargaining tool with Parliament to get their arrears of pay. The infection within the town also guaranteed that Article Eight of the surrender articles, which stated that the townsfolk would 'not be molested in their persons, privileges, goods or estate', was scrupulously observed. In fact, most of the Parliamentarian troops drawn from outside of Nottinghamshire returned home as soon as possible, leaving the control of quarantining the town, as well as the destruction of Royalist defences, to the supervision of the Nottinghamshire forces.

Plague meant that additional conditions had to be added to the movement of those Royalist forces leaving Newark that had to journey beyond the county, to either return to their homes or go to any other 'unblocked' Royalist garrison. In June 1646, plague reappeared in the South Yorkshire town of Doncaster and, by the end of that year, had claimed 136 victims. Robert Ince, the mayor of that town, was blamed for the reintroduction of the pestilence by his neglect and carelessness, and the town corporation successfully petitioned for his removal in September 1646. One of the accusations made against him was:

> That about the 4th of May last past, at which time the garrison of Newark was delivered into the Parliamentary forces and the soldiers which came forth of the said garrison went to their several homes; he, the said mayor, having received commands, and by warrant from the said commissioners about Newark, that

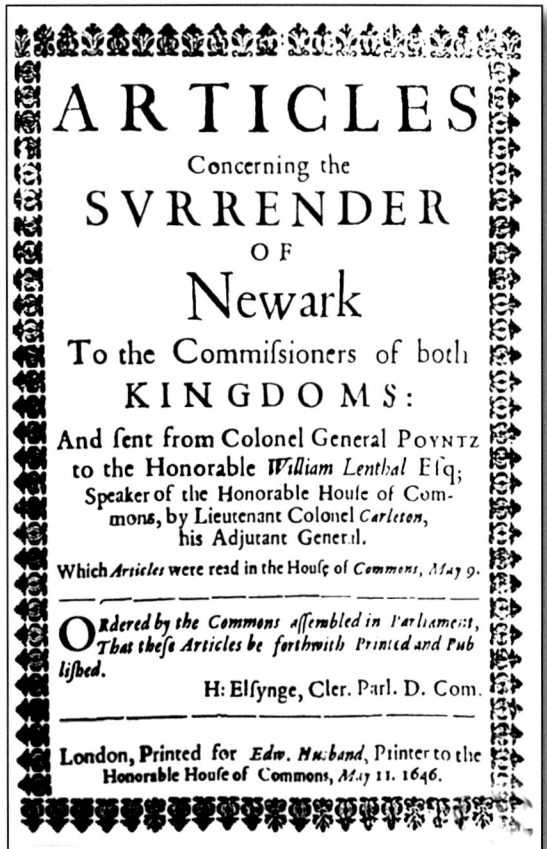

ARTICLES
Concerning the
SVRRENDER
OF
Newark
To the Commissioners of both
KINGDOMS:
And sent from Colonel General POYNTZ to the Honorable *William Lenthal* Esq; Speaker of the Honorable House of Commons, by Lieutenant Colonel *Carleton*, his Adjutant General.

Which *Articles* were read in the House of *Commons, May* 9.

ORdered by the Commons *assembled in Parliament,* That these *Articles* be *forthwith Printed and Published.*

H: Elsynge, Cler. Parl. D. Com.

London, Printed for *Edw. Husband,* Printer to the Honorable House of Commons, *May* 11. 1646.

Articles of surrender for the garrison of Newark. (Author's collection)

19   Thomas Bailey, *Annals of Nottinghamshire: History of the County of Nottingham, including the Borough* (London: Simpkin, Marshall & Co., 1853–1855), vol. II, p.763.
20   Brown, *History of Newark*, vol. II, p.119.

none of the said soldiers should be received or lodged in any town on their march for fear of infection (it being very vehement in the said town of Newark), yet he, not withstanding, did not only suffer certain of the soldiers to remain in the town, for the space of a whole week; but he also himself entertained and harboured in his own house one Thomas Ince, an inhabitant of Newark, who came from thence at that very time, and also his wife, for divers weeks together, to the great fear and imminent danger of the whole town.[21]

The articles of surrender clearly spelt out the conditions that applied to Royalist soldiers leaving the garrison. Both officers and men were allowed to march away 'with their money, clothes and swords', whilst officers and gentlemen were also allowed their horses. Carriages were to be provided in a convoy to allow them to carry away their goods, providing hostages were left to guarantee the safe return of those carriages. The only conditions applied to their march away from the town were that those 'who have no money, to have free quarter' and that they were 'not to march above ten miles in one day umlesse they please' (Article Three). There was no mention of them avoiding being 'received or lodged' in any town as referred to in the warrant received at Doncaster, issued by the commissioners at Newark. Once the town had been surrendered and the ferocity of the pestilence was made clear to the commissioners, they felt it necessary, for the protection of local communities, to add further conditions to the Royalists on their march back to their homes.

The order from Parliament for the defences at Newark to be slighted, so that it could not be used again as a defensive fort, were also severely impacted by the presence of plague. A contemporary letter states:

… the countrie thereabouts are all summoned to come in with spades, shovels, pickaxes and other necessaries, on Monday next, to assist in demolishing the works of Newark. I believe they will come in very joyfully to that worke, which tends to so much and great an ease to all those parts, as they have found by wofull experience, since they felt the oppression of that garrison and others, of all which they are now clear, and all will be buried in the ruins of this, which they are forthwith to level.[22]

This demolition probably began a few weeks after the surrender and is evidenced by a register entry at the parish of North Collingham dated 18 July 1646 that records the burial of Richard Thorneton, 'a labourer who was killed with the falling of stone at the pulling downe of Newarke Castle'.[23]

There can be little doubt that the surrender of Newark, and the subsequent withdrawal of most of the besieging forces, came as a relief

21   C. W. Hatfield, *Historical Notices on Doncaster* (Doncaster: Brooke, White and Hatfield, 1870), pp.113–14. See also Stuart B. Jennings, 'Nottinghamshire 1646; Plague, Disruption of Trade and Commerce and the Cancelling of the Goose Fair in the County Town of Nottingham', *Midland History*, 43:2 (2018), pp.182–84.

22   Cornelius Brown, *The Annals of Newark-upon-Trent: Comprising the History, Curiosities, and Antiquities of the Borough* (London: H. Sotheran & Co., 1879), p.165.

23   Nottinghamshire Archives (NA): PR/16/118: North Collingham Parish Register, 18 July 1646.

to the population across north Nottinghamshire. Though, it would be an exaggeration to claim, as the contemporary witness above did, that those conscripted to come to the pestilence-ridden town to dismantle the defences did so with joy. There was a very real concern that the infection would be carried back to the surrounding parishes. This in fact happened, resulting in the cancellation of the main county fair (Goose Fair) that was to be held at Nottingham in October 1646. The fair, though moved to a different venue within the town, had managed to continue to be held over the previous four years of the Civil War.[24]

The desire to get away from Newark as quickly as possible, so as to avoid catching the plague, probably explains why the slighting of the defences was only partially completed, leaving some of the Royalist defences still visible to this day. The two sconces, one to the north of the town (King's Sconce) and the other to the south (Queen's Sconce), were stripped of their palisades, but the bulk of their earthworks were left untouched. The King's Sconce was finally destroyed in the nineteenth century, but the impressive Queen's Sconce still survives.[25]

The earthwork defences, beyond the dilapidated medieval stone town walls, were substantially dismantled, although a small remnant is just about discernible in the Friary Gardens, but the outer deep ditch was predominantly filled in before the slighting was ended. It is the surviving remains of the castle, though, that raises the most awkward questions about the nature of the slighting. The southern and eastern curtain walls and the part of the north curtain wall that ran from the gatehouse to the southern wall have completely disappeared above the ground level. Yet the western curtain wall and its towers overlooking the Newark branch of the River Trent survived almost to their full height. The impressive twelfth-century gatehouse was stripped of its roof and timbers, but the stone walls substantially remain almost to their full height and still overlook and guard the bridge crossing over the river into the town. Likewise, the Queen's Sconce continues to overlook the crossing over the River Devon. The walls of the castle adjacent to the town were totally dismantled, but the outward facing defences over the river were left almost complete. Possibly, this has as much to do with the stone being used either for rebuilding within the town or, more likely, sold to raise cash rather than for any military reasons. The medieval town walls, within the siege defences, were already somewhat dilapidated and, in places, broken down and had finally disappeared by the start of the eighteenth century, but two of the gates were still standing at the latter part of the eighteenth century: Bar Gate was demolished in 1762, and the East gate in 1784.[26]

Still standing within the town, there remains a significant number of early timber-framed buildings, giving the town its impressive historical ambience.

---

24   See Jennings, 'Nottinghamshire 1646', pp.174–89.

25   RCHM, *Newark Siegeworks*, p.31.

26   Thanks to Kevin Winter at the National Civil War Centre for this information. 'Meet The Experts - Norman & Medieval Newark', *YouTube*, uploaded by National Civil War Centre, 22 May 2020, <https://youtu.be/h1mOjEDOAlM>, accessed 14 Dec. 2022.

Newark North Gate and Bar Gate in the eighteenth century. Plates from William Dickinson's *The History and Antiquities of the Town of Newark in the County of Nottingham*, published in 1819. (National Civil War Centre, Newark, with permission)

Amongst structures built pre-Civil War (fifteenth to early seventeenth century) are buildings in Boar Lane, Castlegate, Kirkgate, the Governors House, Old White Hart Inn (the base for Colonel William Staunton in 1645–1646), Prince Rupert's accommodation, the Old Grammar School (now part of the National Civil War Centre), the impressive parish church of St Mary Magdalene and the castle ruins.[27]

27   Alison Arnold and Victoria McMillan, 'The Development of Newark-on-Trent 1100–1750, as Demonstrated through Its Tree-Ring Dates', *Vernacular Architecture*, 35:1 (2004), pp.50–62.

10

Disease, Wounds and Death: Soldiers at the Garrison[1]

Becoming a Garrison

From the end of 1642 to its surrender in May 1646, the town of Newark had become a significant Royalist garrison. One of the consequences of this was that the population of the community doubled and, on occasions, such as the arrival of forces with the Queen and later Prince Rupert, trebled or even quadrupled. The impact of this upon the civilian population has already been explored in earlier research, but what did it mean for the soldiers at the garrison?[2] This significant growth of the town's population, made up of not only soldiers but also the families of Lincolnshire and Nottinghamshire Royalist sympathisers seeking safety, occurred at a time when the amounts of buildings available for occupation were significantly reduced. Houses and cottages beyond the circuit of defences were either dismantled or burnt to remove any cover for attacking forces. Buildings that abutted the internal walls of the town defences were also demolished for greater security. This resulted in more and more people being crammed into the limited accommodation remaining within the defences. This impacted upon not only civilians but also the soldiers serving at the garrison, especially at times of sieges, when they had to quartered within the defences. At the Restoration of Charles II in 1660, a petition from the town's civic authorities claimed that, in the service of the King's late father, the town had incurred damages amounting to the sum of £40,000 'by the burning of a sixt part of the town when it was made a garrison, by erection of works, money lent and never repaid, [and] quartering of soldiers'.[3]

---

1   Some of this research first appeared in Jennings, 'Controlling Disease', pp.40–54.
2   For the civilian population, see Jennings, *These Uncertaine Tymes*.
3   Anon., *CSPD*, 1661–1662, 27 July 1661, p.45.

Quartering of Troops and the Storage of Munitions and Provisions

At the start of the Civil War, Newark was principally a town of low, thatched-roof, timber-framed houses, some of which still retained large gardens. Fire was a constant risk, and it was probably only the fact that the three sieges of the town occurred over winter or very early spring, when the thatch was still wet, that spared it from extensive fire damage. Within the walled town, there were only three stone buildings: the castle, the church and the grammar school. This was to create difficulties not only in quartering soldiers but also in finding safe and secure premises for the storage of munitions and perishable provisions once Newark was garrisoned with the arrival of Sir John Henderson and 4,000 troopers in December 1642.[4]

Over the course of the sixteenth and early seventeenth centuries, Newark Castle, which in fact had originally been constructed as a fortified episcopal palace, was occupied by a series of tenants who had spent considerable sums of money converting the castle into a comfortable country house. Large windows in the west curtain wall, including an oriel window, installed in the late fifteenth century, additional fireplaces and the adaptation of many of its larger chambers into smaller apartments more convenient for the residents and their families had all been undertaken, reducing both the accommodation capacity and the defensive function of the building. As early as 1536, before many of these alterations had been undertaken, a complaint had been sent to Henry VIII that the castle 'had scant lodgings for a 100 men and no water'.[5] Few of the soldiers making up the garrison after 1642 could be permanently quartered here. The stone undercroft and the castle dungeons still remained and were to prove to be useful for the Royalist defenders. Situated below ground level, they provided a cool and secure storage place, both for munitions and perishable or valuable goods. Here, the regimental quartermasters could obtain supplies of munitions or securely store their provisions gathered in. Surviving graffiti evidence from one of the dungeons at the castle also suggests that, during the third siege, it had been used to accommodate prisoners.

The lack of large buildings and purpose-built barracks, which did not appear in England until the start of the eighteenth century,[6] meant that the quartering of soldiers based at Newark had to be resolved by a variety of measures. Most of those soldiers based permanently at Newark appear to have been accommodated in the homes of the town's residents whilst their officers were usually accommodated in the inns of the town, as was the case for Colonel William Staunton (see Chapter 7). When the King, the Queen or Prince Rupert arrived with their forces at Newark, these arrangements had to be altered so that suitable accommodation for these royals and

4   Wood, *Nottinghamshire in the Civil War*, p.30.
5   See Jennings, 'Controlling Disease', p.42.
6   Paul Pattison, 'History of Berwick-upon-Tweed Barracks', *English Heritage*, <https://www.english-heritage.org.uk/visit/places/berwick-upon-tweed-barracks-and-main-guard/history/>, accessed 16 Dec. 2022.

The undercroft at Newark Castle. (Author's photograph)

Prisoners' graffiti dated 1645/1646 in one of Newark Castle's dungeons. (Photographer Kevin Winter)

their immediate entourage could be found within the security of the town defences. Until the latter part of the war, Royalist cavalry at Newark were often quartered at the villages in the vicinity of the town, or even at the satellite garrisons of Welbeck, Shelford, Wiverton or Belvoir Castle, which provided cover for all the approaches to the town. This arrangement was essential for providing additional fresh pasture for grazing of their horses whilst the troopers were nearby to oversee them. At times, when the Royalist control of these outlying areas was diminished by attacks or sieges, these arrangements could no longer be safely used. This is why, before the third and final siege of Newark closed up the town, the governor had to send away nearly two-thirds of the Newark Horse to the Royalist garrison at Lichfield.[7] At this time, overcrowding in the town became a real problem, as all the Royalist soldiers, probably around 2,000, had to be lodged within the town defences and, by the time of the surrender in 1646, an estimated 1,800 soldiers, who were not from the town, marched out of Newark.[8]

Disease, Wounds and Death amongst the Soldiers

Prior to the surrender of Newark, in May 1646, the Royalist defenders destroyed any documentation that might at a later date be used by Parliament to incriminate individuals within the garrison. Accounts, administrative documents, lists of names or minutes of meetings between officers and the Royalist commissioners of array, who were based at Newark throughout most of the war, were all probably burnt. In many respects, this action makes the survival of the brief accounts for Colonel William Staunton's troop of horse both rare and useful insight.

What has survived, thankfully, is a large amount of documentation generated by the civic and ecclesiastical authorities within the town, possibly spared from destruction by the besiegers because of the presence of the plague.[9] Within both sets of these records, there survives occasional references to military affairs, which impinged upon their respective fields of jurisdiction. Just as significant, though, are the absence of references within these documents to events that one would have expected to find mention of. A good example of this is the parish records of Newark, which survive for the whole of the Civil War period and were generally meticulously kept. From these, it has been possible to identify three outbreaks of typhus within the civilian population, over the years 1643–1645, and an outbreak of plague over the period of late 1645–September 1646. The typhus outbreaks accounted for the deaths of over 15 percent of the civilian population, and the plague for a similar percentage. Probably, over a third of the town's population succumbed to disease over the course of the war.[10] Yet, over the period of the war, the names of only 28 officers and four soldiers appear in the burial records of the church, and, although the churchwarden accounts do occasionally record the purchase of 'winding sheets and inkles' for soldiers who died at parishioners' homes, there are no burial entries for these soldiers. It is most unlikely that soldiers quartered in the homes of parishioners at Newark managed to avoid these periods of infection that so decimated the civilians of the town; in fact, the likelihood is that more soldiers died of disease than of their wounds at the Newark garrison. The answer possibly lies in there being a separate burial

---

7   Wood, *Nottinghamshire in the Civil War*, p.107.
8   Wood, *Nottinghamshire in the Civil War*, p.120.
9   Research on these documents was published in Jennings, *These Uncertaine Tymes*.
10   Jennings, 'Miserable, Stinking, Infected Town', pp.51–70.

plot, or pit, for military casualties separate from the parish graveyard into which ordinary soldiers, not of the parish, were buried. Gentlemen officers and local men appear to have been spared this indignity.

Historians need, though, to focus on what these various civic and ecclesiastical records do unwittingly tell us about garrison soldiers in the town. The largest military action within Nottinghamshire was the breaking of the second siege of Newark in 1644 (see Chapter 4) by forces under the command of Prince Rupert. Royalist newssheets had much to say about this military exploit, but what did it mean for those wounded or killed in the action, both within the garrison as well as those amongst the relieving force? The consequence of this action lasted for several months, and glimpses of some of these survive in, of all places, the churchwarden's accounts for the years 1643–1644 (the new year began on 25 March within the accounts). The following entries for 1643–1644 make mention of events:

> To John Gill by Mr Maiors command for a winding sheet & inkle for a soldier who
>   died at his house – 2s 6d
> To Mr Maior for a winding sheete and inkle for one of Prince Rupert's soldiers
>   – 2s
> To Mr Johnson for the like by Mr Maiors appointment – 2s
> To Mis[tress]Atkinson for two sheets 2s 8d and for an inkle and to a poore woman
>   for winding two soldiers 8d in total – 3s 4d

Early in 1645, payments were still being made for the burial of soldiers 'to Walker and Yoxall for passing Bells and macking of soldiers graves by Mr Maiors command, 3s 4d'.[11] There are several points of interest to be drawn from these entries. First, sick and wounded soldiers appear to have been cared for in people's homes – there is no record of anything resembling a hospital or treatment building, unlike the mention of a 'pesthouse' during the plague of 1645–1646. The large number of soldiers involved, from both the garrison and Prince Rupert's army, probably meant that no household was spared such billeting. Even though the corporation paid for the shrouds and graves of those soldiers who died when the householder was unable to meet the cost, none of these burials are recorded in the registers. An undated bill, most likely from the time of the second siege, records that the corporation paid the sum of £1 'to a surgion'. Each regiment was supposed to have its own surgeon as part of its officer core, but the number of wounded and sick soldiers around the town probably meant that the civic authorities were required to pay for extra cover at this time. This was all occurring just as the town of Newark was coming towards the end of yet another typhus outbreak, to which the additional cost of caring for the casualties of the fighting was also added. It may well be that the presence of infection, as much as other demands, encouraged Rupert not to dwell too long at the town with his exhausted army after their long march across country.

---

11   NA: PR/24810: Newark Churchwarden Accounts, 1640–1660.

The Newark Corporation, as well as the garrison, understandably wanted to celebrate their great deliverance from the siege. The large sum of £5 10s 6d was paid by the corporation to 'Prince Rupert's trumpeters and servants at the raising of the siege'.[12] If the servants were treated so well, there is a strong probability that the senior officers alongside the prince were also entertained with a banquet, gifts and plenty of wine to mark the occasion, though unfortunately the bill for this is missing from the surviving documents. The corporation had previously paid out the sum of £2 7s 8d on 5 January 1643/1644 for 'a banquet for my Lord Withrington [sic]' when he was at Newark.[13] Lord William Widdrington served as governor of Lincoln following Newcastle's success at the Battle of Gainsborough.

By the spring of 1646, plague was raging within Newark. A note on the end board of the parish register records that 'the plague did begin the 2 day of March 1645/6'. The corporation minute book records the implementation of plague orders across the town on 9 March 1646.[14] As noted earlier, the plague had arrived in the town in the autumn of 1645, but the cold winter had curtailed its spread. Now, as the siege began to impact and the weather warmed up, it reappeared with a vengeance. From March to May, some named soldiers and family members appeared in the burial registers with a frequency not seen before, though still in very low numbers, that in no way was a reflection of the size of the garrison of the time. Only the name of one soldier, Thomas Hackney, is recorded, but there are four named captains, a Mr Samuel Reniger, a lieutenant of horse and a daughter-in-law to a Captain Taylor. One of these captains, Edward Twentyman, a relative of John Twentyman, died of gangrene according to the memoirs of the latter, but the others were probably plague victims.[15] The ferocity of the plague amongst Newark's civilian population and the speed with which it spread after the surrender of the town suggest that the infection was also rampant amongst the soldiers much more than the burial entries suggest. It may be the case that the only recorded soldier named in the register, as against officers named, had strong links to the parish, as did Captain Edward Twentyman, but all the other identifiable soldier burials were of officers and gentlemen.

Whilst Royalist soldiers from the garrison who were returning home to the north of the country after their surrender were required to avoid staying in towns on their march, soldiers raised locally in Nottinghamshire were left to make their own way home, with few restrictions. With them, they took the infection, and, within weeks, there were further outbreaks around north-east Nottinghamshire. At the parish of East Stoke, part of which bordered the parish of Newark, though it was a base for the Parliamentarians during the siege, there are entries that display this pattern of spread. On 28 July, it is noted, 'Thomas Pattison, formerly a souldier died of ye plague and was buried in the fields'. Two days later, Peter and John Haselem 'that came from Newark and borded at William Symsons died of the plague'. Whilst it is

---

12   NCWC: NEKMS 2021.19.52: Newark Borough Chamberlain's Accounts, 1644.
13   NCWC: NEKMS 2021.19.31: Newark Bill of Expenses.
14   NA: DC/NW/3/1/1: Borough Minutes, pp.279v–80.
15   NA: PR/27256–257: Newark Parish Registers, entries for 1645 and 1646.

unclear whether these brothers were in arms at Newark, they were certainly in the town over the third siege. Lieutenant Wright, along with 'a youth from Newark', possibly a servant of the former, and both of whom were boarding with Hugh Baguley, died of the plague on 2 September. Hugh Baguley also succumbed to the infection later that month. This pattern of former soldiers carrying plague out to their home villages was most certainly repeated across much of north Nottinghamshire, but the poor survival rate of parish registers for the latter part of the Civil War makes it impossible to quantify the full impact of this.[16]

The death of Captain Edward Twentyman, from gangrene, also underlines another danger that constantly threatened soldiers at the garrison. In an age before antibiotics, infection of wounds was an ever-present danger for soldiers, and it got worse as conditions within the town became increasingly squalid as the final siege progressed. By the time of the Civil War in England, experiences gained in Europe and the publication of military manuals all recommended that a regiment should have, alongside its regular officers, a minimum of one physician (usually university educated), who was judged competent to diagnose internal problems. He was to be supported by a minimum of at least one surgeon, who could assist him in surgery, and an apothecary, who dispensed drugs and might also treat minor ailments.[17] As Newark was an important staging post between the King's capital at Oxford and his northern base at York until 1644, many Royalist regiments passed through, or stayed, at the town, and there would have been occasions when the garrison found it was well provided for with medical care. Those who spent longer periods at Newark providing medical cover for the garrison soldiers are much more difficult to identify because of the scarcity of surviving evidence. One of the main sources for identifying those clearly supporting the Royalist cause with their medical cover, providing they were affluent enough to levy fines from, are the records of the Committee for Compounding. These only identify three named individuals as delinquents at Newark, and they were a Dr Leeming, a 'physician to the garrisons of Newark and Belvoir', John Seele of Cambridge,

Replicas of seventeenth-century surgical equipment. (Newark Civil War Centre, Newark, with permission)

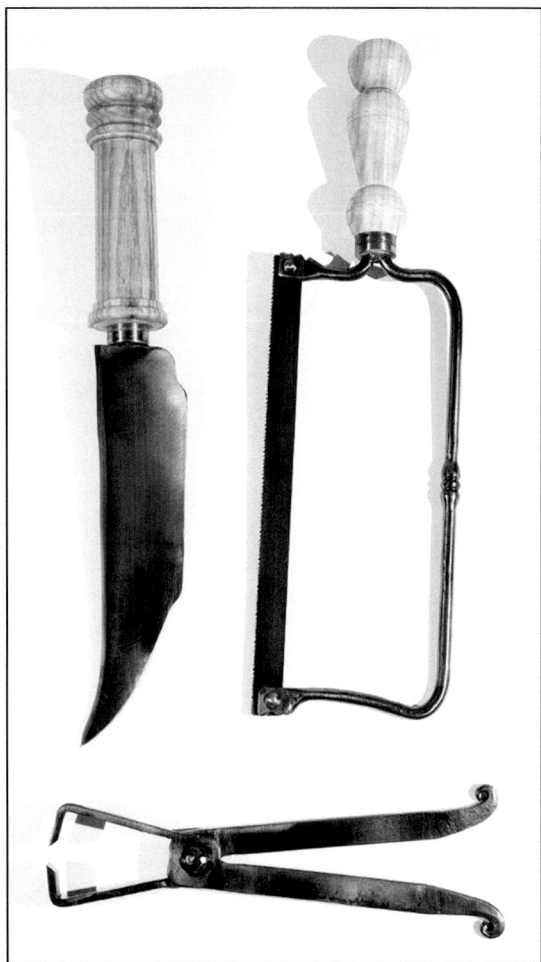

---

16 See Stuart B. Jennings, 'The Anatomy of a Civil War Plague in a Rural Parish: East Stoke, Nottinghamshire, 1646', *Midland History*, 40:2 (2015), pp.201–19.

17 Ismini Pells, 'Reassessing Frontline Medical Practitioners of the British Civil Wars in the Context of the Seventeenth-Century Medical World', *The Historical Journal* (2018), pp.1–27, <https://hdl.handle.net/2381/41486>, accessed 23 Dec. 2022.

'surgeon who went to Newark to assist the king's forces and was still at the garrison at its surrender', and finally a local man from Newark, Henry Cam, who was identified as an apothecary. Each had to compound to retrieve their estates from the sequestration that Parliament had placed on them because of their service to the King's cause.[18]

As we have seen, wounded and sick soldiers appear, from the surviving records, to have been nursed in the homes where they were billeted. Yet, if surgical intervention was required, either through amputation of a limb or the extraction of a musket ball from a wound, a more suitable venue was required, especially if the numbers requiring such treatments were high after military action. The shot from a musket would enter the body, causing internal damage and cavities or, if it struck bone, possibly shattering or breaking a bone. As a musket ball was made of soft lead, it rarely exited the body, as it was usually flattened as it entered the flesh. This meant that it was essential for the musket shot to be removed from the body to avoid infection or septicaemia.[19] Within the town of Newark, there would have been few suitable buildings where surgery could be performed, especially if the numbers requiring surgery were large and availability of surgeons and physicians was limited. Probably, the most suitable venue might have been a chamber set aside at the castle, though there remains no surviving evidence to confirm this.

A physician or surgeon presented with a soldier wounded by a musket shot had two concerns that needed to be addressed immediately if his patient was to survive.[20] First, using a 'bullet extractor', he needed to locate and remove the shot from the wound, and, the ball having been flattened on entry, this was often a difficult task. The chances of the soldier recovering were greatly enhanced by the removal of the lead ball since, if it remained in the wound, over time it would undergo oxidation (rusting) and cause further infection. The second task was to thoroughly cleanse the wound, removing any foreign matter carried into the body by the shot. This might include cloth, metal splinters and dirt, which often led to sepsis if missed. If major infection set in, the only chance of halting its progress, if the wound was in any of the limbs, was by amputation. Captain Edward Twentymen's infection, mentioned earlier in this chapter, began by the simple act of stubbing his toe whilst on duty, and, either through neglect or fear of surgery, he ignored the discomfort. Unfortunately, it quickly turned into gangrene, which was eventually to kill him.

With the musket ball removed, the wound was regularly cleaned, and fresh dressings were applied. The wound was usually kept open under the dressing

---

18   Anon., *CCC*, part II, pp.1399, 1414, 1597.

19   Much of the above is derived from Stephen M. Rutherford, 'The Personal Cost of War: Injuries from Firearms and Their Treatment during the Civil Wars', *Civil War Petitions*, <www.civilwarpetitions.ac.uk/blog/the-personal-cost-of-war-injuries-from-firearms-and-their-treatment-during-the-civil-wars/>, accessed 1 Jan. 2023.

20   For more details, see Stephen M. Rutherford, 'A New Kind of Surgery for a New Type of War: Gunshot Wounds and Their Treatment in the British Civil Wars', in D. J. Appleby and A. Hopper (eds), *Battle-Scarred: Mortality, Medical Care and Military Welfare in the British Civil Wars* (Manchester: Manchester University Press, 2018), pp.57–77.

to allow it to weep, as experience in the Thirty Years' War had shown that this greatly enhanced the healing process, though the reason why was not understood at the time. Modern medical science explains this phenomenon as encouraging the accumulation of lymph at the weeping wound, which fortifies the immune system and limits bacterial growth. With no anaesthetics available at the time, wounded soldiers were often given alcohol before the procedures began to try and dull the pain.

A surviving petition of 1646 from the former Parliamentarian soldier Richard Taylor of Nottingham to the county committee gives us an insight into how painful and expensive such wounds and treatment could be:

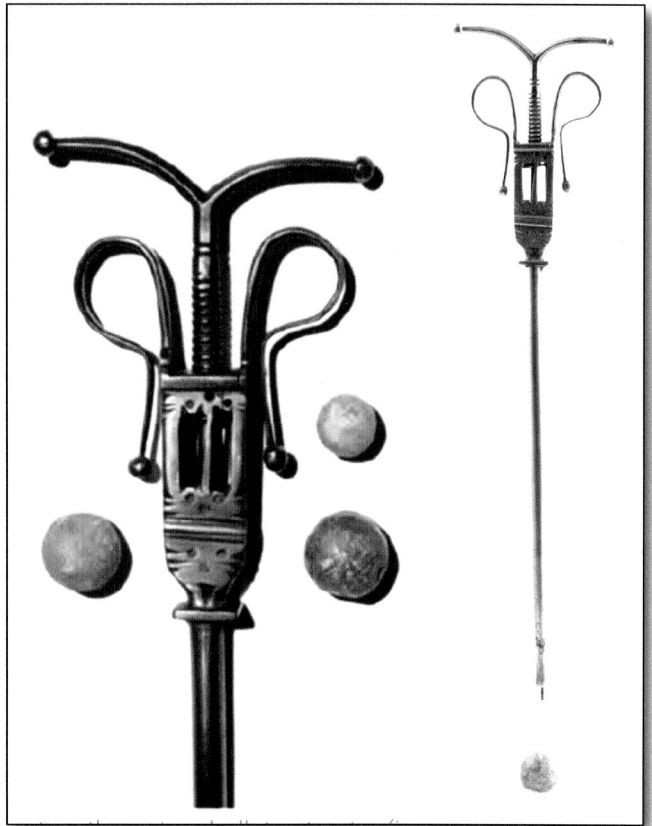

Replica of a seventeenth-century musket ball remover. (National Civil War Centre, Newark, with permission)

> … that at the last siege of Newarke, at the beginning, before it was layd closse hee was sore wounded (being upon the Scout) by the Cavalleers; And shott quite through the raignes of his back, and tuckes, in 7 places of his bodie besides; whereof hee hath lane under Mr Lettins hand the chruigion [sic] 25 weekes; a great part of w[hi]ch time y[ou]r peticoner were no way able to helpe himselfe, nor to turne him in his bed; and hath still a rent 2 inches long in his back; and he knoweth not whether ever hee shall be a sound man againe or not.[21]

As the petition shows, recovery after treatment was sometimes possible, but it was a long and expensive affair. Surgeons and their treatment had to be paid for, and the wounded soldier was often incapacitated and so was unable to earn a wage. Taylor was at least awarded a gratuity of 20s for his pain, a benefit of fighting for the winning side in the First Civil War. Royalist troops wounded in the garrison at Newark generally received little or nothing for their suffering until the Restoration of Charles II in 1660, if they survived that long.

---

21 'The Petition of Richard Taylor, Nottinghamshire, 12 August 1646', *Civil War Petitions*, <www.civilwarpetitions.ac.uk/petition/the-petition-of-richard-taylor-nottinghamshire-12-august-1646/>, accessed 1 Jan. 2023.

Conclusion

After the Battle of Waterloo in 1815, the Duke of Wellington wrote in a letter back to England, 'believe me, nothing except a battle lost can be half so melancholy as a battle won'.[1] The soldiers and civilians of the town of Newark would have identified strongly with the sentiment of this quote. Having endured sieges, disease, hardship, death, destruction and financial devastation, they had surrendered not because of defeat but in response to a direct order of the King they had served so faithfully for nearly four years. They knew not what long-term reckoning that the victorious Parliamentarians at Westminster, or their local supporters across Nottinghamshire, might place upon the town. Perhaps they felt a glimmer of hope with the disappearance of the Scottish army from the area, but the reality was that plague was rampant in the town and quarantine would be expected from them both in the town and for those garrison soldiers marching home beyond the county border. Those citizens of Newark convicted of supporting the Royalist cause, as late as January 1647, petitioned the Committee for Compounding for further time to pay their fines because of the plague and because trade was much curtailed.[2] In the county town of Nottingham, as late as 25 December 1649, the minute book of the corporation records, 'Newark – It is thought fitt that the corne comeinge from Newarke bee Not stopt, but houshold goods to be stopt that come from thence'.[3]

The town of Newark was to witness both the zenith and the nadir of Prince Rupert's military career during the First Civil War. On 12 March 1644, he had received an urgent message from the King to march from Chester to break the siege of Newark. In just nine days, he managed to march the 126 miles, collecting troops from Shrewsbury, Bridgnorth and other smaller Royalist garrisons, before rendezvousing with Lord Loughborough at Ashby-de-la-Zouch in Leicestershire on 18 March. In the early morning of 21 March, with his combined force of 3,500 horse and 3,000 foot, he surprised the besieging army of Sir John Meldrum, enjoying a stunning victory and capturing 3,000

---

1   Edward S. Creasy, *The Fifteen Decisive Battles of the World: From Marathon to Waterloo* (London: Richard Bentley & Son, 1899), p.382.
2   Jennings, *These Uncertaine Tymes*, p.84.
3   W. T. Baker (ed.), *Records of the Borough of Nottingham, 1625–1702* (Nottingham: Nottingham Corporation, 1900), vol. V, p.245.

muskets, 11 cannons and two mortars, most of which ended up in the armoury of the Newark garrison and were a resource well used throughout the rest of the war.[4] Nineteen months later, he was back at Newark on 15 October 1645 and, within a few days, submitted himself to a court martial for his surrender of the city of Bristol. Although he was to be acquitted of the charges, the relationship between Charles and Rupert was to be fractured for the remainder of the Civil War.

Even after the soldiers had left the vicinity of Newark, the demographic and economic consequences of the war were to remain with the town well into the eighteenth century. The three outbreaks of typhus in the town, over the winter months of 1644, 1645 and 1646, and the plague outbreak that ravaged the town from March to September 1646 were to reduce the population of the town by about a third. The 1674 Hearth Tax returns, even allowing for possible under-registration of houses, clearly demonstrate that Newark's population had still not returned to its pre-1640 levels. Unlike the larger mercantile cities of Bristol and Chester, a smaller county town such as Newark had fewer economic opportunities to attract people back into it from the surrounding countryside.[5]

As an important market town for the north-east of Nottinghamshire, the destruction wrought upon the landscape during the war was to have a substantial impact on its economy, long after the fighting had ended. The construction of earthen defences and siege works required large areas of pasture to be dug up in order to provide turf to face these works to prevent their erosion by the harsh weather over the winter months. Before the war, the parishes around Newark, along the Trent Valley, were renowned for both dairy produce and the provision of grazing pasture for the raising of young horses ready for sale at market.[6] The pasture would not be sufficiently recovered for grazing until late spring 1647 at the earliest, and the movement of beasts, as well as people, was only then just beginning again after plague concerns had diminished. This would have considerable impact on the market activities within the town for this period at least, and complete economic recovery would be a long, drawn-out affair.

At the Restoration of Charles II in 1660, the Newark Corporation petitioned the King for the issuing of a new charter to the town, in recognition of its faithful service to his late father. In their appeal, they drew attention to the 'burning of a sixth part of the town when it was made a garrison'.[7] Most of the property that was destroyed by fire was almost certainly of the poorer quality that lay outside the perimeter of the town defences or abutted up to it from the town side. More substantial timber-frame buildings, such as the one 'small tenement consisting of two bayes of building lately erected upon the townes land at Milngate and nere the river of Trent', were ordered to be dismantled 'for the strengthening and better fortifieing of the Bulworks there'

4   See Chapter 4.
5   Jennings, *These Uncertaine Tymes*, pp.62–84.
6   P. R. Edwards, 'The Supply of Horses to the Parliamentarian and Royalist Armies in the English Civil War', *Historical Research*, 68:165 (1995), pp.49–66.
7   Anon., *CSPD*, 1661–1662, 27 July 1661, p.45.

Newark Castle's western curtain wall and gatehouse, c. 1904. They still stand sentinel over the river crossing at the town as a lasting testimony to the town's Civil War history. (Author's collection)

and re-erected elsewhere as specified by the authorities. As the three sieges occurred over the wet months of winter and early spring, damage within the town itself seems to have not been too substantial, as the mortars and grenades fired in were generally unsuccessful in setting fire to the thatched roofs of most of the buildings. Certainly, the more substantial homes of Alderman Hercules Clay and Christopher Wilson, a future mayor of the town, were noted as being destroyed or severely damaged, and a petition also survives from a poorer resident, Charles Piggot, claiming that he and his family were left destitute by the destruction of their home during the second siege.[8] A walk around the town centre of Newark today still presents the visitor with an array of sixteenth- and early seventeenth-century timber-framed homes and inns that survived the war, and a substantial part of the other buildings to be seen are of either the Georgian or Regency period, suggesting that finance for substantial rebuilding, or replacement of damaged or poor quality housing, only became available from the eighteenth century onwards.

Huge sums of money had been borrowed from the more affluent members of the town over the course of the war. According to records amongst the State Papers, a total sum of £11,285 had been loaned, but, by 1661, there was still a sum amounting to £3,212 15s 1d remaining to be paid back by the Royalist commissioners.[9] A long and bitter legal action amongst the surviving Royalist commissioners was instigated to recover this money, which dragged on for most of the decade. This fact alone may well account for some of the economic difficulties that the town encountered over the latter part of the seventeenth century.

---

8   Jennings, *These Uncertaine Tymes*, pp.56–59.
9   Anon., *CSPD*, 1661–1662; Brown, *Annals of Newark-upon-Trent*, p.187.

Appendix I

John Twentyman's Account[1]

(Original spelling is retained, but punctuation has been added.)

Our familie was loyall & true to his late Majestie Charles the First & gave the decision to make that Town of Newarke a Garrison. Thus two troopes of Horse came from Lincoln under command of them who were for the Parliment, & faced the Towne upon Beacon Hill, it was reported in the town that they would come and plunder the towne.

One of my uncles having been Ensign to Captain Rossell & an old drum being in the House, but the head broken, my Grandmother charged my uncle Edward Twentyman upon her blessing to take it out & commanded Edward Foster her grandchild to beat an alarm & see who would stand for king Charles & their own Defence.

They came together unanimously with forks and spitts & what weapons they had, for very few guns were among them & resolved to defend themselves as well as they could & upon what notice or feare I know not those Troopes withdrew & made no attempt.

Upon this they sent to the Duke of Newcastle for aide who sent them some Troopes of Horse & the town Bands were call'd in & they made a garrison of it, takeing in only the round of the Town & leaving out Milngate & the best streete for building Northgate with the Earle of Exeter's House. And most pitifull works they were, very low and thin & a drie ditch which most men might easily leap upon the East & South.

The Parliament forces came against it under the command of Major Generall Ballard, who had served in forreign warrs & such were so renowned that they were thought able to do wonders among us in the beginning of our unhappy discords. Sir John Henderson a Scotchman who had also been abroad in forreign service was then Governor of the Town. The Parliament's forces came to the Spittle or towards it, which occasioned both it and Norgate to be sett on fire. Then they made some attempt to enter at Balderton Gate, but were beat of & the Towns-men won 2 or 3 little peices from them which greatly encouraged them. They attempted some other parts of the Town, but

---

1   NUMD: Me LM 11: Mellish Papers, Twentyman Manuscript.

not in diverse places at once, for they within had so few guns that they were forced who had them to run with them to the place of assault as Colonell Henderson ordered and directed who rode upon a white horse & encouraged the soldiers & kept in continuall motion upon his horse that the enemie might not take mark at him. Low & bad (as I have said) works. God at this time preserved the Town, for the Parliament forces drew of & went away & they imputed the not winning of the Town at this time to the trechery of Major General Ballard.

After this they began to make new works very high and strong & set up a great skonse in my Dove Coate Close called the King's Skonce, a footstep whereof is seen by the ditch left in it & at this time they secured the street called Milngate. These works were begun when his Majesties Forces were Masters of the Field, & according to humane judgment (but the Lord ruleth over all, & further appeared in his anger against us for our sins) they might have marched to London, into the associate Counties & have placed the king in his throne. But his Majestie with his army set down before Glocester & the Duke of Newcastle with his beseiged Kingston upon Hull, where both suffered much losse, gave advantage to the Parliament to recruit their Forces & were compelled to leave them.

Those Forces of his Majestie which belonged to Newark & to Lincoln (which Garrison the Parliament left) had the comands of that county & raised contributions for carrying on the war, but they enjoyed it not long for the Earl of Manchester then General of the Parliament Army for those parts marched with his army out of the associate Counties & Cromwell with him, & 3 miles from Horncastle (my native place) at a Town called Winsby, the Lord Witherington would needes encounter them, though Sir John Henderson was utterly against it who was comander in cheife, untill the other provoked him by telling him he was a coward, & then his judgment yeild to his reputation & honour, but the victory soon fell to the Parlimenteers. Then Manchester marched to Lincoln & took that Garrrison by storm, & it was supposed that if he had marched on to Newarke then he might have taken it, for the works were not finished.

But not long after it was beleagurd by the Forces of Lincoln, Nottingham, Darby etc. Sir Richard (afterward Lord) Byron of Newsteade was Governor. I was in it all that seige. They shott after they had formed their League 13 peices of ordinance every night & 2 Bomballs about 12and one of the clock. Prince Rupert came & raised this seige. I saw the Engagement from the Pinacles or steeple. They of the Parliament drew up their horse into one main Body & 2 wings under the brow of Beacon Hill against that place where Spittle stood, & where all their Infantry were enskonsed & there they had a Bridge of Boats over the Trent. The Prince charged one wing coming with fury upon them from Codington ward, & after the charge both retired that wing to the main body & the Prince with his up the Hill, & presently he came down upon the other wing & they did as before on both sides. Upon the 3d assault the Prince coming with his whole Body upon theirs totally routed them & fell so in with them they made a length from the hill to Spittle; there the Horse would have broke into their own Foot, but they shott to keep them out. Many fled over the Bridge of Boates & all would have gone, but they were forced to stay some that they might make the better Composition for themselves & they were [satisfied], & did leave all their armes behind them & march away. Thus the Lord delivered us this time also. This was the second seige.

After Sir Richard Byron succeeded Sir Richard Willis to be Governor who for his misdemeanours was removed a lewd & debauched person & was corrupted by Oliver Cromwell (…n) Protector[2] with 800 pounds to doe some high Acts of disloyalty after his master had lost his head.

The 3d & last seige was anno 1645 John Bellasis (now Lord Bellasis) Governor before which seige the king's armie decaying & not able to keep the Feild, many betook themselves into the strongest Garrisons. And there was built a very noble & strong worke which the Townsmen kept & built up an house of 3 or 4 Bay of Building in the middle of it, & called it the Royall Sconse or else changed this name with that in my close which in my time when it was made was called the king sconce but it seemes was altered to the Royall Sconce, this new one takeing the old name from it & because at Milngate End upon the south above Markhall Bridge there was another very noble work called the Queen's sconse)

The loyall Townsmen kept the King's Skonce & were formed into a Regiment. My uncle Edward Twentyman was the Eldest or first Captain that Regiment & died of a Gangrene which followed upon Butting of his Toe a little before the surrender of it.

It was a Strong Garrison now & kept of the Enemie at a great distance from them. They were well provided for a siege & were strongly beleagured by the Scotts & many more of the Parliament forces, but his Majestie casting himselfe upon the loyalty of the Scottish rebells he commanded the Town to be surrendered which was done after one or two intreaties before made unto his Majestie that they might still keep their Town for him; for they had those high thoughts that before their store could be spent, some change or another would have appeared to his Majestie's advantage & releife but his majesties continuing his command, they as obedient subjects to their great greife layd down their armes & so was surrendered 1646 The Virgin Garrison of Newarke.

And so it was the mercifull Providence of God to deliver them out of the hands of enraged & unmercifull men, who had long threatened & sought their ruine to take them into his own, the plague being brought in among them by some soldiers which came from some other place proved the only securitie for their goods.

My father was an ironmonger at Horncastle & was imprisoned 6 or 7 Times at Lincoln & Tattershall Castle for his loyalty, he married Sarah Hollinhedge daughter to Mr Robert Hollinhedge, B.D. Minister of Horncastle an eminent Divine by whom he had John,[3] Robert, William, Edward drowned in a voyage to the East Indies.

---

2 Mellish added a note in his margin explaining that the manuscript is torn at this place.

3 A note in the margin identifies John as 'the author of this account'.

Appendix II

The Accounts for Colonel William Staunton's Regiment at Newark, 1644–1645[1]

[folio 1] Received by me from ye 10th of December 1644 till April 20th 1645 as by particular receipts as do appear as followeth.

December	10	And first from my Colonel	12	14	0	
	17	And borrowed of my Colonel	1	10	0	
	26	And of my Colonel for ye souldiers	17	0	0	
		Of Thomas Clifton of Bradmore	1	19	6	
		Of ye constable of Bradmore	1	10	0	
		Of John Chamberlin	7	0	0	
January	3	Of ye constable of Bradmore	10	17	5	
		Of Mr Long	2	0	0	
	8	Of ye constable of Upton	2	1	0	
	8	Of ye constable of Morton	5	0	0	
	10	Of Mr Long	3	0	0	Total
	15	Of Tho: Speed of Basford	3	3	6	£ s d
	15	Of ye constable of Morton		14	0	111 9 1
	16	Of Mr Milford of Bradmore	6	15	0	
	17	Of my Colonel		10	0	
	20	Of Captaine Bright from my Col	15	0	0	
	20	For one horse that I sould		19	0	
	23	Of Mr Long	5	0	0	
	23	Of ye constable of Upton	1	4	0	
	27	Of John Speed of Basford	3	0	0	
	27	Of ye constable of Morton	1	10	0	
	27	Of Tho Higden of Selston	1	10	0	
	28	Of John Harrot of Selston		14	8	
	28	Of Robt Streete of Selston		3	8	
	28	Of William Rawson of Selston		14	4	
		Of ye constable of Upton	5	0	0	

---

1   I am indebted to my friend and colleague Professor Martyn Bennett, with whom I transcribed these accounts, and to Mr and Mrs Staunton of Staunton for allowing us both to do so. These accounts were originally published as part of Bennett, Jennings, and Whyld, 'Two Military Account Books', pp.107–21.

Gervase Hewet

[folio 2] Received

January	29	Of Mr Bristow	1	0	0	
	29	Of ye constable of Upton	1	4	0	
February	5	Of ye constable of Morton	1	0	0	
	10	Of ye constable of Upton	4	8	0	
	11	Of Mr Draper	47	14	0	
	18	Of my Colonel	4	0	0	
	27	Of ye constable of Morton		17	0	
March	4	Of ye constable of Morton	1	16	0	
	5	Of my Colonel	1	0	0	
	12	Of ye constable of Morton	2	4	0	
	12	Of Rich Farneworth of Selston	10	18	0	Total
	27	Of ye constable of Upton	3	0	8	£ s d
	28	Of Mr Long	10	0	0	195 8 2
	30	Of ye constable of Upton	4	13	4	
	31	Of ye constable of Upton	2	2	10	
April	1	Of ye constable of Morton in hay	1	4	0	
	2	Of ye constable in Morton	1	16	0	
	6	Of Mr Draper	30	0	0	
	8	Of Rich Lawrence of Selston		13	6	
	8	Of Fran Granger of Underwood		5	0	
	8	Of Ed Richards of Underwood		3	4	
	8	Of William Burton of Underwood		3	6	
	8	Of Anne Hardy of Bagthorpe		3	8	
	8	Of James Mosse of Bagthorpe	3	14	8	
	8	Of Tho Ryley of Bagthorpe		14	8	
	11	Of Mr Draper by ye Qt'r master	59	16	0	

Gervase Hewet

[folio 3] Disbursed by me from ye 10th of December 1644 till 22 of April 1645 as followeth

Decem.	10	And first to ye souldiers as by ye weekly list doe appear	12	14	0	
	27	And also to ye souldiers as by a second list appear	21	8	0	
January	9	And more to ye souldiers as by a third list appear	14	10	0	
		And to my Colonel	1	10	0	
		More to my Colonel		5	0	
		To ye Qt'r master	1	0	0	
		For red Mr Longs cloke		14	0	£ s d
		For two horses that I brought for ye souldiers	3	0	0	99 19 0
		For two souldiers for getting in hey		1	0	
		To a man of Thrumpton		1	0	
		To a guard		1	0	
	10	To my Colonel at ye Hart	2	0	0	
	10	To Tom Kirchevile of picking of hey		1	0	

January					
January		For clenging ye yeard at ye Angell		2	0	
		For clenging street against wid Teylers		2	0	
		To my Colonel		5	0	
	15	To ye Qt'r master for oats	3	9	6	
	15	To my Colonel	1	0	0	
	17	To ye Qt'r Master for pease	2	0	0	
		To ye guide to Selston	0	[?]	0	
	20	To ye Qt'r Master for hey	1	10	0	
	24	To ye souldiers as by a fourth list appeare	27	18	9	
	24	To ye Qt'r Master for Hey		13	6	
	24	To ye constable of Morton for one horse	2	0	0	
	24	To Robt Ward for one qtr and di of oats	1	4	0	
	24	To ye Qt'r Master for hey	1	4	0	
	26	To Robt Ward for one Qt'r and di of oats	1	4	0	

[folio 4]

January					
January	26	For one peare of chuis		1	0	
		For ye carriage of one load of hey		1	0	
		For teeming of ye same hey			6	
	27	To ye Qt'r Master	2	0	0	
	27	To RobtWard for one qt'r and di of oats	1	4	0	
		To Barn Kooke for one qt'r of oats		16	0	
		To ye Qt'r Master for hey	2	5	0	
	28	To ye Qt'r Master towards his pay	1	0	0	
	29	To ye souldiers at Werton		2	0	
Feb	12	To Barn Kooke for two qt'r of hey	1	12	0	
	12	To ye Qtr Master for ye carriage of 10 loads of hey		10	0	
	11	To Mr Draper for Col Hollis at Oxford	15	0	0	
	11	And to him for his allowance for ye receipts	4	15	6	
	14	To Robt Ward for one Qt'r and di of oats	1	3	3	£ s d
	13	To ye souldiesr by a fift weekly list appeare	22	13	0	
	1	To John Chamberlin for a horse	1	0	0	
	15	To ye Qt'r Master for ye stable at Mar't Creams		2	0	
	20	To Edm Whitwand to arrange load of hey		3	0	
	20	To my Colonel		1	6	
	20	To ye Qt'r Master		4	6	
	20	To John Clarke and Mr Wright in ye time of their imprisonment at Nottingham		10	0	
	20	To George Whitlen for to by things for use of 2 horses		2	0	

			£	s	d	
Feb	27	To George Turner for ye carriage of 2 loads of hey		6	0	
	27	To Robt Ward for oats		10	0	
	29	To Robt Ward for one qt'r and di of oats	1	3	3	
	29	To Mr Bristow for one horse	1	10	0	
March	6	To ye Qt'r Master towards his pay		10	0	
	6	To ye Qt'r Master for peases	2	0	0	
	6	To Mr Mansfield for to buy one horse	1	0	0	

[folio 5]

			£	s	d	
March	12	To ye Qt'r Master		10	0	
	16	To Robt Ward for oats		14	0	
	16	To ye Qt'r Master		2	6	
	27	To ye Qt'r Master for pease	2	0	0	
	28	To ye Qt'r Master for oats and pease & for yr repaireing of ye stables at ye Angell		5	0	
	30	To ye souldiers at Upton given		1	0	
		To ye carpenters for repaireing ye stable at ye Angell		13	6	
		To ye Qt'r Master for pease	1	0	0	
	31	To ye Qt'r Master for pease	2	10	0	
April	1	To a man of Sutton for one load of hey		11	0	
	2	To a man of Collingham for one load of hey		11	6	
	2	To ye constable of Morton for 2 loads of hey	1	4	0	
	2	For ye burial of Edw Kitchen	1	0	0	
	[ ]	To ye souldiers as by a sixt list doe appeare	79	0	0	£ s d
	12	To Mr Crust for one qt'r of pease	1	0	0	123 12 6
	12	To ye Qt'r Master for three qt'r of pease	3	0	0	
	12	To ye Qt'r Master		5	0	
	5	To ye Guide to Selston		5	0	
	5	To ye Quartermaster	1	0	0	
	7	To my Colonel	10	0	0	
	13	To John Arsedale for three loads of hey	2	2	0	
	13	To John Gamble for a horse for ye trumpet	1	0	0	
	14	To ye souldiers at ye sconce for bread and chees		3	0	
	16	To ye Qt'r master		5	0	
	17	To Joseph Christ for a horse	1	10	0	
		For one qr of pease March 18	1	0	0	
	18	To Sr Gervase Clifton	8	0	0	
	19	To my Colonel ye cornet	4	0	0	

[folio 6]

1645 Disburst							
April	19	To Robt Ward for one Qt's of oats	1	0	0	£ s d	
	20	To Colonel Staunton	6	0	0	8 0 0	
	20	To Porter for teaching ye trumpeter to sound	1	0	0		
[From] April 20 til July Disburst							
	21	To ye Qt'r master	[		]		
	23	To ye Qt'r master for pease & oats	[	8	0]		
	23	For a peace of beefe and [ ] [ ]					
		To ye Qt'r Master					
	26	To ye trumpet & for ye [ ]				£ s d	
	26	To Rich Lightfoot of [ ]				[54 18 6]	
	26	To ye souldiers as doe appeare by ye weekly list	[14	0	0]		
May	22	To ye cornet	[1	0	0]		
	22	To ye souldiers for ye weekly list by [ ] of [ ] [ ]	3	3	6		
	25	To ye Qt'r Master	1	0	0		
		To Corporall Wright	1	10	0		
	28	To Tho: Johnson			6		
	28	To Mr Tooks		5	0		
	28	To Rowland Henderson		2	0		
June	16	To Will Wagstaff		1	0		
	16	To [ ]		1	0		
	17	To Christo: Chopham		1	0		
	18	To Rob Wright		1	0		
	30	To Will Wagstaff		1	0		
July	1	To Christo: Chopham		1	0		

[folio 7]

April	25	Of William Rason for ye sessementes	3	11	8
		Of John Harret for fine sessements	3	13	0
		Of William Watnall for ye Sessement	6	6	0
		Of Francis Cussels for two sessementes		16	0
		Of Francis Magson for one Sessemente	1	0	6
		Of Rob Street for two sessements		7	4
		Of Gervase Saxton for one sessemente		7	4
		Of James Weightman for foure sessementes	3	13	4
		Of William Fellow for six sessementes	8	5	0
		Of William Howet for eight sessementes and more	7	6	8
		Of Rich Clarke for one sessement	1	6	6
		Of [ ] Hallfor two sessementes & upwards	1	7	4
		Of Charles Shepherd for eight sessementes for his lande	10	14	0
		Of Jo: Clarke for foure Sessementes	6	4	8
		Of William Farneworth for five sessementes	1	12	0
		Of George Weightman for two sessementes	1	16	8
		Of Charles Shepherd for six sessementes	8	0	0
		Of Francis Granger for one sessemente	3	18	0
		Of Charles Harrot for one ses & [ ]	4	0	0

Selston		Of Gervase Saxton for eight Sessementes	2	18	0
		Of ye constables of Morton		9	10
		Of Colonel Staunton	12	0	0
		Of Mr Johnson	6	0	0
		Of ye constables of Morton by Robt White	2	14	7
		Of Rich Widowson of Thrumpton	2	10	0
		From Lincolne Castearn ye Townes men	6	12	10

[folio 8]

July	16	Of Fran Magson of Selston	15	6

Appendix III

The Petition of Anne Staunton, Widow[1]

(Original spelling is retained, but punctuation has been added.)

July 1660
To the kings most excellent Ma[jes]ty

The humble petition of Anne Staunton widow of Col. William Staunton humble sheweth

That her deceased Husband did faithfully serve yo[u]r Ma[jest]ie's Royal Father from the time of his setting up the standard at Nottm during all the times of the war, and at his owne charges, and raysed Regiment of Foot and a Troop of Horse and served at Edgehill, Branford [Brentford?] and in the Garrison at Newark til the place [sur]rendered, and by this meanes was enforced to expose his house, estate & family to the cruelty of the enemy & to contract great debts by composition & other pressures wch chiefly occasioned the sale of most of his Ancient paternal fortunes, and yo'r petitioner's jointure, so that she and her children are left in a deplorable condition.

Your petitioner being thus disabled to support her self and children. She humbly beeecheth yo'r Ma[jes]tie to be graciously pleased to confer upon Ralph Staunton, one of her younger sons, a Scholarship in the Charter house at the next election. And she shall ever pray for your Ma[jes]tie's long and prosperous Reign etc.

I know all this to be most true
Gilb. Sheldon

---

1   TNA: SP 29/9/159: Petition of Anne Staunton, July 1660.

Appendix IV

The Articles of Surrender for Newark, 1646

Articles agreed & concluded the sixth of May 1646, betweene the Commissioners here under named Authorised by the Committee of the Parliament of both kingdoms, of England and Scotland, on the one part, and the Commissioners hereunder named, authorised by the Governour of Newarke, Lieutenant General to His Majestie, of the Counties of Nottingham, Lincolne, and Rutland, and Governour of the Towne and Castle of Newarke of the other party, touching the yielding and surrendering of that Garrison and the Castle, Forts, and Sconces hereunto belonging, to the Committee of both Kingdomes, for the use of the Parliament of England.

1. That the Towne and Garrison of Newarke, with the Castle, Forts, Sconces, Ordinance, Mortar-peeces, Armes, Ammunition, and Provisions, and necessaries of warre, (not hereafter expressed) be surrendered on Saturday next at ten of the clock, into the hands of the Committee of both Kingdomes, or whom they shall appoint for the use of the Parliament of England, without imbezling any of them.
2. That the Governour of the said Garrison, shall march away with his Servants, Horses, Armes, and proper goods to any Garrison he shall name, not besieged or blockt up, or to his owne house there to remaine unmolested, submitting to all Ordinances of Parliament: And also, that the said Governour shall have liberty upon desire, any time within three months to passé beyond seas, and to have passes granted for himselfe, and servants accordingly.
3. That all Officers in Commission, or that have beene formerly in Commission, shall march away with their Horses, Armes, and their proper goods, the common Souldiers of Horse and Foot, with their Money, clothes and Swords, to any Garrison not besieged or blockt up, or to their owne houses as they shall make choice of; and those that have not money, to have free quarter in their march and not to march above ten miles in one day unlesse they please, and to have a Convoy and Carriages provided for the carrying away their goods. Hostages being given for their returne of the Convoy and Carriages, and such goods

as cannot be removed, the Owners shall have three months libertie to dispose them.

4. That all such Officers and Gentlemen, now in the Garrison who shall desire to depart this Kingdome, shall upon signification thereof to the Commissioners, of both Kingdomes, any time in three months have Passes for that purpose, for themselves and servants, engaging themselves during their stay, to doe no dis-service to the Parliament.

5. That all such Officers and Souldiers, as by reason of Sicknesse, Wounds, or otherwise, as are not able to march out at the same time appoynted, shall have libertie to stay in the Towne, or some other convenient place, till they be recovered, and such as are not able to provide maintenance for themselves, shall have care taken of them.

6. That all Noblemen and Gentlemen in the said Garrison, shall have libertie to march forth the same with their Horses and Armes, and their knowne meniall servants, with their Horses and Swords to their own houses, there to remaine unmolested, submitting to all Ordinances of Parliament, and have libertie to carry away their own proper goods, then, or at any time within three months, or to have Passes for themselves and servants to goe beyond Sea upon desire within three months; and in the meane time to engage themselves to doe nothing to the dis-service of the Parliament.

7. That all Clergy-men in the Garrison, shall have libertie, with their Horses, Servants, and their owne proper goods, to march to any Garrison unblockt up or not besieged, or to their owne houses, there to remaine unmolested, submitting to all Ordinances of Parliament.

8. That the Maior, Aldermen, and Inhabitants of the said Garrison, shall not be molested in their persons, priviledges, goods, or estate, (submitting to all Ordinances of Parliament) and to enjoy the same libertie, and to have the same protection as all other Townes have which are in the power of the Parliament.

9. That the Ladies, Gentlewomen, Wives, Widowes, Children and Servants, belonging to any of the persons mentioned in the former Articles, or any other, shall have libertie to march forth of the said Garrison, with their Coaches, Horses, and proper goods, as in the sixth Article: And if any of them, by reason of sicknesse or any other just reason, cannot march forth, then they shall have libertie to stay there till their recovery, and then to depart unmolested.

10. That all prisoners now in the said Garrison, Castle, or Forts, or any other prisoners of warre, taken by either party since the siege began, shall forthwith upon signing these Articles be set at liberty, unlesse they be detained for criminall offences charged upon them, not as souldiers.

11. That all persons comprised with these Articles, grounded upon the summons of the 27 of April, which began this present Treaty, be recommended to compound with the Parliament for Their estates, as coming in before 1[4] of May, so as they doe effectually prostrate any compositions within two months next ensuing the date hereof.

12. If any of the persons above-mentioned shall violate any of these Articles, or any part of them, they shall loose the benefit of all the said Articles.

13. That for the performance of these Articles Hostages may be mutually given, and that a cessation of Armes continued by both sides till the time of surrender, according to the Articles; and the guards and convoys be appointed to protect the Gentry and souldiers (in their march) from violence.

Signed by us the Comissioners of the L. Bellasis.
Thomas Ingram
Bryan Balmes
Jarvis Nevill
Robert Sutton
Simon Fansshaw
[Anthony] Eyre
[Anthony] Gilby
Darsie
Atkins
[Edward] Standish

Signed by us authorized by the Commissioners of both Kingdoms.
Alexander Popham
Francis Thornhagh
John Hutchinson
Henry Gray
Richard Thornton
Twisleton
John Archer
Walter Scot
Gilbert Carre.
Archibald Douglas

Thomas Bristow cler.

Vera copia.

FINIS.

Bibliography

Primary Manuscript Sources

British Library (BL)
A Continuation of True Intelligence from the Army under the Command of the Earl of Manchester from July 27th to August 16th 1644 (London: Wood Street, 1644)
Add. MS 16730: Plans of fortified towns and battlefields in England
Add. MS 30305: Fairfax Family Correspondence, 1518–1700
Add. MS 37344: Whitelocke's Annals
E1 (1)–E1920 (3): Thomason Tracts [Individual items are referenced in footnotes.]
Harley MSS 164–66: Sir Simonds D'Ewes parliamentary diary, 1642–1645 transcribed by YCPH
Harley MS 6390: Fairfax Actions in the Civil War

National Civil War Centre – Newark Museum (NCWC)
NEKMS 2021.19.12–86: Newark Borough Miscellaneous Papers

Nottingham University Manuscripts Department (NUMD)
A24: Archdeaconry of Nottingham Act Book
Me LM 11: Mellish Papers, Twentyman Manuscript
Ne A 98: Account Papers Relating to the Estates of the Duke of Newcastle

Nottinghamshire Archives (NA)
DC/NW/3/1/1: Newark Borough Council Minutes, 1640–1660
DC/NW D48.74: Newark Military Documents, 1642–1648
PR/16/118: North Collingham Parish Register, 18 July 1646
PR/346: East Stoke Parish Registers
PR/1531: Coddington Constable Accounts, 1641–1769
PR/1549: Coddington Town Levies, 1639–1702
PR/1710: Upton Constable Accounts, 1640–1666
PR/5767: Thorpe by Newark Account Book of Parish Officers including Constables' Accounts
PR/21774: Farndon Parish Registers
PR/24810: Newark Churchwarden Accounts, 1640–1662
PR/27256–257: Newark Parish Registers, 1640–1660
PR/NW 22 October 1645: Will of Thomas Waite

The National Archives (TNA; formerly the Public Record Office (PRO))
PROB 11/200/390: Will of Francis Hacker of Colston Bassett, dated 20 May 1647
SP 23/185/386: Committee for Compounding with Delinquents, Royalists Composition Papers
SP 28/1–120: Army Pay and Supply Warrants, 1624–1651
SP 28/174, ff. 82–89: Parliamentarian Accounts for Broxtowe Hall
SP 28/240: Nottingham County Committee Treasurers Accounts, 1645–1648
SP 29/9/159: Petition of Anne Staunton, July 1660

Printed and Digitised Primary Sources

Anon., *Calendar of State Papers Domestic* [*CSPD*] (London: HMSO, 1860–1897)

Anon., *Calendar of the Proceedings of the Committee for Compounding etc., 1643-1660* [*CCC*] (London: HMSO, 1889–1892)

Anon., *Journal of the House of Commons, 1640–1653* [*HC Journal*] (London: HMSO, 1802), vols III–VII

Anon., *Journal of the House of Lords, 1640–1649* [*HL Journal*] (London: HMSO, 1767–1830), vols V–X

Baker, W. T. (ed.), *Records of the Borough of Nottingham, 1625–1702* (Nottingham: Nottingham Corporation, 1900), vol. V

Bell, Robert (ed.), *The Fairfax Correspondence* (London: Richard Bentley, 1849), vols III–IV

Bennett, Martyn (ed.), *A Nottinghamshire Village in War and Peace: The Accounts of the Constables of Upton, 1640-1666* (Nottingham: Thoroton Society, 1995)

Bodleian Library: Peter Heylyn, *A Brief Relation of the Remarkable occurrences in the Northern parts: viz. The Landing of the Queenes Maiestie In the Bay of Burlington: And the repulse given unto the Rebels of the Town of Newark, 'both signified by severell Letters on the same day, being Friday March 1642'* (March 1642/1643)

Bury, Lieutenant Colonel, *A Briefe Relation of the Siege at Newark …* (London: Peter Cole, 1644)

Copnall, H. H., *Nottinghamshire County Records of the 17th Century* (Nottingham: Henry B. Saxton, 1915)

De la Pryme, Abraham, *The Diary of Abraham de la Pryme, the Yorkshire Antiquary* (Durham: Andrews & Co., 1870)

'Early English Books Online (EEBO)', *ProQuest*, <https://proquest.libguides.com/eebopqp>, accessed 20 May 2024

Firth, C. H. (ed.), *Memoirs of the Life of Colonel Hutchinson by His Widow Lucy* (London: George Routledge & Sons, 1906)

Firth, C. H. (ed.), *The Life of William Cavendish, Duke of Newcastle* (London: George Routledge & Sons, 1890)

Firth, C. H., and Rait, R. S. (eds), *Acts and Ordinances of the Interregnum, 1642-1660* (London: HMSO, 1911), vol. I

Firth, J. B., *Highways and Byways in Nottinghamshire* (London: Macmillan & Co., 1924)

Gardiner, Samuel R. (ed.), *The Constitutional Documents of the Puritan Revolution* (Oxford: Clarendon Press, 1979) [First published in 1889.]

Hodgkinson, R. F. B. (ed.), *Extracts from the Records of the Borough of Newark-upon-Trent* (Newark: Newark Herald, 1921)

Hyde, Edward, *The History of the Rebellion and Civil Wars in England* (Oxford: Oxford University Press, 1828), vol. V

Keeble, Neil H. (ed.), *Memoirs of the Life of Colonel Hutchinson* (London: J. Dent, 1995)

Kenyon, J. P., *The Stuart Constitution, 1603–1688* (Cambridge: Cambridge University Press, 1986)

Lomas, S. C. (ed.), *The Letters and Speeches of Oliver Cromwell, with Elucidations by Thomas Carlyle* (London: Methuen & Co., 1904), vols I–III

Long, C. E. (ed.), *Richard Symond's Dairy of the Marches of the Royal Army* (Cambridge: Cambridge University Press, 1998) [Originally published in 1859.]

Rushworth, John (ed.), *Historical Collections of Private Passages of State* (London: D. Browne, 1742), vols I–VII

Slingsby, Sir Henry, *The Diary of Sir Henry Slingsby of Scriven, Bart* (London: Longman Rees, 1836)

Train, K. S. S. (ed.), *Nottinghamshire Visitation, 1662-1664* (Nottingham: Thoroton Society, 1950)

Webster, W. F. (ed.), *Nottinghamshire Hearth Tax Returns, 1664, 1674* (Nottingham: Thoroton Society, 1986)

Webster, W. F. (ed.), *Protestation Returns 1641/2, Nottinghamshire and Derby* (West Bridgford: Publisher unknown, 1980)

Whitelock, Bulstrode, *Memorials of English Affairs from the Beginning of the Reign of Charles I to the Restoration of Charles II* (Oxford: Oxford University Press, 1853), vols I–IV

Wing, Donald (ed.), *Short-Title Catalogue of Books Printed in England, Scotland, Ireland, Wales, and British America and of English Books Printed in Other Countries, 1641-1700* (2nd edition, New York: Modern Language Association of America, 1998), vols I–IV

Secondary Sources

Books

Adair, John, *By the Sword Divided: Eyewitnesses to the English Civil War* (London: Century Press, 1983)

Appleby, David J., and Hopper, Andrew (eds), *Battle-Scarred: Mortality, Medical Care and Military Welfare in the British Civil Wars* (Manchester: Manchester University Press, 2018)

Ashton, Robert, *The English Civil War: Conservatism and Revolution, 1603–1649* (London: Phoenix, 1997) [Originally published in 1978.]

Aylmer, G. E., and Morrill, J. S., *The Civil War and Interregnum: Sources for Local Historians* (London: Bedford Square Press, 1979)

Bailey, Thomas, *Annals of Nottinghamshire: History of the County of Nottingham, including the Borough* (London: Simpkin, Marshall & Co., 1853–1855), vols I–IV

Beckett, John (ed.), *A Centenary History of Nottingham* (Manchester: Manchester University Press, 1997)

Beckwith, Ian, *The Book of Gainsborough* (Buckingham: Barracuda Books, 1988)

Bennett, Martyn, *Cromwell at War: The Lord General and His Military Revolution* (London: I. B. Tauris, 2017)

Bennett, Martyn, *In the Midst of the Kingdom: The Royalist War Effort in the North Midlands, 1642-1646* (Warwick: Helion & Company, 2021)

Bennett, Martyn (ed.), *Society, Religion and Culture in Seventeenth-Century Nottinghamshire* (Lampeter: Edwin Mellen Press, 2005)

Bennett, Martyn, *The Civil Wars in Britain and Ireland, 1638–1651* (Oxford: Blackwell, 1997)

Bennett, Martyn, *The English Civil War: A Historical Companion* (London: W. H. Smith, 1992)

Blackmore, David, *Arms and Armour of the English Civil Wars* (London: Royal Armouries, 1990)

Braddick, Michael, *God's Fury, England's Fire: A New History of the English Civil Wars* (London: Penguin, 2009)

Briggs, Asa, *A Social History of England* (London: Penguin, 1985)

Bristow, Joy, *The Local Historian's Glossary and Vade Mecum* (2nd edition, Nottingham: University of Nottingham, 1994)

Brown, Cornelius, *A History of Newark-on-Trent: Being the Life Story of an Ancient Town* (Nottingham: Nottinghamshire County Council, 1995), vols I–II [Originally published in 1904.]

Brown, Cornelius, *A History of Nottinghamshire* (London: Elliot Stock, 1891)

Brown, Cornelius, *The Annals of Newark-upon-Trent: Comprising the History, Curiosities, and Antiquities of the Borough* (London: H. Sotheran & Co., 1879)

Cantor, Leonard, *The Changing English Countryside, 1400–1700* (London: Routledge & Kegan Paul, 1987)

Carlton, Charles, *Going to the Wars: The Experience of the British Civil Wars, 1638–1651* (London: Routledge, 1992)

Clark, Peter, and Slack, Paul, *English Towns in Transition, 1500–1700* (Oxford: Oxford University Press, 1976)

Cooke, David, *The Civil War in Yorkshire: Fairfax versus Newcastle* (Barnsley: Pen and Sword, 2004)

Cooke, David, *Yorkshire Sieges of the Civil Wars* (Barnsley: Pen and Sword, 2011)

Coward, Barry (ed.), *A Companion to Stuart Britain* (Oxford: Blackwell, 2003)

Coward, Barry, *The Stuart Age: England, 1603–1714* (4th edition, Harlow: Pearson Education, 2012)

Cust, Richard, and Hughes, Ann (eds), *The English Civil War* (London: Arnold, 1997)

Defoe, Daniel, *A Tour through the Whole Island of Great Britain* (London: Penguin, 1971)

Dowen, Keith, *Arms and Armour of the English Civil Wars* (Leeds: Royal Armouries, 2019)

Duffy, Christopher, *Siege Warfare: The Fortress in the Early Modern World, 1494–1660* (London: Routledge, 1996)

Durston, Christopher, *Cromwell's Major-Generals: Godly Government during the English Revolution* (Manchester: Manchester University Press, 2001)

Edwards, Peter, *Dealing in Death: The Arms Trade and the British Civil Wars, 1638–52* (Stroud: Sutton, 2000)

Firth, C. H., *Cromwell's Army: A History of the English Soldier during the Civil Wars* (3rd edition, London: Methuen, 1921)

Firth, Sir Charles, and Davies, Godfrey, *The Regimental History of Cromwell's Army* (Oxford: Clarendon Press, 1940), vols I–II

Fox, Malcolm, *Newark in the Civil War* (Newark: Newark and District Council, 1985)

Gardiner, Samuel R., *History of the Great Civil War, 1642–1649* (Moreton-in-Marsh: Windrush Press, 1991), vols I–IV [Originally published in 1893.]

Gaunt, Peter, *Oliver Cromwell* (Oxford: Blackwell, 1996)

Gaunt, Peter, *The Cromwellian Gazetteer; An Illustrated Guide to Britain in the Civil War and Commonwealth* (Stroud: Alan Sutton Publishing, 1987)

Gaunt, Peter, *The English Civil War: A Military History* (London: I. B. Tauris, 2014)

Gentles, Ian, *The English Revolution and the Wars in the Three Kingdoms, 1638–1652* (Harlow: Pearson Education, 2007)

Gittings, Clare, *Death, Burial and the Individual in Early Modern England* (London: Routledge, 1988)

Gurnham, Richard, *A History of Lincoln* (Chichester: Phillimore & Co., 2009)

Gurnham, Richard, *A History of Nottingham* (Andover: Phillimore & Co., 2010)

Harrington, Peter, *English Civil War Archaeology* (London: B. T. Batsford, 2004)

Heal, Felicity, and Holmes, Clive, *The Gentry in England and Wales, 1500–1700* (Basingstoke: Palgrave Macmillan, 1994)

Hey, David, *Journeys in Family History* (London: National Archives, 2004)

Hill, Christopher, *The Century of Revolution, 1603–1714* (2nd edition, London: Routledge, 1980)

Hill, Sir Francis, *Tudor and Stuart Lincoln* (Cambridge: Cambridge University Press, 1956)

Holmes, Clive, *Seventeenth-Century Lincolnshire* (Lincoln: Society for Lincolnshire History and Archaeology, 1980)

Houlbrooke, Ralph, *Death, Religion and the Family in England, 1480–1750* (Oxford: Clarendon Press, 1998)

Houston, R. A., *The Population History of Britain and Ireland 1500–1750* (Cambridge: Cambridge University Press, 1995)

Hughes, Ann, *The Causes of the English Civil War* (2nd edition, London: Macmillan Press, 1998)

Hunt, Tristram, *The English Civil War at First Hand* (London: Phoenix, 2002)

Hutton, Ronald, *The Royalist War Effort, 1642–1646* (London: Routledge, 1999)

Ingham, Sharon (ed.), *Discovering the Civil War in Nottinghamshire* (Nottingham: Nottinghamshire County Council, 1992)

Jennings, Stuart B., *A Very Gallant Gentleman: Colonel Francis Thornhagh (1617-1648) and the Nottinghamshire Horse* (Warwick: Helion & Company, 2022)

Jennings, Stuart B., 'Controlling Disease in a Civil-War Garrison Town: Military Discipline or Civic Duty? The Surviving Evidence for Newark-upon-Trent, 1642–1646', in D. J. Appleby and A. Hopper (eds), *Battle-Scarred: Mortality, Medical Care and Military Welfare in the British Civil Wars* (Manchester: Manchester University Press, 2018), pp.40–54

Jennings, Stuart B., 'These Uncertaine Tymes': Newark and the Civilian Experience of the Civil Wars, 1640–1660* (Nottingham: Nottinghamshire County Council, 2009)

Kenyon, John, *The Civil Wars of England* (London: Weidenfeld & Nicolson, 1988)

Kenyon, John, and Ohlmeyer, Jane (eds), *The Civil Wars: A Military History of England, Scotland and Ireland, 1638–1660* (Oxford: Oxford University Press, 1998)

Laslett, Peter, *The World We Have Lost: Further Explored* (3rd edition, London: Routledge, 1983)

Liddiard, Robert, *Castles in Context: Power, Symbolism and Landscape, 1066 to 1500* (Macclesfield: Windgather Press, 2005)

Lindley, Keith, *The English Civil War and Revolution: A Sourcebook* (London: Routledge, 1998)

Lynch, John, *For King and Parliament: Bristol and the Civil War* (Stroud: Sutton Press, 1999)

Macinnes, Allan I., *The British Revolution, 1629–1660* (Basingstoke: Palgrave Macmillan, 2005)

McRae, Alisdair, *How the Scots Won the English Civil War: The Triumph of Fraser's Dragoons* (Stroud: Spellmount, 2011)

Morrill, John, *Revolt in the Provinces: The People of England and the Tragedies of War, 1630–1648* (2nd edition, Harlow: Pearson Education, 1999) [First published in 1976.]

Morrill, John (ed.), *The Impact of the English Civil War* (London: Collins & Brown, 1991)

Morrill, John, *The Nature of the English Revolution* (London: Longman, 1993)

Newman, Peter R., *Companion to the English Civil Wars* (Oxford: Facts on File, 1990)

Page, William (ed.), *Victoria County History of Nottinghamshire* (London: Victoria County History, 1910), vols I–II

Pask, Brenda M., *Newark Parish Church of St. Mary Magdalene* (Newark: District Church Council of St. Mary Magdalene, 2000)

Polkey, Andrew, *The Civil War in the Trent Valley* (Derby: J. H. Hall & Sons, 1992)

Richardson, R. C., *The Debate on the English Revolution* (3rd edition, Manchester: Manchester University Press, 1998)

Richardson, R. C. (ed.), *The English Civil Wars: Local Aspects* (Stroud: Sutton Publishing, 1997)

Roberts, Keith, *Cromwell's War Machine: The New Model Army, 1645–1660* (Barnsley: Pen and Sword, 2005)

Roots, Ivan, *The Great Rebellion, 1642–1660* (2nd edition, Stroud: Alan Sutton, 1995)

Royal Commission on Historical Monuments [RCHM], *Newark on Trent: The Civil War Siegeworks* (London: HMSO, 1964)

Rutherford, Stephen M., 'A New Kind of Surgery for a New Type of War: Gunshot Wounds and Their Treatment in the British Civil Wars', in D. J. Appleby and A. Hopper (eds), *Battle-Scarred: Mortality, Medical Care and Military Welfare in the British Civil Wars* (Manchester: Manchester University Press, 2018), pp.57–77

Saunders, Andrew, *Fortress Builder: Bernard de Gomme, Charles II's Military Engineer* (Liverpool: Liverpool University Press, 2004)

Scott, Miriam, *Prerogative Court of Canterbury: Wills and Other Probate Records* (London: PRO Publications, 1997)

Seel, Graham E., *The English Wars and Republic, 1637–1660* (London: Routledge, 1999)

Sherwood, Roy, *The Civil War in the Midlands, 1642–1651* (Stroud: Alan Sutton, 1992)

Smith, Nigel, *Literature and Revolution in England, 1640–1660* (New Haven, CT: Yale University Press, 1994)

Staunton, George W., and Stenton, Frank M., *The Family of Staunton of Staunton, Nottinghamshire: An Essay* (Newark: S. Whiles, 1911), <http://www.nottshistory.org.uk/books/staunton1911/preface.htm>, accessed 22 Nov. 2022

Thirsk, Joan, *The Rural Economy of England* (London: The Hambledon Press, 1984)

Thompson, M. W., *The Decline of the Castle* (Cambridge: Cambridge University Press, 2008)

Thoroton, Robert, *The Antiquities of Nottinghamshire* (London: Robert White, 1677)

Tincey, John, *Soldiers of the English Civil War (2): Cavalry* (London: Osprey Publishing, 1990)

Trotter, Eleanor, *Seventeenth Century Life in the Country Parish* (London: Frank Cass & Co., 1919)

Wanklyn, Malcolm, *Decisive Battles of the English Civil War* (Barnsley: Pen and Sword, 2006)

Wanklyn, Malcolm, and Jones, Frank, *A Military History of the English Civil War* (Harlow: Pearson Education, 2005)

Warner, Tim, *Newark: Civil War and Siegeworks* (Nottingham: Nottinghamshire County Council, 1992)

West, John, *The Battle of Gainsborough, 1643* (Nottingham: DP Publishing, 2021)

Wheeler, James S., *The Irish and British Wars, 1637–1654* (London: Routledge, 2002)

Wilshere, Jonathan, and Green, Susan, *The Siege of Leicester–1645* (Leicester: Leicester Research Department, 1984)

Wood, Alfred C., *A History of Nottinghamshire* (Wakefield: S. R. Reprint, 1971) [Originally published in 1947.]

Wood, Alfred C., *Nottinghamshire in the Civil War* (Wakefield: S. R. Reprint, 1971) [Originally published in 1937.]

Woolrych, Austin, *Battles of the English Civil War: Marston Moor, Naseby, Preston* (London: Phoenix, 1991)

Wrightson, Keith, *English Society, 1580–1680* (London: Routledge, 1990)

Young, Peter, *Civil War England* (London: Longman Group, 1981)

Young, Peter, *Marston Moor 1644: The Campaign and the Battle* (Kineton: Roundwood Press, 1970)

Young, Peter, and Holmes, Richard, *The English Civil War: A Military History of the Three Civil Wars, 1642–1651* (London: Eyre Methuen, 1974)

Journal Articles

Appleby, David J., 'Fleshing Out a Massacre: The Storming of Shelford House and Social Forgetting in Restoration England', *Historical Research*, 93:260 (2020), pp.286–308

Arnold, Alison, and McMillan, Victoria, 'The Development of Newark-on-Trent 1100–1750, as Demonstrated through Its Tree-Ring Dates', *Vernacular Architecture*, 35:1 (2004), pp.50–62

Barley, M. W., 'Newark in the Sixteenth Century', *Transactions of the Thoroton Society*, 53 (1949), pp.15–25

Barratt, John, 'The Battle of Rowton Heath, 1645', *Journal of the Society for Army Historical Research*, 54:220 (1976), pp.208–24

Beats, Lynn, 'The East Midland Association 1642–1644', *Midland History*, 4:3 (1978), pp.160–74

Bennett, Martyn, 'Contribution and Assessment: Financial Exactions in the English Civil War, 1642-1646', *War and Society*, 5:1 (1986), pp.1–11

Bennett, Martyn, '"He Would Not Meddle against Newark…" Cromwell's Strategic Vision, 1643–1644', *British Journal for Military History*, 5:1 (2019), pp.3–23

Bennett, Martyn., '"My Plundered Townes, My Houses Devastation": The Civil War and North Midlands Life, 1642-1646', *Midland History*, 22:1 (1997), pp.35–50

Bennett, Martyn, 'The Civil War at Cotes Bridge', *Leicestershire Historian*, 3:3 (1984/1985), pp.15–21

Bennett, Martyn, 'The King's Gambit: Charles I and Nottingham in the Summer of 1642', *Transactions of the Thoroton Society of Nottinghamshire*, 6 (1992), pp.133–45

Bennett, Martyn, Jennings, Stuart, and Whyld, Martin, 'Two Military Account Books for the Civil War in Nottinghamshire', *Transactions of the Thoroton Society of Nottinghamshire*, 100 (1996), pp.107–21

Brown, Angela., '"Truth is a Thing Desirable": Propaganda and Nottinghamshire during the English Civil War', *Transactions of the Thoroton Society of Nottinghamshire*, 100 (1996), pp.95–106

Butler, R. M., 'The Civil War Defences at Nottingham', *Transactions of the Thoroton Society of Nottinghamshire*, 53 (1949), pp.26–33

Cressy, David, 'Saltpetre, State Security and Vexation in Early Modern England', *Past and Present*, 212 (2011), pp.73–111

Edwards, P. R., 'The Supply of Horses to the Parliamentarian and Royalist Armies in the English Civil War', *Historical Research*, 68:165 (1995), pp.49–66

Engberg, Jans, 'Royalist Finances during the English Civil War, 1642-1646', *Scandinavian Economic History Review*, 14:2 (1966), pp.73–96

Gordon, M. D., 'The Collection of Ship-Money in the Reign of Charles I', *Transactions of the Royal Historical Society*, 4 (1910), pp.142–62

Guilford, E. L., 'The Surrender of King Charles I to the Scots', *Transactions of the Thoroton Society of Nottinghamshire*, 26 (1922), pp.81–95

Hill, Christopher, 'Colonel John Hutchinson, 1615-1664: A Tercentenary Tribute', *Transactions of the Thoroton Society of Nottinghamshire*, 69 (1965), pp.79–87

Hoskins, W. G., 'Harvest Fluctuations and English Economic History, 1620–1759', *The Agricultural History Review*, 16:1 (1968), pp.15–31

Jennings, Stuart B., '"A Miserable, Stinking, Infected Town": Pestilence, Plague and Death in a Civil War Garrison, Newark, 1640-1649', *Midland History*, 28:1 (2003), pp.51–70

Jennings, Stuart B., 'Nottinghamshire 1646; Plague, Disruption of Trade and Commerce and the Cancelling of the Goose Fair in the County Town of Nottingham', *Midland History*, 43:2 (2018), pp.174–89

Jennings, Stuart B., 'The Anatomy of a Civil War Plague in a Rural Parish: East Stoke, Nottinghamshire, 1646', *Midland History*, 40:2 (2015), pp.201–19

Jennings, Stuart B., 'The Third and Final Siege of Newark (1645-1646) and the Impact of the Scottish Army upon Nottinghamshire and Adjacent Counties', *Midland History*, 37:2 (2012), pp.142–62

Jones, G. F. T., 'The Payment of Arrears to the Army of the Covenant', *English Historical Review*, 73 (1958), pp.459–65

Kishlansky, Mark A., 'The Army and the Levellers: The Road to Putney', *The Historical Journal*, 22:4 (1979), pp.795–824

Pells, Ismini, 'Reassessing Frontline Medical Practitioners of the British Civil Wars in the Context of the Seventeenth-Century Medical World', *The Historical Journal* (2018), pp.1–27, <https://hdl.handle.net/2381/41486>, accessed 23 Dec. 2022

Race, Sydney, 'The British Museum Manuscript of the Life of Colonel Hutchinson, and Its Relation to the Published Memoirs', *Transactions of the Thoroton Society of Nottinghamshire*, 18 (1914), pp.35–58

Samuels, John, Charles, F. W. B., Henstock, Adrian, and Sidall, Philip, '"A Very Old and Crasey Howse": The Old White Hart Inn, Newark, Nottinghamshire', *Transactions of the Thoroton Society*, 100 (1996), pp.19–54

Seddon, P. R., 'Colonel Hutchinson and the Disputes between Nottinghamshire Parliamentarians, 1643-1645: New Evidence Analysed', *Transactions of the Thoroton Society of Nottinghamshire*, 98 (1994), pp.71–81

West, John, 'Oliver Cromwell and the Battle of Gainsborough, July 1643', *Cromwelliana* (1993), pp.9–15

Wood, Alfred C., 'A Note on the Population of Nottingham in the 17th Century', *Transactions of the Thoroton Society of Nottinghamshire*, 40 (1936), pp.109–13

Wood, Alfred C., 'A Young Nottinghamshire Soldier of the Civil War', *Transactions of the Thoroton Society of Nottinghamshire*, 36 (1932), pp.125–33

Young, Peter, 'The Royalist Army at the Relief of Newark', *Journal of the Society for Army Historical Research*, 30:124 (1952), pp.145–48

Unpublished Theses

Fox, Malcolm, *Urban Elite and Town Government: Newark on Trent in the Mid-Seventeenth Century*. 1985. Unpublished. Nottingham University, MA

Jennings, Stuart B., *Bunny and Bradmore, 1640–1690: Change and Continuity in an Age of Revolutions*. 1991. Unpublished. University of Nottingham, MA

Young, Charlotte, *A Study of English Civil War Sequestration*. 2019. Unpublished. Royal Holloway, PhD

About the author

Stuart Jennings is a historian specialising in the Early Modern period, a retired Methodist minister, and a Fellow of the Royal Historical Society. He holds an MA in History from Nottingham University and earned his PhD in Early Modern British History at Nottingham Trent University. Dr Jennings has published extensively on Newark and the Civil War and is the author of four books, most recently Royalist Newark (Helion, 2024). For nearly a decade, Dr Jennings served as a coordinator and lecturer of Historical Studies at the University of Warwick's Centre for Lifelong Learning.

About the artist

Marco Capparoni is a fine artist and illustrator for wargames, fiction & nonfiction publishers, and private commissions. Specialising in history and military history, Marco's works also include natural history, portraiture, and book illustrations.

Other titles in the Century of the Soldier series